*A Treatise on
Political Economy*

Antoine Louis Claude
Destutt de Tracy

A Treatise on Political Economy

Antoine Louis Claude Destutt de Tracy

TRANSLATED BY
THOMAS JEFFERSON

ᏽ

EDITED AND WITH AN INTRODUCTION
BY JEREMY JENNINGS

LIBERTY FUND
Indianapolis

This book is published by Liberty Fund, Inc., a foundation established to encourage study of the ideal of a society of free and responsible individuals.

The cuneiform inscription that serves as our logo and as the design motif for our endpapers is the earliest-known written appearance of the word "freedom" (*amagi*), or "liberty." It is taken from a clay document written about 2300 B.C. in the Sumerian city-state of Lagash.

Introduction, editorial annotations, and index © 2011 by Liberty Fund, Inc.

The text of this edition is the translation by Thomas Jefferson, published in 1817 by Joseph Milligan.

Frontispiece is an engraving, circa 1761–1790, by Victor Texier after Charles Toussaint Labadye, from the Réunion des Musées Nationaux / Art Resource, NY.

c 10 9 8 7 6 5 4 3 2 1
p 10 9 8 7 6 5 4 3 2 1

Library of Congress Cataloging-in-Publication Data
Destutt de Tracy, Antoine Louis Claude, comte, 1754–1836.
A treatise on political economy / Antoine Louis Claude Destutt de Tracy; translated by Thomas Jefferson; edited and with an introduction by Jeremy Jennings.
p. cm.
"The text of this edition is the translation by Thomas Jefferson, published in 1817 by Joseph Milligan [published as: A treatise on political economy: to which is prefixed a supplement to a preceding work on the understanding: or Elements of ideology: with an analytical table, and an introduction on the faculty of the will]."
A Treatise on political economy appears as the fourth part of the Élémens d'idéologie, entitled Traité de la volonté et de ses effets.
Includes bibliographical references and index.
ISBN 978-0-86597-812-6 (hbk.: alk. paper)—
ISBN 978-0-86597-813-3 (pbk.: alk. paper)
1. Economics. I. Jefferson, Thomas, 1743–1826. II. Jennings, Jeremy, 1952– III. Title.
HB163 .D413 2011
330—dc23   2011032107

LIBERTY FUND, INC.
8335 Allison Pointe Trail, Suite 300
Indianapolis, Indiana 46250-1684

Contents

Acknowledgments

I am indebted to the staff of Liberty Fund for their invaluable support and encouragement and wish, in particular, to thank Christine Henderson. In addition, I would also like to thank Henry Clark for his helpful suggestions with regard to the introduction and translation of the text. Finally, my thanks go to the staff of the Rare Books Room at the British Library.

Introduction to the Liberty Fund Edition

Antoine Louis Claude Destutt de Tracy was born in 1754, the son of a distinguished aristocratic and military family that traced its lineage back to 1419, the year in which four Scottish brothers named Strutt joined the army of the future Charles VII of France to fight against the English. At his father's deathbed, the young Antoine promised to pursue a military career. This he duly did, joining the company of the Black Musketeers at the age of 14, later attending the school of artillery in Strasbourg, and eventually serving in the Revolutionary army as second-in-command of the cavalry under Lafayette in the war against Austria. After inheriting the lands of his family estate, in 1779 he married Emilie-Louise de Durfort de Civrac, a cousin of the Duke of Orleans. The king and queen of France signed their marriage certificate.

As the first stages of the French Revolution began to unfold, Destutt de Tracy was elected to represent the nobility of the Bourbonnais at the Estates General, called by Louis XVI to meet at Versailles in May 1789. We know little of his actions or views at this time, but it seems that he was in favor of the reform of the old monarchical and feudal system. This became clear in April 1790, when, first in a brief parliamentary speech and then in a short pamphlet, he sought to refute Edmund Burke's charge that the Revolution would end in bloodthirsty disaster.[1] Contrary to the claims of his illustrious adversary, Destutt de Tracy maintained that France was in the process of establishing a constitutional and hereditary monarchy that would guarantee the liberties of the individual. He was not of the opinion that France should slavishly imitate English institutions.

1. *M. de Tracy à M. Burke* (Paris: Imprimerie Nationale, 1790).

This early optimism was quickly dissipated as the Revolution pursued a course closer to the one predicted by Burke. On the grounds of his aristocratic birth, Destutt de Tracy was arrested and imprisoned in November 1793, securing his release the following October in the wake of the overthrow of Maximilien Robespierre and the end of the Reign of Terror. He had been lucky to escape the guillotine. It is in this experience that the origins of Destutt de Tracy's attempt to outline what he came to describe as the science of "ideology" can be first discerned.

Despite pursuing a military career, Destutt de Tracy did not neglect his academic studies. Moreover, as a parliamentary representative in Paris, he joined the elegant and influential *Société de 1789,* and it was here that he was to meet many of the great minds of his generation and many of those with whom he was to work closely in later years. In 1792 Destutt de Tracy moved his household to what was then the small village of Auteuil, on the western outskirts of Paris. The philosopher Condorcet likewise moved there in September 1792, and it was here that the widow of Helvétius held her famous literary and philosophical salon. At the home of Madame Helvétius, the spirit of the *philosophes* and of enlightenment still reigned supreme, and it was here that Destutt de Tracy began to absorb the sensationalist psychology of Condillac and the precepts of Helvétius's morality of self-interest. He also became close friends with the physiologist Cabanis, from whom he learnt that human nature was the proper object of study for both doctors and moralists. Together both might improve the nature of the human species.

Destutt de Tracy, therefore, became one of a group of intellectuals—later to be known by the collective name of the *Idéologues*—who sought to formulate a philosophical response to the violence and frenzied rhetoric of the Terror.[2] To explain the Terror, they believed, the springs of human

---

2. For further reading on Destutt de Tracy and the Idéologues, see Emmet Kennedy, *A Philosophe in the Age of Revolution: Destutt de Tracy and the Origins of "Ideology"* (Philadelphia: American Philosophical Society, 1978); Cheryl B. Welch, *Liberty and Utility: The French Idéologues and the Transformation of Liberalism* (New York: Columbia University Press, 1984); B. W. Head, *Ideology and Social Science: Destutt de Tracy and French Liberalism* (Dordrecht: Martinus Nijhoff, 1985); and Martin S. Staum, *Minerva's Message: Stabilizing the French Revolution* (Montreal: McGill-Queen's University Press, 1996).

action had to be fully explored and the workings of our intellectual faculties soundly analyzed. Only then could the questions that had so divided opinion during the Revolution be settled. Philosophy would put an end to revolutionary barbarism and provide a solid foundation upon which the Republic could be established.

With a new constitution and the establishment of the Directory in 1795, it appeared that the Idéologues would have the opportunity to turn their ideas into practice. That same year saw the foundation of the *Institut National,* within which was to be housed a Class of Moral and Political Sciences. This itself was to contain the Section of the Analysis of Sensations and Ideas, and it was to this body that Destutt de Tracy was elected in February 1796. Now, for the first time, he came to formulate the goals and methods of "ideology," or the "science of thought." Upon the achievements of this new discipline, he believed, rested the possibility of all human advance. At a minimum it entailed an almost limitless enthusiasm for the possibilities of conceptual reform, a characterization of religious belief and speculative metaphysics as obsolete sources of wisdom, and the search for means of perfecting our intellectual capacities. The intellectual possibilities and practical applications of this new science appeared unbounded. Beginning with an analysis of the self, it would explore grammar (the science of communicating ideas) and logic (the science of discovering new truths) before moving on to investigate education, morality, and, ultimately, politics. Ideology, not religion or the discredited prejudices of the past, was to be our infallible guide.

The political thrust of this message was not unduly difficult to discern. Destutt de Tracy, like his fellow Idéologues, was against monarchy and the Church; he was for a secular morality and moderate republican institutions; he believed in progress through the diffusion of knowledge and educational reform. In brief, he defended the bourgeois republic established after the Thermidorian Reaction of 1795.

How, then, did he respond to the rise of Napoléon Bonaparte and the establishment, first, of the Consulate and then the Empire in 1804? Initially the Idéologues and Napoléon seemed to see each other as natural allies, but the emperor soon concluded that they were a disruptive and unwelcome presence. He came to see them as metaphysicians, prone to idle speculation and eager to meddle in the affairs of government. Moreover, in the interests of stability and order, Napoléon was prepared to reach a compromise with the Roman Catholic Church. Accordingly, Napoléon closed down the Class of Moral and Political Sciences, thereby indicating that political theory would not be tolerated, and promoted the condemnation of the Idéologues as conspirators and atheists.

Faced with this new and hostile climate, Destutt de Tracy and his colleagues retired from public life and comforted themselves with their scientific and philosophical investigations. In Destutt de Tracy's particular case, this encouraged his resolve to complete his monumental inquiry into the component parts that, in his view, made up the various elements of ideology. Fortunately the investigation began at a level of abstraction that would ensure that all matters of practical application could be safely left aside for some time to come, as questions relating to politics and political economy could be answered only when the arduous philosophical groundwork of attaining "a complete knowledge of our intellectual faculties" (*A Treatise on Political Economy,* 9) had been finished.[3]

It is this that explains why *A Treatise on Political Economy* appears as the fourth part of the *Elements of Ideology* and why, on several occasions in the text, Destutt de Tracy insists that his is "not properly a treatise on political economy" but the "first part of a treatise on the will," which itself is "but the sequel of a treatise on the understanding" (*TPE,* 252). For us better to understand our text, therefore, we might briefly pause to consider the content of the first three parts of the *Elements of Ideology.* The first part appeared initially in 1801 and was subsequently republished in 1804 under the title *Idéologie proprement dite.* Destutt de Tracy here sought to establish, following Condillac, that the source of all knowledge lay in our sense impressions. From this he went on to analyze the four mental faculties of simple sensation, memory, judgment and will. The second part of the *Elements of Ideology* appeared in 1803 and was entitled *Grammaire.* According to Destutt de Tracy, grammar was not only the science of signs but also a continuation of the science of ideas. Accepting that it would not be possible to create a perfect language that would always accurately reflect reality, the

---

3. Page references to *A Treatise on Political Economy* are to the Liberty Fund edition and are cited in the text as *TPE.*

ambition was a more modest one of correcting and improving our present vulgar language in order that we might more clearly and correctly express our ideas. Destutt de Tracy was here partly inspired by a reaction against what he saw as the verbal excesses of the French Revolution. The third part of the *Elements of Ideology,* entitled *Logique,* was published in 1805. At this point Destutt de Tracy's purpose was nothing less than to establish a universal principle of certitude. Put simply, he did this by arguing that sense experience was free of error. As he explained in the "Supplement to the First Section of the *Elements of Ideology*" found in the present volume, he had reduced the whole science of logic to two facts: "we are perfectly, completely, and necessarily sure of all that we actually feel" and "none of our judgments, taken separately, can be erroneous" (32).

Thus it was that Destutt de Tracy began his examination of political economy by restating the previously established philosophical premises upon which this investigation was to be built. The first part of his argument was therefore as follows: Our needs and means, rights and duties, derived from the faculty of the will. Since to want something was to possess something, it followed that the idea of property and our conception of the self and of personality arose naturally. Thus, the concepts *yours* and *mine* were derived directly from the faculty of the will and the injunction to love thy neighbor as thyself was "inexecutable" (64). Our desires were the source of our needs, and from this derived our ideas of riches and poverty, for "to be rich is to possess the means of supplying our wants, and to be poor is to be deprived of these means" (72). Liberty was understood as the power to execute our will, to act according to our desires, and therefore was "the remedy of all our ills, the accomplishment of all our desires, the satisfaction of all our wants" (78). Constraint was the opposite of liberty and was "the cause of all our sufferings" (78). As such, liberty was to be equated with happiness and was "our only good" (80). It was our duty to satisfy our needs "without any foreign consideration" (87). The goal of the "true society," accordingly, was "always to augment the power of every one, by making that of others concur with it, and by preventing them from reciprocally hurting one other" (90). Only when these points had been established did Destutt de Tracy feel that he could move on to an analysis of the mechanisms of production and distribution.

Destutt de Tracy, like Thomas Jefferson, saw the difficulties that this approach might pose to his readers, fearing that they "will be impatient at being detained so long in generalities" and that his treatment of the subject might appear "too abstract" (10). He was, on the other hand, unrepentant. He would be very sorry, he avowed in the "Advertisement," if anyone "should be able to accuse me of having passed over some links in the chain of ideas" (11).

However, life in Napoleonic France for a dissident philosopher was never without its difficulties. Destutt de Tracy's original intention had been to supplement the first three volumes of the *Elements* with a further three volumes on the moral, economic, and political sciences. But views critical of the Imperial government were subject to rigorous censorship. In 1806–7, therefore, Destutt de Tracy interrupted the completion of the *Elements* and wrote an extended critique of Montesquieu intended to serve as the basis for his projected discussion of economics and politics. With no hope of its publication in France, Destutt de Tracy sent the manuscript to Thomas Jefferson, with whom he was already in correspondence. The latter, despite minor reservations over the nature of executive power, was sufficiently impressed with the text to secure its translation and anonymous publication in 1811 under the title *A Commentary and Review of Montesquieu's "Spirit of the Laws."*[4] In general terms, Destutt de Tracy recommended a system of what he termed "national government," resting upon free but indirect elections, civil liberty (including freedom of the press and from arbitrary arrest), legal but not economic equality, and a society in which every citizen would benefit from the liberalization of commerce and industry. Crucially, liberty was defined not (following Montesquieu) as doing what one ought to want but as the ability to do as one pleases. Moreover, he argued that the American constitution far better exemplified the principle of the division of powers than did its English counterpart admired by his illustrious predecessor. It is not difficult to understand why Jefferson was impressed by Destutt

---

4. On this episode see Gilbert Chinard, *Jefferson et les Idéologues d'après sa correspondance inédite* (Baltimore: Johns Hopkins University Press, 1925), 31–96. In 1817 a French version appeared in Belgium without Destutt de Tracy's permission. The authorized edition was published in Paris in 1819.

de Tracy's manuscript, since it harmonized quite remarkably with his own political philosophy and gave external confirmation of the soundness of the famed principles of Jeffersonian democracy. In a letter to Destutt de Tracy dated January 26, 1811, Jefferson wrote that he considered it "the most precious gift the present age has received" (Chinard, 74).

Encouraged by Jefferson's lavish praise, Destutt de Tracy resumed work on the proposed fourth part of the *Elements,* under the title *A Treatise on Political Economy.* In doing so he reproduced (at times verbatim) the arguments relating to luxury, taxation, public debt, and money to be found in the later sections of the *Commentary.* Again the text was sent to Jefferson with a view to securing its translation in the United States, and again it met with the enthusiastic approval of the American. To the publisher of the *Commentary,* W. Duane, Jefferson wrote on January 22, 1813: "The present volume is a work of great ability; it may be considered as a review of the principles of the Economists, of Smith, and of Say. . . . As Smith has corrected some principles of the economists and Say some of Smith's; so Tracy has done as to the whole. He has in my view corrected fundamental errors in all of them" (Chinard, 105). Nevertheless, publication in America was seriously delayed. The volume finally appeared in 1817, some two years after the French version was brought out under the title *Élémens d'Idéologie, IV partie: Traité de la Volonté.* The interminable delay in securing publication had many causes, but when, finally, Jefferson received the manuscript in English translation he found it, as his correspondence reveals, to be "wretched," "abominable," and "mutilated" (Chinard, 138, 141, and 140). To Lafayette, he remarked that it "had been done by a person who understood neither French nor English" (Chinard, 150). By his own account, therefore, Jefferson was obliged to revise it as best he could. Working up to five hours a day for two months or more during the spring of 1816, he eventually produced a translation that, if "unexceptional," was at least "faithful" to Destutt de Tracy's original version (Chinard, 138 and 141). It was, however, Jefferson who decided to depart from the pagination adopted by the author in order, as he told John Adams, "to prepare the reader for the dry, and to most of them, uninteresting character of the preliminary tracts" (Chinard, 145). Nonetheless, Jefferson did not begrudge his arduous labors on Destutt de Tracy's behalf. To the Frenchman he confided that "this, I believe, is the country which will profit most from your lessons" (Chinard, 170). For his part, Destutt de Tracy returned the compliment, indicating that, as an inhabitant of a Europe where the spirit of liberty had been oppressed and broken, all his hopes and affections lay with the United States (Chinard, 179).

What, then, were the distinguishing features of Destutt de Tracy's outline of political economy? Most obviously he disputed the theory of production associated with the physiocratic orthodoxy of the eighteenth century. This entailed, first, a rejection of the physiocratic notion that agriculture was the primary source of wealth and, second, a repudiation of the attachment of the physiocrats to a centralized state as a vehicle of economic progress. At issue was a fundamental disagreement about the nature of productive activity, for Destutt de Tracy wished to argue that to produce was to give to things a utility they did not previously possess and, therefore, that all labor from which utility arose was productive. This meant, in contradiction to physiocratic doctrine, that agriculture could be reduced to a branch of manufacturing industry possessing no distinctive characteristics. A farm was "a real manufactory" and a field was "a real tool" (*TPE*, 106). All those who labored and who belonged to "the laborious class" (107), be they manufacturers or merchants, were producers of utility and, therefore, of riches or wealth. This had a further radical implication: whereas the physiocrats had been prepared to argue that the "sterile" class was largely composed of those not engaged in agriculture, Destutt de Tracy overturned this idea, countering that "the truly sterile class is that of the idle, who do nothing but live, nobly as it is termed, on the products of labours executed before their time, whether these products are realized in landed estates which they lease . . . or that they consist in money or effects which they lend for a premium" (107).

Viewed thus, society could be described as "nothing but a succession of exchanges" (95) from which all the contracting parties can be said to benefit. "It is," Destutt de Tracy clarified, "this innumerable crowd of small particular advantages, unceasingly arising, which composes the general good, and which produces at length the wonders of perfected society, and the immense difference we see between it and a society imperfect or almost null, such as exists amongst savages" (97). This multiplicity of exchanges rested upon three causes of prosperity: the concurrence or uniting of men to labor in a common endeavor, the increase and preservation of knowledge, and the division of labor. Accordingly, the richest society was one where those who worked were "the most laborious and the most skillful" and who produced the greatest utility (109).

Following Jean-Baptiste Say, Destutt de Tracy believed that all productive activity could be divided into three operations: "theory, application and execution" (113). Seldom in advanced societies were these three activities now performed by the same person, and, consequently, it was possible to identify three species of laborer: the savant or man of science concerned with invention, the entrepreneur who directed and financed the enterprise, and the workman who executed the physical labor required to complete the process of fabrication. All three were entitled to financial reward, but the savant and the workman would always be in the pay of the entrepreneur. Such, Destutt de Tracy declared, "decrees the nature of things" (116), and it was, therefore, only just that the entrepreneur should be rewarded for "the quantity of utility which he will have produced" (116). Next, Destutt de Tracy extended this analysis to include the activity of trade or commerce, arguing that the merchant, being "neither a parasite nor an inconvenient person" (133), was also, exactly like the industrial entrepreneur, a producer of utility. It was thus no exaggeration to say of these two groups that they were "really the heart of the body politic, and their capitals are its blood" (201).

Having explained how wealth was created and who created it, Destutt de Tracy turned his attention to issues of consumption. Consumption, in his view, was the contrary of production and we were all consumers. However, consumption came in various forms, and Destutt de Tracy was eager in particular to make a distinction between that of "idle" and "active" capitalists (199). The expenditure of the former, he contended, largely deriving from a fixed income in the form of rent or interest on capital, was devoted to their personal satisfaction and, as such, was "absolutely pure loss" and "sterile" (199). In its extreme form it degenerated into "unbridled luxury" (199), the excessive and superfluous expenditure that was both "repugnant to good sense" (204) and damaging to the economy. In contrast, the active capitalist was modest in his consumption patterns. "Industrious men," Destutt de Tracy wrote, "are commonly frugal, and too often not very rich" (200). They spent little to satisfy personal and family needs and returned their capital to the productive process, thereby increasing the growth and circulation of wealth throughout society.

Patterns of consumption were linked to questions of distribution. This, in turn, raised the issue of the unequal possession of wealth. According to Destutt de Tracy, a natural inequality existed between individuals, deriving from their differing faculties and abilities. This natural inequality was extended as our material wealth increased. Conflicts of interest were inherent to this situation. Did this mean that class conflict was inevitable and permanent? Destutt de Tracy did not think so. First, although we each had particular interests, these were frequently changing. Next, all of us—employers and employees—were united by the "common . . . interests of proprietors and consumers" (167). In brief, we all benefited if property was respected and industry prospered. This was best attained through "the free disposition" (189) of labor and, in Destutt de Tracy's view, if wages were both sufficient and constant. As he commented: "humanity, justice and policy, equally require that of all interests, those of the poor should always be the most consulted" (179), but to this he added that "the real interests of the poor" were "always conformable to reason and the general interest" (180). For example, to reduce the lowest class of society to "extreme misery" would be to encourage "the death of industry" (182–83).

It was clearly no part of Destutt de Tracy's plan that government should seek to eradicate the consequences of natural inequality. To attempt to do so would be vain. Rather, in his view, "in every society the government is the greatest of consumers" (217) and its expenditure, even when necessary, was unproductive and thus sterile. To the extent that taxes encroached on productive consumption and took "from individuals the wealth which was at their disposition" (220), it should be reduced to a minimum. It was even more desirable that governments should not contract debts as the evidence of the recent past proved that "public credit is the poison which rapidly enough destroys modern governments" (250). Destutt de Tracy similarly lamented the government issue of paper currency, seeing it as a form of theft and a cause of inflation.

Destutt de Tracy was never to finish his *Elements of Ideology.* Around 1815 he started to go blind, and his plan to extend his inquiries from economy to morality got no further than an essay on love (duly sent to Jefferson but first published in Italy in 1819). He lived until 1836, sitting in the Chamber of Peers and maintaining a distinguished salon frequented by both Benjamin Constant and the novelist Stendhal. Long before his death the philosophical climate had turned against the scientific aspirations of idéologie, but this could not detract from the fact that in his *Treatise on Political Economy* Destutt de Tracy had written one of the classics of nineteenth-century French economic liberalism.

Note on the Text

As the introduction makes clear, when Thomas Jefferson finally received the translation of Destutt de Tracy's text, he was not pleased with what he found and thus set about revising and correcting it as best he could. "The claim of the present translation," he wrote in the Prospectus, "is limited to its duties of fidelity and justice to the sense of the original." In preparing this edition I have sought to approach Destutt de Tracy's text and Jefferson's translation in the same spirit and have, therefore, kept revisions to a minimum.

Certain changes have been made in terms of presentation. I have restored the paragraph structure of the original French text. I have done the same with the use of italics and capitalization, as the English version used these randomly. I have similarly removed the vast number of dashes deployed needlessly in the translation. I have likewise endeavored to correct typographical errors and, upon a few occasions and where necessary, have corrected the translation. I have retained the page order of the English translation, where the Abstract or Analytical Table appears at the beginning rather than at the end of the book.

All translations present the translator and editor with dilemmas. Destutt de Tracy's text in its Jeffersonian version is no exception to this rule. As far as possible I have modified the translation of key terms only when if left unchanged they would confuse the modern reader or obscure the meaning of the text. Below I set out the specific decisions I have made with regard to key terms.

Agriculteur: Rather than the original "agricolist," I have chosen the more familiar "farmer."

Besoin: Although we might more normally translate this as "need," I have retained its translation as "want."

Commerçan: Rather than the original "commercialist," I have chosen "merchant."

Entrepreneur: In the Jefferson edition this is translated as "undertaker." To avoid an obvious misunderstanding I have chosen "entrepreneur."

Fabrican: Rather than the original "fabricator," I have chosen "manufacturer." Similarly, for the verb "fabriquer," I have chosen "to manufacture" rather than "to fabricate."

Impôt: In the original text this is translated as both "impost" and "tax." I have decided to leave this unchanged.

Métairie: Rather than the original "half-shares," I have chosen "sharecropper" and "tenant farm."

Rentier: Rather than the original "annuitant," I have chosen "rentier" as it now has an accepted English usage.

Salarié: Rather than the original "hireling," I have chosen "wage earner."

*A Treatise on
Political Economy*

A TREATISE

ON

POLITICAL ECONOMY;

TO WHICH IS PREFIXED

A SUPPLEMENT TO A PRECEDING WORK

ON THE UNDERSTANDING,

OR ELEMENTS OF IDEOLOGY;

WITH AN

ANALYTICAL TABLE,

AND AN

INTRODUCTION ON THE FACULTY OF THE WILL.

❧

BY THE COUNT DESTUTT TRACY,

MEMBER OF THE SENATE AND INSTITUTE OF FRANCE, AND OF
THE AMERICAN PHILOSOPHICAL SOCIETY.

❧

TRANSLATED FROM THE UNPUBLISHED FRENCH ORIGINAL.

GEORGETOWN, D. C.
PUBLISHED BY JOSEPH MILLIGAN.
1817.
W. A. Rind & Co. Printers.

Letter from Thomas Jefferson
to Joseph Milligan

❧

Monticello, October 25, 1818.

Sir,

I now return you, according to promise, the translation of M. Destutt Tracy's Treatise on Political Economy, which I have carefully revised and corrected. The numerous corrections of sense in the translation, have necessarily destroyed uniformity of style, so that all I may say on that subject is that the sense of the author is every where now faithfully expressed. It would be difficult to do justice, in any translation, to the style of the original, in which no word is unnecessary, no word can be changed for the better, and severity of logic results in that brevity, to which we wish all science reduced. The merit of this work will, I hope, place it in the hands of every reader in our country. By diffusing sound principles of Political Economy, it will protect the public industry from the parasite institutions now consuming it, and lead us to that just and regular distribution of the public burthens from which we have sometimes strayed. It goes forth therefore with my hearty prayers, that while the Review of Montesquieu, by the same author, is made with us the elementary book of instruction in the principles of civil government, so the present work may be in the particular branch of Political Economy.

Thomas Jefferson.

Mr. Milligan.

Joseph Milligan was a Georgetown bookseller and publisher with whom Jefferson appears to have had extensive contacts. In 1817 he published the first English edition of the *Treatise.*

Prospectus.

❧

Political Economy, in modern times, assumed the form of a regular science, first in the hands of the political sect in France, called the Economists. They made it a branch only of a comprehensive system, on the natural order of Societies. Quesnay first, Gournay, Le Trosne, Turgot, & Dupont de Nemours, the enlightened, philanthropic, and venerable citizen now of the United States, led the way in these developments, and gave to our enquiries the direction they have since observed. Many sound and valuable principles, established by them, have received the sanction of general approbation. Some, as in the infancy of a science, might be expected, have been brought into question, and have furnished occasion for much discussion; their opinions on production, and on the proper subjects of taxation, have been particularly controverted; and whatever may be the merit of their principles of taxation, it is not wonderful they have not prevailed, not on the questioned score of correctness, but because not acceptable to the people, whose will must be the supreme law. Taxation is, in fact, the most difficult function of government, and that against which, their citizens are most apt to be refractory. The general aim is, therefore, to adopt the mode most consonant with the circumstances and sentiments of the country.

Adam Smith, first in England, published a rational and systematic work on Political Economy; adopting generally the ground of the Economists, but differing on the subject before specified. The system being novel, much argument and detail seemed then necessary to establish principles which now are assented to as soon as proposed. Hence his book admitted to be able, and of the first degree of merit, has yet been considered as prolix and tedious.

In France, John Baptist Say has the merit of producing a very superior work on the subject of Political Economy. His arrangement is luminous, ideas clear, style perspicuous, and the whole subject brought within half the volume of Smith's work; add to this, considerable advances in correctness, and extension of principles.

The work of Senator Tracy, now announced, comes forward with all the lights of his predecessors in the science, and with the advantages of further experience, more discussion and greater maturity of subject. It is certainly distinguished by important traits; a cogency of logic which has never been exceeded in any work, a rigorous enchainment of ideas, and constant recurrence to it, to keep it in the reader's view, a fearless pursuit of truth, whithersoever it leads, and a diction so correct, that not a word can be changed but for the worse; and, as happens in other cases, that the more a subject is understood, the more briefly it may be explained, he has reduced, not indeed all the details, but all the elements and the system of principles, within the compass of an 8vo. of about 400 pages; indeed, we might say within two thirds of that space, the one third being taken up with preliminary pieces now to be noticed.

Mr. Tracy is the author of a Treatise on the elements of Ideology, justly considered as a production of the first order in the science of our thinking faculty, or of the understanding. Considering the present work but as a second section to those elements under the titles of Analytical Table, Supplement, and Introduction, he gives in these preliminary pieces a supplement to the Elements, shows how the present work stands on that as its basis, presents a summary view of it, and, before entering on the formation, distribution and employment of property, he investigates the question of the origin of the rights of property and personality, a question not new indeed, yet one which has not hitherto been satisfactorily settled. These investigations are very metaphysical, profound and demonstrative, and will give satisfaction to minds in the habit of abstract speculation. Readers, however, not disposed to enter into them, after reading the summary view, entitled "On our actions," will probably pass on at once to the commencement of the main subject of the work, which is treated of under the following heads:

Of Society.

Of Production, or the Formation of our Riches.

Of Value, or the Measure of Utility.

Of Change of Form, or Fabrication.

Of Change of Place, or Commerce.

Of Money.

Of the Distribution of our Riches.

Of Population.

Of the employment of our Riches or Consumption.

Of Public Revenue, Expenses and Debts.

Although the work now offered is but a translation, it may be considered in some degree, as the original, that having never been published in the country in which it was written; the author would there have been submitted to the unpleasant alternative either of mutilating his sentiments, where they were either free or doubtful, or of risking himself under the unsettled regimen of their press. A manuscript copy communicated to a friend here has enabled him to give it to a country which is afraid to read nothing, and which may be trusted with any thing, so long as its reason remains unfettered by law.

In the translation, fidelity has been chiefly consulted; a more correct style would sometimes have given a shade of sentiment which was not the author's, and which in a work standing in the place of the original, would have been unjust towards him. Some Gallicisms have therefore been admitted, where a single word gives an idea which would require a whole phrase of Dictionary English; indeed, the horrors of neologism, which startle the purist, have given no alarm to the translator; where brevity, perspicuity, and even euphony can be promoted by the introduction of a new word, it is an improvement of the language. It is thus the English language has been brought to what it is; one half of it having been innovations, made at different times, from the Greek, Latin, French, and other languages—and is it the worse for these? Had the preposterous idea of fixing the language been adopted in the time of our Saxon ancestors, Pierce, Plowman, of Chaucer, of Spenser, the progress of ideas must have stopped with that of the progress of the language. On the contrary, nothing is more evident than that, as we advance in the knowledge of new things, and of new combinations of old ones, we must have new words to express them. Were Van Helmont, Stahl, Scheele, to rise from the dead at this time, they would scarcely understand one word of their own science. Would it have been better, then, to have abandoned the science of Chemistry, rather than admit innovations in its terms? What a wonderful accession of copiousness and force has the French language attained by the innovations of the last thirty years? And what do we not owe to Shakespear for the enrichment of the language by his free and magical creation of words? In giving a loose to neologism, indeed uncouth words will sometimes be offered; but the public will judge them, and receive or reject, as sense or sound shall suggest, and authors will be approved or condemned, according to the use they make of this license, as they now are from their use of the present vocabulary. The claim of the present translation, however, is limited to its duties of fidelity and justice to the sense of its original; adopting the author's own word only where no term of our own language would convey his meaning.

Advertisement.

❦

At the end of my logic I have traced the plan of the *Elements of Ideology,* such as I conceived they ought to be, to give a complete knowledge of our intellectual faculties, and to deduce from that knowledge the first principles of all the other branches of our knowledge, which can never be founded on any other solid base. It has been seen that I divide these elements into three sections. The first is properly the history of *our means of knowledge,* or of what is commonly called our understanding. The second is the application of this study to *that of our will and its effects,* and it completes the history of our faculties. The third is the application of this knowledge of our faculties to the study of those beings which are not ourselves, that is to say of all the beings which surround us. If the second section is an introduction to the moral and political sciences, the third is that to the physical and mathematical; and both, preceded by a scrupulous examination into the nature of our certitude and the causes of our errors, appear to me to form a respectable whole, and to compose what we ought really to call the *first philosophy.* I even believe this to have been proved in my third volume, chapter the ninth.

If I cannot flatter myself with the hope of bringing so important a work to perfection, I wish at least to contribute to it as much as is in my power; and I hope to contribute to it, perhaps even by the faults from which I shall not have been able to guard myself. My three first volumes of *ideology, grammar* and *logic,* compose the first section, or the history of our means of knowledge.

I am now about to commence the second section or the *Treatise on the will and its effects;* but before entering on this new subject I think it right

9

to add yet something to that which I have said on the first. Here then will be found, under the name of a supplement to the first section, something further supporting by some new observations my manner of conceiving the artifice of judgment and reasoning.

I hope it will not be displeasing to the amateurs of this research; because in condensing and bringing more closely together the most important of my logical principles, I present them under a new aspect, and have more-over added some considerations on the theory of probabilities, which are not without interest, considering the little progress this science has hitherto made. Those too who are not curious as to the latter article, and who may be sufficiently satisfied with my theory of logic and convinced of its justice, may save themselves the trouble of reading this supplement, which is but a superabundance of proof.

Afterwards follows the Treatise on the will and its effects; the first part of which I now submit to the public. It is to contain three. The first, which treats of our actions; the second, which treats of our sentiments; and the third, which treats of the manner of directing our actions and our senti-ments. These three parts are very distinct in their foundation, although closely connected with one another; and I shall be very careful not to con-found them, notwithstanding the numerous relations which unite them, and to avoid as much as possible all repetitions. But it will readily be per-ceived that there are general considerations which are common to them; and that before speaking of the effects and consequences of our *willing faculty,* and of the manner of directing it, we must speak of this faculty it-self. This will be the subject of a preliminary discourse, composed of seven chapters or paragraphs. I fear it will appear too abstract; and that many readers will be impatient at being detained so long in generalities which seem to retard the moment of real entry on our subject. I can agree that I could have abridged them. If I have not done it, it is because I have been well persuaded that I should gain time under the appearance of losing it.

In effect I pray that it may be considered, that wishing really to place the moral and political sciences on their true basis, a knowledge of our intellectual faculties, it was necessary to begin by considering our faculty or will under all its aspects; and that this preliminary examination being once made, almost all the principles will find themselves established naturally, and we shall advance very rapidly afterwards, because we shall never be obliged to retrace our steps. If any one wishes to satisfy himself of the advantage of this course, he has only to commence reading the book after the preliminary discourse. He will see every instant that he has need of an incidental dissertation, to obviate the difficulties which will have been solved before; and so much the worse for those who should not experience this necessity, for such are capable of being persuaded without sufficient reason. There are but too many readers endowed with this kind of indulgence; but it is not of their suffrages I am most ambitious. I consent then that they shall accuse me of having said too much; but I should be very sorry if those who are more difficult, should be able to accuse me of having passed over some links in the chain of ideas. It is especially in the commencement that this fault would be most unpardonable, for then it might lead to the most serious errors; and it is thence that arise all those erroneous systems which are the more deceiving, inasmuch as the defect is hidden in the foundation, and all that appears is consequent and well connected. Should the last reproach be urged, my only answer would be that I have made every effort not to deserve it; and I can at the same time protest, that I have not sought beforehand any of those results to which I have been conducted, and that I have only followed the thread which guided me, the series of ideas exerting all my attention not to break it. The judgment of the public will teach me whether I have succeeded, and I will not forestall it by any other preface than this simple advertisement.

My plan, my motives, and my manner of proceeding have been sufficiently explained in the preceding volumes.

Abstract, or Analytical Table.

❧

Advertisement.

Before commencing the second section of the elements of Ideology, which treats of the *will and its effects,* I am going to give a supplement to the first, which embraces *the history of our means of knowledge.*

Then will come the introduction to the treatise on the will, which presents the general considerations common to the three parts of which this treatise is composed.

The introduction will be followed by the first of these three parts, that which treats specially of our actions.

Supplement
To the first section of the Elements of Ideology.

I have previously reduced the whole science of logic to two facts.

The first is that our perceptions being every thing for us, we are perfectly, completely, and necessarily sure of whatever we actually feel.

The second is that consequently none of our judgments, separately taken, can be erroneous: inasmuch as we see one idea in another it is actually there; but their falsity, when it takes place, is purely relative to anterior judgments, which we permit to subsist; and it consists in this, that we believe the idea in which we perceive a new element to be the same as that we have always had under the same sign, when it is really different, since the new element which we actually see there is incompatible with some of those which we have previously seen; so that to avoid contradiction we must either take away the former or not admit the latter.

From these two facts or principles I deduce here fourteen aphorisms or maxims, which constitute in my opinion the whole art of logic, such as it proceeds from the true science of logic.

According to the last of these aphorisms, which enjoins us to abstain from judging while we have not sufficient data, I speak of the theory of probability.

The science of probability is not the same thing as the calculation of probability. It consists in the research of data and in their combination. The calculation consists only in the latter part: it may be very just, and yet lead to results very false. Of this the mathematicians have not been sufficiently aware. They have taken it for the whole science.

The science of probability is not then a particular science; as a research of data it makes a part of each of the sciences on which these data depend; as a calculation of data it is an employment of the science of quantity.

The science of probability is properly the conjectural part of each of the branches of our knowledge, in some of which calculation may be employed.

But it is necessary to see well what are those of which the ideas are, from their nature, susceptible of shades sufficiently precise and determinate to be referred to the exact divisions of the names of numbers and of cyphers, and in order that in the sequel we may apply to them the rigorous language of the science of quantities. To this again the mathematicians have not paid sufficient attention. They have believed that every thing consisted in calculation, and this has betrayed them into frightful errors.

In the state in which the science of probability is as yet, if it be one, I have thought I should confine myself to this small number of reflections, intended to determine well its nature, its means, and its object.

Second Section
of the
*Elements of Ideology, or a treatise on the will
and its effects.*

Introduction.

SECTION 1.

The faculty of will is a mode and a consequence of the
faculty of perception.

We have just finished the examination of our means of knowledge. We must employ them in the study of our faculty of will to complete the history of our intellectual faculties.

The faculty of willing produces in us the ideas of *wants* and *means*, of *riches* and *deprivation*, of *rights* and *duties*, of *justice* and *injustice*, which flow from the idea of *property*, which is itself derived from the idea of *personality*.

It is necessary therefore first to examine this latter, and to explain beforehand with accuracy what the faculty of willing is.

The faculty of willing is that of finding some one thing preferable to another.

It is a mode and a consequence of the faculty of feeling.

SECTION 2.

From the faculty of will arise the ideas
of personality and property.

The *self* of every one of us is for him his own sensibility.

Thus sensibility alone gives to a certain point, the idea of *personality*.

But the mode of sensibility, called the *will* or willing faculty, can alone render this idea of personality complete; it is then only that it can produce the idea of *property* as we have it.

The idea of property arises then solely from the faculty of will; and moreover it arises necessarily from it, for we cannot have an idea of *self* without having that of the property in all the faculties of *self* and in their effects.

If it was not thus, if there was not amongst us a natural and necessary property, there never would have been a conventional or artificial property.

This truth is the foundation of all economy, and of all morality; which are in their principles but one and the same science.

SECTION 3.

From the faculty of will arise all our wants and all our means.

The same intellectual acts emanating from our faculty of will, which cause us to acquire a distinct and complete idea of *self,* and of exclusive property in all its modes, are also those which render us susceptible of *wants,* and are the source of all our *means* of providing for those wants.

For 1st. Every desire is a want, and every want is never but the need of satisfying a desire. Desire is always in itself a pain.

2d. When our sensitive system re-acts on our muscular system these desires have the property of directing our actions, and thus of producing all our means.

Labour, the employment of our force, constitutes our only treasure and our only power.

Thus it is the faculty of will which renders us proprietors of *wants* and *means,* of *passion* and *action,* of *pain* and *power.*

Thence arise the ideas of *riches* and *deprivation.*

SECTION 4.

From the faculty of will arise also the ideas of riches and deprivation.

Whatsoever contributes, mediately or immediately, to the satisfaction of our wants is for us a *good;* that is to say, a thing the possession of which is a good.

To be rich is to possess these goods; to be poor is to be without them.

They arise all from the employment of our faculties, of which they are the effect and representation.

These goods have all two values amongst us; the one is that of the sacrifices they cost to him who produces them, the other that of the advantages which they procure for him who has acquired them.

The labour from which they emanate has then these two values.

Yes, labour has these two values. The one is the sum of the objects necessary to the satisfaction of the wants that arise inevitably in an animated being during the operation of his labour. The other is the mass of utility resulting from this labour.

The latter value is eventual and variable.

The first is natural and necessary. It has not however an absolute fixity; and it is this which renders very delicate all economical and moral calculations.

We can scarcely employ in these matters but the considerations drawn from the theory of limits.

Section 5.

From the faculty of will arise also the ideas of *liberty* and *constraint.*

Liberty is the power of executing our *will.*

It is our first good. It includes them all. A *constraint* includes all our evils, since it is a deprivation of the power to satisfy our wants and accomplish our desires.

All constraint is sufferance; all liberty is enjoyment.

The total value of the liberty of an animated being is equal to that of all his faculties united.

It is absolutely infinite for him and without a possible equivalent, since its entire loss imports the impossibility of the possession of any good.

Our sole duty is to augment our liberty and its value.

The object of society is solely the fulfilment of this duty.

Section 6.

Finally, from the faculty of will arise our ideas of rights and duties.

Rights arise from wants, and duties from means.

Weakness in all its kinds is the source of all rights, and power the source of all duties; or in other words of the general duty to employ it well, which comprehends all the others.

These ideas of rights and duties are not so essentially correlative as is commonly said. That of rights is anterior and absolute.

An animated being by the laws of his nature has always the right to satisfy his wants, and he has no duties but according to circumstances.

A sentient and willing being, but incapable of action, would have all rights and no duties.

This being supposed capable of action, and insulated from every other sensible being, has still the same plenitude of rights, with the sole duty of properly directing his actions and well employing his means for the most complete satisfaction of his wants.

Place this same being in contact with other beings who develop to him their sensibility too imperfectly to enable him to form conventions with them; he has still the same rights, and his duties or rather his sole duty is only changed, so far as he must act on the will of these beings, and is under a necessity to sympathise more or less with them. Such are our relations with animals.

Suppose this same sensible being in relation with beings with whom he can completely communicate and form conventions, he has still the same rights unlimited in themselves, and the same sole duty.

These rights are not bounded, this duty is not modified by the conventions established; but because these conventions are so many means of exercising these rights, of fulfilling this duty better and more fully than before.

The possibility of explaining ourselves and not agriculture, grammar and not Ceres, is our first legislator.

It is at the establishment of conventions that the *just* and *unjust,* properly speaking, commence.

SECTION 7.

Conclusion.

The general considerations just read begin to diffuse some light over the subject with which we are occupied, but they are not sufficient. We must see more in detail what are the numerous results of our actions; what are the different sentiments which arise from our first desires, and what is the best possible manner of directing these actions and sentiments. Here will be found the division which I have announced.

I shall begin by speaking of our actions.

First Part
of the
Treatise on the Will and Its Effects.
Of Our Actions.

CHAPTER I.

Of Society.

In the introduction to a treatise on the will it was proper to indicate the generation of some general ideas which are the necessary consequences of this faculty.

It was even incumbent on us to examine summarily,

1st. What are inanimate beings, that is to say beings neither *sentient* nor *willing.*

2d. What *sentient* beings would be with indifference *without will.*

3d. What are *sentient* and *willing* beings but isolated.

4th. Finally, what are *sentient* and *willing* beings like ourselves, but placed *in contact with similar beings.*

It is with the latter we are now exclusively to occupy ourselves, for man can exist only in *society.*

The necessity of reproduction and the propensity to sympathy necessarily lead him to this state, and his judgment makes him perceive its advantages.

I proceed then to speak of *society.*

I shall consider it only with respect to *economy*, because this first part concerns our *actions* only and not as yet our *sentiments*.

Under this relation society consists only in a continual succession of exchanges, and exchange is a transaction of such a nature that both contracting parties always gain by it. (This observation will hereafter throw great light on the nature and effects of commerce.)

We cannot cast our eyes on a civilized country without seeing with astonishment how much this continual succession of small advantages, unperceived but incessantly repeated, adds to the primitive power of man.

It is because this succession of exchanges, which constitutes society, has three remarkable properties. It produces *concurrence* of *forces, increase* and *preservation* of *intelligence* and *division* of *labour.*

The utility of these three effects is continually augmenting. It will be better perceived when we shall have seen how our riches are formed.

CHAPTER II.

Of Production, or the formation of our Riches.

In the first place what ought we to understand by the word *production?*

We create nothing. We operate only changes of *form* and of *place.*

To *produce* is to give to things a *utility* which they had not before.

All labour from which utility results is *productive.*

That relative to agriculture has in this respect nothing particular.

A farm is truly a manufactory.

A field is a real tool, or in other words a stock of first materials.

All the laborious class is *productive.*

The truly *sterile* class is that of the idle.

Manufacturers fabricate, merchants transport. This is our industry. It consists in the production of *utility.*

CHAPTER III.

Of the measure of Utility, or of Value.

Whatever contributes to augment our enjoyments and to diminish our sufferings, is useful to us.

We are frequently very unjust appreciators of the real utility of things.

But the measure of utility which, right or wrong, we ascribe to a thing is the sum of the sacrifices we are disposed to make to procure its possession.

This is what is called the price of this thing, it is its real value in relation to riches.

The mean then of enriching ourselves is to devote ourselves to that species of labour which is most dearly paid for, whatever be its nature. This is true as to a nation as well as to an individual.

Observe always that the conventional value, the market price of a thing, being determined by the balance of the resistance of sellers and buyers, a thing without being less desired becomes less dear, when it is more easily produced.

This is the great advantage of the progress of the arts. It causes us to be provided for on better terms, because we are so with less trouble.

Chapter IV.

Of the change of form, or of manufacturing Industry, comprising Agriculture.

In every species of industry there are three things: theory, application and execution.

Hence three kinds of labourers; the man of science, the entrepreneur, and the workman.

All are obliged to expend more or less before they can receive, and especially the entrepreneur.

These advances are furnished by anterior economies, and are called *capitals*.

The man of science and the workman are regularly compensated by the entrepreneur; but he has no benefit but in proportion to the success of his manufacturing.

It is indispensable that the labors most necessary should be the most moderately recompensed.

This is true most especially of those relative to agricultural industry.

This has moreover the inconvenience that the agricultural entrepreneur cannot make up for the mediocrity of his profits by the great extension of his business.

Accordingly this profession has no attractions for the rich.

The proprietors of land who do not cultivate it are strangers to agricultural industry. They are merely lenders of funds.

They dispose of them according to the convenience of those whom they can engage to labor them.

There are four sorts of entrepreneurs; two with greater or smaller means, the lessees of great and small farms; and two almost without means, those who farm as sharecroppers and labourers.

Hence four species of cultivation essentially different.

The division into great and small culture is insufficient and subject to ambiguity.

Agriculture then is the first of arts in relation to necessity, but not in regard to riches.

It is because our means of subsistence and our means of existence are two very different things, and we are wrong to confound them.

CHAPTER V.

Of the change of place, or of Commercial Industry.

The isolated man might manufacture but could not trade.

For commerce and society are one and the same thing.

It alone animates industry.

It unites in the first place inhabitants of the same canton. Then the different cantons of the same country, and finally different nations.

The greatest advantage of external commerce, the only one meriting attention, is its giving a greater development to that which is internal.

Merchants, properly so called, facilitate commerce, but it exists before them and without them.

They give a new value to things by effecting a change of place, as manufacturers do by a change of form.

It is from this increase of value that they derive their profits.

Commercial industry presents the same phenomena as manufacturing industry; in it are likewise theory, application and execution. Men of science, entrepreneurs and workmen; these are compensated in like manner; they have analogous functions and interests, &c. &c.

Chapter VI.

Of Money.

Commerce can and does exist to a certain degree without money.

The values of all those things, which have any, serve as a reciprocal measure.

The precious metals, which are one of those things, become soon their common measure, because they have many advantages for this purpose.

However they are not yet *money*. It is the impression of the sovereign which gives this quality to a piece of metal, in establishing its *weight* and its *fineness*.

Silver money is the only true common measure.

The proportion of gold and silver vary according to times and places.

Copper money is a false money, useful only for small change.

It is to be desired that coins had never borne other names than those of their weight; and that the arbitrary denominations, called monies of account, such as livres, sous, deniers, &c. &c. had never been used.

But when these denominations are admitted and employed in transactions, to diminish the quantity of metal to which they answer, by an alteration of the real coins, is to *steal*.

And it is a theft which injures even him who commits it.

A theft of greater magnitude, and still more ruinous, is the making of paper *money*.

It is greater, because in this money there is absolutely no real value.

It is more ruinous, because by its gradual depreciation, during all the time of its existence, it produces the effect which would be produced by an infinity of successive deteriorations of the coins.

All these iniquities are founded on the false idea that money is but a sign, while it is *value* and a true *equivalent* of that for which it is given.

Silver being a value, as every other useful thing, we should be allowed to hire it as freely as any other thing.

Exchange, properly so called, is a simple barter of one money for another.

Banking, or the proper office of a banker, consists in enabling you to receive in another city the money which you deliver him in that in which he is.

Bankers render also other services, such as discounting, lending, &c. &c.

All these bankers, exchangers, lenders, discounters, &c. &c. have a great tendency to form themselves into large companies under the pretext of rendering their services on more reasonable terms, but in fact to be paid more dearly for them.

All these privileged companies, after the emission of a great number of notes, end in obtaining authority to refuse payment at sight; and thus forcibly introduce a *paper money.*

CHAPTER VII.

Reflections on what precedes.

Thus far I believe myself to have followed the best course for the attainment of the object which I propose.

This not being a treatise expressly of political economy, but a treatise on the will, the sequel of one on the understanding, we are not here to expect numerous details, but a rigorous chain of principal propositions.

What we have seen already overturns many important errors.

We have a clear idea of the *formation* of our riches.

It remains for us to speak of their *distribution* amongst the members of society, and of their *consumption.*

CHAPTER VIII.

Of the distribution of our Riches amongst Individuals.

We must now consider man under the relation of the interests of individuals.

The species is strong and powerful, the individual is essentially *miserable.*

Property and inequality are insuperable conditions of our nature.

Labour, even the least skilful, is a considerable property as long as there are lands not occupied.

It is an error in some writers to have pretended there were *non-proprietors.*

Divided by many particular interests, we are all re-united by those of *proprietors* and of *consumers.*

After agriculture the other arts develop themselves.

Misery commences when they can no longer satisfy the calls for labour, which augment.

The state of great ease is necessarily transitory; the fecundity of the human species is the cause.

CHAPTER IX.

Of the multiplication of Individuals, or of Population.

Man multiplies rapidly wherever he has in abundance the means of existence.

Population never becomes retrograde, nor even stationary, but because these means fail.

Amongst savages it is soon checked, because their means are scanty.

Civilized people have more, they become more numerous in proportion as they have more or less of these means, and make better use of them. But the increase of their population is arrested also.

Then there exists always as many men as can exist.

Then it is also absurd to suppose they can be multiplied otherwise than by multiplying their means of existence.

Then finally it is barbarous to wish it, since they always attain the limits of possibility, beyond which they only extinguish one another.

CHAPTER X.

Consequences and development of the
two preceding Chapters.

Let us recollect first, that we all have separate interests, and unequal means.

Secondly. That nevertheless we are all united by the common interests of *proprietors* and *consumers.*

Thirdly. That, consequently, there are not in society classes which are constantly enemies to one another.

Society divides itself into two great classes, *wage earners* and *employers.*

This second class contains two species of men, namely the *idle* who live on their revenue.

Their means do not augment.

And the *active* who join their industry to the capitals they may possess. Having reached a certain term their means augment but little.

The funds on which the stipendiaries live become therefore with time nearly a constant quantity.

Moreover the class of wage earners receives the surplus of all the others.

Thus the extent which that surplus can attain determines that of the total population of which it explains all the variations.

It follows thence that whatever is really useful to the poor, is always really useful to society at large.

As *proprietors* the poor have an interest, first that property be respected. The preservation even of that which does not belong to them, but from which they are remunerated is important to them. It is just and useful also to leave them masters of their labour, and of their abode.

Secondly. That wages be sufficient. It is of importance also to society that the poor should not be too wretched.

Thirdly. That these wages be steady. Variations in the different branches of industry are an evil. Those in the price of grain are a still greater one. Agricultural people are greatly exposed to the latter. Commercial people are rarely exposed to the former, except through their own fault.

As *consumers* the poor have an interest that manufacturing should be economical, the means of communication easy, and commercial relations numerous. The simplification of process in the arts, the perfection of method are to them a benefit and not an evil. In this their interest is also that of society in general.

After the opposition of our interests let us examine the inequality of our means.

All inequality is an evil, because it is a mean of injustice.

Let us distinguish the inequality of power from inequality of riches.

Inequality of power is the most grievous. It is that which exists among savages.

Society diminishes the inequality of power; but it augments that of riches, which carried to an extreme reproduces that of power.

This inconvenience is more or less difficult to avoid, according to different circumstances. Thence the difference in the destinies of nations.

It is this vicious circle which explains the connexion of many events which have been always spoken of in a manner very vague and very unexact.

Chapter xi.

Of the employment of our riches, or of Consumption.

After having explained how our riches are formed, and how they are distributed, it is easy to see how we use them.

Consumption is always the reverse of production.

It varies however according to the species of consumers, and the nature of the things consumed. First let us consider the consumers.

The consumption of the hired ought to be regarded as made by the capitalists who employ them.

These capitalists are either the idle who live on their revenue, or the active who live on their profits.

The first remunerate only sterile labour. Their entire consumption is a pure loss, accordingly they cannot expend annually more than their revenue.

The others expend annually all their funds, and all those which they hire of the idle capitalists; and sometimes they expend them several times in the year.

Their consumption is of two kinds.

That which they make for the satisfaction of their personal wants is definitive and sterile, as that of idle men.

That which they make in their quality of industrious men returns to them with profit.

It is with these profits they pay their personal expenses, and the interest due to idle capitalists.

Thus they find that they pay both the wage earners whom they immediately employ, and the idle proprietors and their wage earners; and all this returns to them by the purchases which all those people make of their productions.

It is this which constitutes circulation, of which productive consumption is the only fund.

In regard to the nature of things consumed, consumption the most gradual is the most economical; the most prompt is the most destructive.

We see that luxury, that is to say superfluous consumption, can neither accelerate circulation nor increase its funds. It only substitutes useless for useful expenses.

It is like inequality, an inconvenience attached to the increase of riches; but it can never be the cause of their augmentation.

History plainly shows what happens wherever useless expenses have been suppressed.

All theories contrary to this reduce themselves to this untenable proposition. That *to destroy is to produce.*

CHAPTER XII.

Of the revenues and expenses of government and its debts.

The history of the consumption of government is but a part of the history of general consumption.

Government is a very great consumer, living not on its profits but on its revenues.

It is good that the government should possess real property. Independently of other reasons it calls for so much the less of taxes.

A tax is always a sacrifice which the government demands of individuals.

While it only lessens every one's personal enjoyments, it only shifts expenses from one to another.

But when it encroaches on productive consumption it diminishes public riches.

The difficulty is to see clearly when taxes produce the one or the other of these two effects.

To judge well of this we must divide them into six classes.

We show in the first place that the taxes of each of these six classes are injurious in ways peculiar to themselves.

We show afterwards who in particular are injured by each of them.

Is a conclusion asked? Here it is. The best taxes are, first, the most moderate, because they compel fewer sacrifices and occasion less violence. Secondly, The most varied, because they produce an equilibrium amongst themselves. Thirdly, The most ancient, because they have already mixed with all prices, and every thing is arranged in consequence.

As to the expenses of government they are necessary but they are sterile. It is desirable that they be the smallest possible.

It is still more desirable that government should contract no debts.

It is very unfortunate that it has the power of contracting them.

This power, which is called *public credit,* speedily conducts all the governments which use it to their ruin; has none of the advantages which are attributed to it; and rests on a false principle.

It is to be desired that it were universally acknowledged that the acts of any legislative power whatsoever cannot bind their successors, and that it should be solemnly declared that this principle is extended to the engagements which they make with the lenders.

CHAPTER XIII.

Conclusion.

This is not properly a treatise on political economy, but the first part of a treatise on the will; which will be followed by two other parts, and which is preceded by an introduction common to all the three.

Thus we ought not to have entered into many details, but to ascend carefully to principles founded in the observation of our faculties, and to indicate as clearly as possible the relations between our physical and moral wants.

This is what I have endeavoured to do. Incontestible truths result from it.

They will be contested however, less through interest than passion.

A new bond of union between economy and morality; a new reason for analizing well our different sentiments, and for enquiring with care whether they are founded on just or on false opinions.

Let us now consider our sentiments.

Supplement
to the
First Section of the Elements of Ideology.

ↄↄ

In proportion as I advance in the composition of these elements, I am incessantly obliged to return to objects, of which I have already treated. At the commencement of the grammar it was necessary to recall the attention of the reader to the analysis of judgment, to render still more precise the idea of that intellectual operation, and of its results, and to repeat several of the effects already recognized in the signs, and several of their relations, with the nature of the ideas which they represent.

At the commencement of the volume which treats more especially of logic, I of necessity looked back on the ancient history of science, to show, that true logic is absolutely the same science with that of the formation, the expression, and combination of our ideas; that is to say, that which has been since called *Ideology, general grammar,* or *analysis of the understanding;* and to show that my two first volumes are but the restoration, more or less fortunate, of the two first parts of the ancient logics, and the supplement of that which has always been wanting to these very important preliminaries. I have moreover been under the necessity of insisting also on the explication of the idea of existence, and on that of the reality of our preceptions, and of their necessary concordance with the reality of the beings which cause them, when they are all legitimately deduced from the first and direct impressions, which these beings make on us.

At present I find myself, in like manner, constrained to speak again of the conclusions of this logic, before advancing further, and not to apply my theory of the causes of certitude and error, to the study of the will and its effects, without having given it some new developements. The reader ought to pardon these frequent retrospects; for they arise almost necessarily from the nature of the subject, from the manner in which it has been treated hitherto, and from the necessity we are under, of anticipating a crowd of objections, when we wish to render a new opinion acceptable.

Let me be permitted then to mention here again, that I have reduced the whole science of logic to the observation of two facts, which result manifestly from the scrupulous examination of our intellectual operations. The first is, that our perceptions being every thing for us, we are perfectly, completely, and necessarily sure of all that we actually feel. The second, which is but a consequence of that, is that none of our judgments, taken separately, can be erroneous, since, for the very reason that we see one idea in another, it must be actually there; but that their falsity, when it takes place, is purely relative to all the anterior judgments, which we permit to subsist, and consists in this, that we believe the idea, in which we see a new element, to be the same we have always had under the same sign, while it is really different, since the new element we actually see there is incompatible with some of those which we have previously seen there. So that, to avoid contradiction, it would be necessary either to take away the former, or not to admit the latter.

After having established these two principles, or rather these two facts, I have given some elucidations, I have met in advance some objections, I have shown that these two objections are equally true, whatever be the nature of our ideas, and whatever the use we make of them; and hence I have concluded, that all the rules whatsoever which have been prescribed for the form of our reasonings, to assure us of their justice, are absolutely useless and illusory; and that our sole and only means of preserving ourselves from error, is to assure ourselves well that we comprehend the idea of which we judge, and if it be doubtful, to make the most complete enumeration possible of the elements which compose it, and principally of those which may either implicitly contain or exclude that whose admission or exclusion is in question.

It is here that, without more details, I have terminated my treatise on logic, which consequently finishes almost at the point at which all the others commence. This ought so to be, as I meant to speak only of the science; while other logicians, neglecting the science almost entirely, have occupied themselves only with the art. I confess my belief, that my labour is more useful than theirs; because, in every matter, it is always very difficult, from premature consequences, to remount to the principles which ought to have served as their foundation. Whereas, when we have well established the first truths, it is easy to deduce the consequences which flow from them. Yet this second operation is important also, and as a subject is not completely treated of, but when it is executed, I will present, before proceeding further, summarily, but methodically, the series of practical maxims, which result from my method of considering our means of knowledge. The use I shall afterwards make of these same means, in the study of the will and its effects, will be an example of the manner in which these rules are applied in all our researches.

Aphorism First.*

We know our existence only by the impressions we experience, and that of beings other than ourselves, but by the impressions which they cause on us.

OBSERVATION.

In like manner, as all our propositions may be reduced to the form of enunciative propositions, because at bottom they all express a judgment, so all our enunciative propositions may afterwards be always reduced to some one of these: *I think, I feel,* or *I perceive, that such a thing is in such a manner, or that such a being produces such an effect;* propositions of which we are ourselves the subject, because in fact we are always the subject of all our judgments, since they never express but the impression which we experience.

---

* I have employed the form of aphorisms, observations and corollaries, in order to say the most in the fewest words.

Corollary.

From hence it follows: 1st. That our perceptions are all of them always such as we feel them, and are not susceptible of any error, taken each separately, and in itself.

2dly. That if in the different combinations, we make of them, we add to them nothing which is not primitively comprised in them, implicitly or explicitly, they are always conformable to the existence of the beings which cause them, since that existence is not known to us but by them, and consists for us only in those perceptions.

3dly. That we know nothing but relatively to ourselves, and to our means of receiving perceptions.

4thly. That these perceptions are every thing for us; that we know nothing ever but our perceptions; that they are the only things truly real for us, and that the reality which we recognize in the beings that cause them is only secondary, and consists only in the permanent power of always causing the same impressions under the same circumstances, whether on ourselves, or on other sensible beings, who give us an account of them (also by the impressions which they cause in us) when we have become able to hold communication with them by signs.

Aphorism Second.

Since our perceptions are all of them always such as we feel them, when we perceive one idea in another, it is actually and really there, from the very circumstance of our perceiving it there: hence no one of our judgments taken separately and detached, is false. It has always and necessarily the certitude which belongs inevitably to each of our actual perceptions.

Corollary.

None of our judgments then can be false, but relatively to anterior judgments, and that suffices to render them false relatively to the existence of beings, the causes of our impressions, if these anterior judgments were just, relatively to that existence.

Aphorism Third.

When we see in an idea, or a perception, an element incompatible with those which it included before, this idea is different from what it was, for, such as it was, it excluded this new element which we see there; and, such as it is, it excludes those which are incompatible with it.

Corollary.

That it may then be the same idea which it was before, we must exclude from it the element which we see there at present, or if those which are repugnant to it, are misplaced in this idea, they must themselves be excluded from it; that is to say, it must be rendered such as it was, when they were erroneously admitted into it, which is to restore it again to the same state in which it was, before it was changed by a false judgment, without our perceiving it.

Aphorism Fourth.

When we form a judgment of an idea, when we see in it a new element, one of these four things must necessarily happen:

Either the judgment which we now form is consequent to a just idea, in which case it is just; and the idea without changing its nature has only developed and extended itself.

Or it is inconsequent to a just idea, in which case it is false; and the idea is changed, and is become false.

Or it is consequent to an idea already false, then it is false, but the idea is not changed; it is when it has become false previously, that it has changed in relation to what it was primitively.

Or it is inconsequent to a false idea, then it may be just or false; but never certain, for the idea is changed. But it may have become just, such as it was originally, or false, in a manner different from the preceding.

Observation.

Remark always, that an idea infected with false elements, and consequently meriting the name of *false, taken in mass,* may also contain many true elements. We may form then, in consequence of these true elements, just judgments, and then they will be completely true; as we may also form from them false judgments, which shall be completely false; but these judgments will not be formed from that idea, inasmuch as it is false, and in consequence of that which it has of falsity; they ought therefore to be considered as formed from a true idea, and enter into what we have said of these.

This is what most frequently happens to us, so few compound ideas have we which are perfectly pure, and without mixture of imperfection. Perhaps we have none. Perhaps it would suffice for us to have one alone, to render all our others the same, by the sole force of their relations and combinations, proximate or remote.

Aphorism Fifth.

Thus all our perceptions are originally just and true, and error is only introduced to them at the moment when we admit an element which is opposed to them. That is to say, which denaturalises and changes them, without our perceiving it.

Aphorism Sixth.

This would never happen to us, if we had always present to the mind, that which the idea comports, of which we judge. Thus all our errors really come from this: that we represent the idea imperfectly to ourselves.

Aphorism Seventh.

What precedes not appertaining to any circumstance peculiar to any one of our perceptions rather than to another, agrees generally with all.

COROLLARY.

Hence it follows, 1st. That our manner of proceeding is the same for our ideas of every kind.

2dly. That all our errors originate from the basis of our ideas, and not from the form of our reasonings.

3dly. That all the rules which can be prescribed for the forms of these reasonings, can contribute nothing to avoid error; or at least can contribute to it but accidentally.

Aphorism Eighth.

We have then no other effectual means of avoiding error, but to assure ourselves well of the comprehension of the idea of which we judge, that is to say, of the elements of which it is composed.

OBSERVATION.

That is not possible, unless we commence by well determining the extension of this idea, for it contains many elements in certain degrees of its extension, which it does not in others, that is to say, it is not exactly similar to itself, it is not rigorously the same idea in their different degrees of extension.

Aphorism Ninth.

This general and only method embraces several others, and first that of studying with care the object, or objects, from which the idea in question emanates, and afterwards that of guarding ourselves with the same care from the affections, passions, prejudices, dispositions, habits and manners of being, by which the idea could be altered.

OBSERVATION.

These two precautions are necessary, the first to assemble, as far as possible, all the elements which really appertain to the idea in question, the second to separate from it in like manner all those which are foreign to it, and which might mingle themselves with it, and alter it, without our perceiving it.

Aphorism Tenth.

After these two necessary preliminaries, if we are still in doubt as to the judgment we are to form, the most useful expedient of which we can avail ourselves, is to make an enumeration the most complete possible of the elements composing the idea, which is the subject of the judgment, and principally of those which have relation to the idea which we propose to attribute to it, that is to say, to the attribute of the contemplated judgment.

Observation.

The effect of this operation is to recall to ourselves, or to those whom we wish to convince of the truth or falsity of a proposition, the elements of the subject which implicitly comprehend the proposed attribute, or which on the contrary may exclude it.

It is the object which the logicians propose to attain by what they call *definitions;* but in my opinion they fall into several errors relatively to definitions, and they greatly mistake their effects and properties.

1st. They believe that there are definitions of words, and definitions of things, while in truth there are none but definitions of ideas. When I explain the sense of a word, I do nothing but explain the idea which I have when I pronounce that word, and when I explain what a being is, I still do nothing but explain the idea I have of that being, and which I express when I pronounce its name.

2d. They aver that definitions are principles, and that we cannot dispute about definitions. These two assertions are contraries, and yet both of them false.

In the first place they are contradictory, for if definitions are principles, we can and we ought frequently to question their truth, as we ought never to recognise any principle as true without a previous examination, and if we cannot contest definitions, they cannot be principles, since every principle should be proved before it is admitted.

Again, these two assertions are both false. Definitions are not principles; for facts are the only true principles; and definitions are not facts, but simple explanations founded on facts, as all our other propositions whatsoever. Now we may contest a definition, as every other proposition; for when I explain the idea that I have of a being, I do not pretend to say merely that I have this idea; I pretend also to affirm that this idea agrees with that being, and that we may so conceive it without error; now this is what may be false, and what may be contested. So also when I explain the idea which I have of the sense of a word, I do not solely pretend that I have this idea, I pretend further that it does not affect the real relations of this word with an infinity of others, that we may employ it in this sense without inconvenience and without inconsequence; now this is what again may be contested with reason. In fine, if I should pretend by a definition only to explain the complex and compound idea that I have actually in my head, yet it should always be allowed to show me that this idea is badly formed, that it is composed of judgments inconsequent the one to the other, and that it includes contradictory elements.

Then definitions never are principles, and yet they always are contestible.

3dly. The logicians have believed that the definition is good, and that the idea defined is perfectly explained when they have determined it, *per genus proximum et differentiam specificam,* as they say; that is to say, when they have expressed that one of its elements which constitutes it of such a genus, and the one which in this genus distinguishes it from the ideas of the neighbouring species. Now this is still false, and is only founded on the fantastical doctrine, in virtue of which they believed they were able to distribute all our ideas into different arbitrary classes called *categories.*

That is false, first, because these arbitrary classifications never represent nature. Our ideas are connected the one to the other by a thousand different relations. Seen under one aspect they are of one genus, and under another they are of another genus; subsequently each of them depends on an innumerable multitude of proximate ideas, by an infinity of relations, of natures so different that we cannot compare them together, to decide which is the least remote. Thus we can never, or almost never find really *the proximate genus or specific difference* which deserves exclusively to characterise an idea.

Moreover, if we should have found in this idea the elements which in fact determine the genus and species in which it is reasonably permitted to class it, the idea would still be far from sufficiently explained, to be well known.

These two elements might even be absolutely foreign to the decision of the question which may have given place to the definition. Assuredly when I say that gold is a metal, and the heaviest of metals except platina, I have correctly ranged gold in the genus of beings to which it belongs, and I have distinguished it by a characteristic difference from those nearest to it in that genus. Yet this does not help me to know whether the use of gold, as money, is useful to commerce, or pernicious to morality, nor even whether it is the most ductile of metals. The two first questions depend on ideas too foreign to those which fix gold in a certain place amongst metals; and though the latter may be less distant, yet we do not know the direct and necessary relation between weight and ductility.

Logicians have been mistaken respecting the nature, the effects and properties of definitions. They are incapable of answering the end which they propose to attain by their means, that of presenting the idea of which we are to judge in such a manner that we cannot avoid forming a just judgment. The only mean of attaining this is to make the best description possible of the idea, and with the precautions which we have indicated.

Remark.

It is necessary to observe that all that we have advised in the 8th, 9th and 10th aphorisms, and also what we shall advise hereafter to be done, to know well the idea, the *subject* of the judgment in question is equally applicable to the idea which is the *attribute* of the same judgment, a knowledge of which is equally essential, and can only be acquired by the same means.

Aphorism Eleventh.

The means indicated above of knowing well the idea of which we are to judge, are the only really efficacious ones in bringing us to the formation of just judgments; but they may very possibly be insufficient to give us a certitude of having succeeded. We must therefore add subsidiary means.

Aphorism Twelfth.

The best and most useful of our secondary means is to see, on the one hand, if the judgment we are to form is not in opposition to anterior judgments, of the certitude of which we are assured; and on the other if it does not necessarily lead to consequences manifestly false.

REMARK.

The first point is that which has so strongly accredited the usage of general propositions; for, as we can confront them with a number of particular propositions, we have frequently had recourse thereto, and we have habituated ourselves to remount no further, and to believe that they are the primitive source of truth. The second is the motive of all those reasonings which consist in a reduction to what is absurd.

OBSERVATION.

The process recommended in this aphorism is a species of proof to which we submit the projected operation. It is very useful to avoid error, for if the judgment we examine is found in opposition to anterior ones which are just, or necessarily connected with false consequences, it is evidently necessary to reject it; but this same process does not lead us directly and necessarily to truth, for it may be that no determining motive for the affirmative may result from the research.

Aphorism Thirteenth.

In a case in which we want decisive reasons to determine us, no other resource is left us but to endeavour to obtain new lights, that is to say, to introduce new elements into the idea which is the subject of the judgment we are to form. This can be done in two ways only, either by seeking to collect new facts, or by endeavouring to make of those already known combinations which had not previously occurred to us, and thence to draw consequences which we had not before remarked.

OBSERVATION.

The advice contained in this aphorism, is only the developement of the first part of aphorism 9th, and it can be nothing else; for when we are assured that we are not sufficiently acquainted with a subject to judge of it, there is no other resource but to study it more.

Aphorism Fourteenth.

Finally, when the motives of determination fail us invincibly, we should know how to remain in complete doubt, and to suspend absolutely our judgment, rather than rest it on vain and confused appearances, since in these we can never be sure that there are not some false elements.

REMARK AND CONCLUSION.

This is the last and most essential of logical principles; for in following it we may possibly remain in ignorance, but we can never fall into error; all our errors arising always from admitting into that which we know elements which are not really there, and which lead us to consequences which ought not to follow from those that are there effectively.

In effect, if from our first impressions the most simple to our most general ideas, and their most complicated combinations, we have never recognized in our successive perceptions but what is there, our last combinations would be as irreproachable as the first act of our sensibility. Thus, in logical rigour, it is very certain that we ought never to form a judgment but when we see clearly that the subject includes the attributes: that is to say, that the judgment is just.

But at the same time it is also very certain that in the course of life we seldom arrive at certitude, and are frequently obliged, nevertheless, to form a resolution provisionally; to form none being often to adopt one of the most decisive character, without renouncing the principle we have just laid down, or in any manner derogating from it. It is now proper to speak of the theory of probability. It is a subject I encounter with reluctance. First, because it is very difficult, and as yet very little elucidated; next, because one cannot hope to treat it profoundly when one is not perfectly familiar with the combinations of the science of quantities, and of the language proper to them. Finally, because even with these means the nature of the subject deprives us of the hope of arriving at almost any certain result, and leaves us only that of a good calculation of chances. Let us, however, endeavour to form to ourselves an accurate and just idea of it; this will perhaps be already to contribute to its progress.

The science of probability is not a part of logic, and ought not even to be regarded as forming a supplement to it. Logic teaches us to form just judgments, and to make series of judgments: that is to say, of reasonings which are consequent. Now, properly speaking, there are no judgments or series of judgments which are probable. When we judge that an opinion or a fact is probable, we judge it positively; and this judgment is just, false, or presumptuous, according as we have perfectly or imperfectly observed the principles of the art of logic. But it will be said, that the science of probability in teaching us to estimate this probability of an opinion, teaches us to judge justly whether this opinion is or is not probable. I admit it: but it produces this effect as the science of the properties of bodies, physics, teaches us to form the judgment that such a property appertains to such a body; as the science of extension teaches us to form the judgment that such a theorem results from the properties of such a figure; as the science of quantity teaches us that such a number is the result of such a calculation; finally, as all the sciences teach us to form sound judgments of the objects, which belong to their province. Nevertheless we cannot say, and we do not say, that they are but parts of logic, nor even that they are supplements to it. They all on the contrary throw light on the subjects of which they treat only in consequence of the means and processes with which they are furnished by sound logic. This is useful to all the sciences; but none of them either aid it immediately, supply its place, make a part of it, or are supplements to it. The science of probability has in this respect no particular privileges under this aspect; it is a science similar to all the others.

But I go further; the science to which we have given the name of the *science of probability,* is not a science: or to explain myself more clearly, we comprehend erroneously under this collective and common name a multitude of sciences or of portions of sciences quite different among themselves, strangers to one another, and which it is impossible to unite without confounding them all. In effect, that which is called commonly the *science of probability* comprehends two very distinct parts, of which one is the research, and the valuation of data, the other is the calculation, or the combination of these same data.

Now the success of the research and valuation of data, if the question is on the probability of a narration, consists in a knowledge of the circumstances, proper to the fact in itself, and to all those who have spoken of it: thus it depends on and forms a part of the science of history. If the question is on the probability of a physical event, this research of data consists in acquiring a knowledge of anterior facts and of their connection: thus it appertains to physics. If the question is on the probable results of a social institution, or of the deliberations of an assembly of men, the anterior facts are the details of the social organization, or of the intellectual dispositions and operations of these men: thus it depends on social and moral science, or on ideology. Finally, when it is only to foresee the chances of the play of *cross* and *pile,* the data would be the construction of the piece, the manner of resistance of the medium in which it moves, that of the bodies against which it may strike, the motion proper to the arm which casts it, and which are more or less easy to it. Thus these data would still depend on the physical constitution of animate and inanimate bodies. Then as to the research of data, and to the fixation of their importance, the pretended science of probability is composed of a multitude of different sciences, according to the subject on which it is employed; and consequently it is not a particular science.

As to the combination of the data once established, the science of probability is nothing, when we employ calculation therein, but the science of quantity or of calculation itself; for the difficulty does not consist in giving to abstract unity any concrete value whatever, and sometimes one and sometimes another, but in knowing all the resources which perfect calculation furnishes to make of this unity and of all its multiplied combinations the most complicated, and to connect them regularly without losing their thread.

We see then that neither in regard to the research and valuation of data, nor in regard to the combinations of these same data, the pretended science of probability is not a particular science distinct from every other.

We might rather consider it either as a branch of the science of quantities, and as an employment which we make of it in certain parts of several different sciences which are susceptible of this application, or as the reunion of scattered portions of many sciences, strangers the one to the other, which have only so much in common as to give place to such questions as can only be resolved by a very learned and very delicate employment of the admirable means of calculation furnished by the science of quantities in the state of perfection which it has at this time attained; but this is not seeing the theory of probability in its full extent, for we cannot always employ calculation in the estimation of probability. Nevertheless this manner of considering and decomposing what is called the *science of probability* explains to us already many of the things which concern it, and puts us in the way of forming to ourselves an accurate and complete idea of it.

We see first why it is the mathematicians who have had the idea of it, and who have, if we may so say, created and made it entirely. It is because such as they have conceived it, it consists principally in the employment of a powerful agent which was at their disposal; they have been able to push to a great length speculations which other men have been obliged to abandon in consequence of a want of means to pursue them.

We also see why these mathematicians principally and almost entirely employed themselves on subjects of which the data are very simple, such as the chances of games of hazard, and of lotteries, or the effects of the interest of money lent; it is because their principal advantage consisting in their great skill in calculation, they have with reason preferred the objects where this art is almost every thing, and where the choice and valuation of data present scarcely any difficulty; and it is in fact in cases of this kind that they have obtained a success both curious and useful.

We moreover see why it is that all the efforts of these mathematicians, even the most skilful, when they have undertaken to treat in the same manner subjects of which the data were numerous, subtile and complicated, have produced little else than witty conceits which may be called *difficiles nugae,* learned trifles. It is because the farther they have pursued the consequences resulting from the small number of data which they have been able to obtain, the farther they have departed from the consequences which these same data would have produced, united with all those often more important, which they have been obliged to neglect from inability to unravel and appreciate them. This is the cause why we have seen great calculators, after the most learned combinations, give us forms of balloting the most defective, not having taken into account a thousand circumstances, inherent in the nature of men and of things, attending only to the circumstance of the number of the one and of the other. It is the reason why Condorcet himself,[1] when he undertook to apply the theory of probabilities to the decisions of assemblies, and particularly to the judgments of tribunals, either has not ventured to decide any thing on actual institutions, and has confined himself to reasoning on imaginary hypothesis, or has often been led to expedients absolutely impracticable, or which would have inconveniencies more serious than those he wished to avoid.

Whatever respect I bear to the great intelligence and high capacity of this truly superior and ever to be regretted man, I do not fear to pass so bold a sentence on this part of his labors, for I am in some measure authorized to do it by himself. The title of Essay which he has given to his treatise, and the motto which he has prefixed to it, prove how much he doubted of the success of such an enterprise, and what confirms it is, that in his last work, composed on the eve of an unfortunate death, in which he has traced with so firm a hand the history of the progress of the human mind, and in which he has assigned to the theory of probabilities so great a part in the future success of the moral sciences, he uses with all the candour which characterises him these expressions, page 362—"This application, notwithstanding the happy efforts of some geometricians, is still, if I may so say, but in its first elements, and it must open to following generations a source of intelligence truly inexhaustible." Yet he had then made not only the learned essay of which we are speaking, but also a work greatly superior, the *Elements of the Calculation of Probabilities and of its Application to games of chance, to lotteries and to the judgments of men,* which were not published till the year 1805.

I believe, then, that I have advanced nothing rash in observing that in subjects difficult by the number, subtility, complexity and intimate

---

1. Marie-Jean-Antoine-Nicolas de Caritat, marquis de Condorcet (1743–94), French philosopher, mathematician, and political scientist. In 1785 he published his *Essay on the Application of Analysis to the Possibility of Majority Decisions.*

connexion of the circumstances to be considered, without the omission of any of them, the great talent of well combining those, not sufficiently numerous, which have been perceived, has not been sufficient to preserve the most skilful calculators from important errors and great misreckonings. We perceive that that was to be expected. But now I must go further, and all this leads me to a last reflection, which flows from the nature of things, like those which have just been read, which confirms several important principles established in the preceding volumes, which far from annihilating the great hopes of Condorcet tends to assure and realise them, by restraining them within certain limits; but which appear to me to show manifestly, how far the calculation of probabilities is from being the same thing with the theory of probability. Observe in what this observation consists.

The principal object of the theory of probability and its great utility, is in setting out from the reunion of a certain number of given causes, to determine the degree of the probability of the effects which ought to follow; and setting out from the reunion of a certain number of known effects, to determine the degree of the probability of the causes, which have been able to produce them. We may even say that all the results of this theory are but different branches of this general result, and may be traced to be nothing more than parts of it.

Now we have previously seen, and on different occasions, that for beings of any kind, to be successfully submitted to the action of calculation, it is necessary they should be susceptible of adaptation to the clear, precise and invariable divisions of the ideas of quantity, and to the series of the names of numbers and of cyphers, which express them. This is a condition necessary to the validity of every calculation from which that which has probability for its object, cannot be any more exempt, than that which conducts to absolute certainty.

Hence it rigorously follows, that there is a multitude of subjects of which it would be absolutely impossible to calculate the data, if even (which is not always the case) it should be possible to collect them all without overlooking any.

Assuredly the degrees of the capacity, of the probity of men, those of the energy and the power of their passions, prejudices and habits, cannot possibly be estimated in numbers. It is the same as to the degrees of influence of certain institutions, or of certain functions, of the degrees of importance of certain establishments, of the degrees of difficulty of certain discoveries, of the degrees of utility of certain inventions, or of certain processes. I know that of these quantities, truly inappreciable and innumerable in all the rigour of the word, we seek and even attain to a certain point, in determining the limits, by means of number, of the frequency and extent of their effects; but I also know that in these effects which we are obliged to sum and number together as things perfectly similar, in order to deduce results, it is almost always and I may say always impossible to unravel the alterations and variations of concurrent causes, of influencing circumstances, and of a thousand essential considerations, so that we are necessitated to arrange together as similar a multitude of things very different, to arrive only at those preparatory results which are afterwards to lead to others which cannot fail to become entirely fantastical.

Is an example desired, very striking, drawn from a subject which surely does not present as many difficulties of this kind as moral ideas? Here is one. Certainly none of those who have undertaken to estimate the effort of the muscles of the heart, have erred against the rules of calculation, nor, what is more, against the laws of animated mechanics, the certainty of which should still preserve them from many errors. Yet some have been led to estimate this effort at several thousands of pounds, and others only at some ounces; and nobody knows with certainty which are nearest to truth. What succour then can we derive from calculation, when even availing ourselves properly of it we are subject to such aberrations and to such prodigious incertitudes?

It is then true, and I repeat it, that there is a multitude of things to which the calculation of probabilities like every other calculation is completely inapplicable. These things are much more numerous than is generally believed, and even by many very skilful men, and the first step to be taken in the science of probability is to know how to distinguish them. It is for the science of the formation of our ideas, for that of the operations of our intelligence, in a word for sound ideology, to teach us the number of these things, to enable us to know their nature, and to show us the reasons why they are so refractory. And it is a great service which it will render to the human mind, by preventing it in future from making a pernicious use of one of its most excellent instruments. It already shows us that the science of probability is a thing very distinct from the calculation of probability with which it has been confounded, since it extends to many objects to which the other cannot attain. This is what I principally proposed to elucidate.

Finally, as I have before announced, this observation does not destroy the great hopes which the piercing genius of Condorcet had made him conceive from the employment of calculation in general, and from that of probability in particular, in the advancement of the moral sciences; for if the different shades of our moral ideas cannot be expressed in numbers, and if there are many other things relative to social science, which are equally incapable of being estimated and calculated directly, these things depend on others which often render them reducible to calculable quantities, if we may use the expression. Thus for example, the degrees of the value of all things useful and agreeable, that is to say, the degrees of interest we attach to their possession cannot be noted directly by figures, but all those which can be represented by quantities of weight or extension of a particular thing, become calculable and even comparable the one with the other; in like manner the energy and durability of the secret springs which cause and preserve the action of the organs constituting our life are not susceptible of direct appreciation, but we judge of them by their effects. Time and different kinds of resistance and waste are susceptible of very exact divisions. This is sufficient for us, and we derive thence a great multitude of results and of valuable combinations; now there is an infinity of things in the moral sciences which offer us similar resources; but there are also many which offer none, and once more it is of great importance to discriminate perfectly between them: For first, in respect to these latter, every employment of calculation is abusive; and moreover there are often species of quantities presented which appear calculable, but which are inextricably complicated by mixture with those other species of quantities which I permit myself to call *refractory,* and then if calculation be applied thereto, the most skilful mathematicians are inevitably led into enormous errors; against this in my opinion they have not always been sufficiently on their guard. As to these two latter cases we may say of calculation what has been said of the

syllogistic art as to all our reasonings whatsoever; that is, that it conducts
our mind much less correctly than the simple light of good sense aided by
sufficient attention.

This is all I had to observe on the science and calculation of probability,
and I draw from it the following consequences: The theory of probability
is neither a part of nor a supplement to logic. This theory moreover is not a
science separate and distinct from all others. All sciences have a positive and
a conjectural part. In all of them the positive part consists in distinguishing the effects which always and necessarily follow certain causes, and the
causes which always and necessarily produce certain effects. In all of them
also the conjectural part consists in proceeding from the reunion of a certain number of given causes to determine the degrees of probability of
the effects which ought to follow from them, and in proceeding from the
reunion of a certain number of known effects to determine the degree of
probability of the causes which have been able to produce them. In these
two parts, when the ideas compared are not of a nature to comport with the
application of the names of numbers and of figures, we can only employ
the ordinary instruments of reasoning, that is to say our vulgar languages,
their forms, and the words which compose them. In these two parts equally
when the ideas compared by the clearness, constancy, and precision of their
subdivisions are susceptible of adaptation to the divisions of the series of
the names of numbers, and of figures, we can employ with great advantage,
instead of the ordinary instruments of reasoning, the instruments proper
to the science of the ideas of quantity, that is to say, the language of calculation, its formulas, and its signs. It is this which constitutes in respect to the
conjectural part the calculation of probability. It is necessary to distinguish
it carefully from the science of probability; for the one is of use in all cases
in which the object is a likelihood of any kind whatsoever; it is properly
the conjectural part of all other sciences, whereas the other calculation has
place only in those cases in which we can employ the language of calculation; it is but an instrument, of which unhappily the science of probability
cannot always avail itself.

The science of probability consists in the talent and sagacity necessary to
know the data, to chuse them, to perceive their degrees of importance, to
arrange them in convenient order, a talent to which it is very difficult
to prescribe precise rules, because it is often the product of a multitude of

unperceived judgments. On the contrary, the calculation of probability, properly so called, consists only in following correctly the general rules of the language of calculation in those cases in which it can be employed.

This calculation is often extremely useful and extremely learned; but it is necessary carefully to distinguish the occasions on which we can avail ourselves of it, for however little the ideas which we attempt to calculate are mingled with those which I have named *refractory,* and which are truly incalculable, we are inevitably led into the most excessive miscalculations. It is what I think has happened but too frequently to skilful men, who by their knowledge, and even by their mistakes, have put us into the way of discovering their cause.

I will limit myself to this small number of results. I perceive that it is to diffuse but little direct light on a subject, which is so much the more important and the more extensive, as unfortunately certitude is for the most part far from us. But if I have contributed to the formation of a just and clear idea of it I shall not have been useless. I have much more reason than Condorcet for saying *"I have not thought that I was giving a good work, but merely a work calculated to give birth to better ones, &c."*

Not wishing to occupy myself longer with the conjectural part of our knowledge, and not believing it necessary to add to the small number of principles which I have established before this long digression, and which embrace in my opinion every thing of importance in the logical art, such as it proceeds from true logical science; it only remains for me to endeavour to make a happy application of this art to the study of our *will and its effects.* It is this I am going to undertake, with a hope that my instruments being better, I may better succeed than perhaps men more skilful but not so well armed.

---

* See page 183 of the preliminary discourse to the essay on the application of analysis to the probability of decisions, given by a plurality of votes, 1785, à l'Imprimerie royale.

This discourse, and the Elements of the same author which I have already cited,[2] and the excellent lesson of M. Delaplace, which are to be found in the collection of the Normal schools, are, in my opinion, the three works in which we are best able to see the general spirit and process of the calculation of probabilities, and where we can the most easily discover the causes of its advantages and inconveniences, although they are not yet there completely developed.

2. The next two subclauses are not found in the French edition.

Second Section
of the
Elements of Ideology, or a treatise on the will and its effects.

ⷯ

Introduction.

SECTION FIRST.

The faculty of willing is a mode and a consequence of the faculty of feeling.

What has been now read is the end of all that I had to say of human intelligence, considered under the relation of its means of knowing and understanding. This analysis of our understanding, and of that of every other animated being, such as we conceive and imagine it, is not perhaps either as perfect or as complete as might be desired; but I believe at least that it discovers clearly to us the origin and the source of all our knowledge, and the true intellectual operations which enter into its composition, and that it shows us plainly the nature and species of certitude of which this knowledge is susceptible, and the disturbing causes which render it uncertain or erroneous.

Strengthened with these data we can therefore endeavour to avail ourselves of them, and employ our means of knowledge either in the study of the will and its effects to complete the history of our intellectual faculties, or in the study of those beings which are not ourselves; in order to acquire a just idea of what we are able to know of this singular universe delivered to our eager curiosity.

I think for the reasons before adduced, that it is the first of these two researches which ought to occupy us in the first place. Consequently I shall go back to the point at which I endeavoured to trace the plan; and I shall permit myself to repeat here what I then said in my logic, chap. 9th, page 432. Obliged to be consequent, I must be pardoned for recalling the point from whence I set out.

This second manner I have said of considering our individuals, presents us a system of phenomena so different from the first, that we can scarcely believe it appertains to the same beings, seen merely under a different aspect. Doubtless we could conceive man as only receiving impressions, recollecting, comparing and combining them always with a perfect indifference. He would then be only a being, *knowing and understanding* without *passion*, properly so called (relatively to himself) and without *action* relatively to other beings, for he would have no motive to *will*, and no reason and no means to *act*; and certainly on this supposition whatever were his faculties for judging and knowing they would rest in great stagnation, for want of a stimulant and agent to exercise them. But this is not man; he is a being *willing* in consequence of his impressions and of his knowledge, and *acting* in consequence of his will.* It is that which constitutes him on the one part susceptible of sufferings and enjoyments, of happiness and misery, ideas correlative and inseparable, and on the other part capable of influence and of power. It is that which causes him to have *wants* and *means*, and consequently *rights* and *duties*, either merely when he has relation with inanimate beings only, or more still when he is in contact with other beings, susceptible also of enjoying and suffering; for the rights of a sensible being are all in its wants, and its duties in its means; and it is to be remarked that weakness in all its forms is always and essentially the principle of rights; and that power, in whatsoever sense we take this word, is not and can never be but the source of duties, that is to say of rules for the manner of employing this power."[1]

Where there is nothing, the old proverb justly says the king loses his right: but a king as another person cannot lose his rights, but in as much as another

---

* We may say as much of all animated beings which we know, and even of all those we imagine.

1. The remaining lines of this paragraph are not found in the French edition.

individual loses his duties in regard to him; which is saying in an inverse sense, that he who can do nothing, has no more duties to fulfil, has no longer any rule to follow for the employment of his power, since it has become null. That is very true.

Wants and *means, rights* and *duties,* arise then from the faculty of will; if man willed nothing he would have nothing of all these. But to have wants and means, rights and duties, is to *have,* is to *possess,* something. These are so many species of *property,* taking this word in its most extensive signification: They are things which appertain to us. Our means are even a real property, and the first of all, in the most restrained sense of the term. Thus the ideas, *wants* and *means, rights* and *duties,* imply the idea of *property;* and the ideas of *riches* and *deprivation, justice* and *injustice,* which are derived from them, could not exist without that of *property.* We must begin then by explaining this latter; and this can only be done by returning to its origin. Now this idea of *property* can only be founded on the idea of *personality.* For if an individual had not a consciousness of his own existence, distinct and separate from every other, he could possess nothing, he could have nothing peculiar to himself. We must first therefore examine and determine the idea of *personality;* but before proceeding on this examination, there is yet a necessary preliminary; it is to explain with clearness and precision what the willing faculty is, from which we maintain that all these ideas arise, and on account of which we wish to give its history. We have no other means of seeing clearly how this faculty produces these ideas, and how all the consequences which result from it may be regarded as its effects. It is thus that always by returning, or rather by descending step by step, we are inevitably led to the study and observation of our intellectual faculties, whenever we wish to penetrate to the bottom of whatever subject engages us. This truth is perhaps more precious in itself than all those we shall be able to collect in the course of our work. I will commence then by an exposition of that in which the *willing* faculty consists.

This faculty, or the *will,* is one of the four primordial faculties, which we have recognized in the human understanding, and even in that of all animated beings, and into which we have seen that the faculty of *thinking* or of *feeling* necessarily resolves itself when we decompose it into its true elements, and when we admit into it nothing factitious.

We have considered the faculty of willing as the fourth and last of these four primitive and necessary subdivisions of sensibility; because in every desire, in every act of willing or volition, in a word, in every propensity whatsoever, we can always conceive the act of experiencing an impression, that of judging it good either to seek or avoid, and even that of recollecting it to a certain point, since by the very nature of the act of judging we have seen that the idea, which is the subject of every judgment, can always be considered as a representation of the first impression which this idea has made. Thus more or less confusedly, more or less rapidly, an animated being has always felt, recollected and judged, previously to willing.

It must not be concluded from this analysis that I consider the willing faculty as only that of having definitive and studied sentiments which are specially called *desires,* and which may be called *express and formal acts of the will.* On the contrary I believe that to have a just idea of it, we must form one much more extensive; and nothing previously established prevents us from it: for since we have said that even in a desire the most mechanical, and the most sudden, and in a determination the most instinctive, the most purely organic, we ought always to conceive the acts of feeling, recollecting and judging, as therein implicitly and imperceptibly included, and as having necessarily preceded it, were it only for an inappreciable instant, we can without contradicting ourselves regard all these propensities, even the most sudden and unstudied, as appertaining to the faculty of willing; though we have made it the fourth and the last of the elementary faculties of our intelligence. I even think it is necessary to do so, and that the will is really and properly the general and universal faculty of finding one thing preferable to another, that of being so affected as to love better such an impression, such a sentiment, such an action, such a possession, such an object, than such another. *To love* and *to hate* are words solely relative to this faculty, which would have no signification if it did not exist; and its action takes place on every occasion on which our *sensibility experiences any attraction or repulsion whatsoever.* At least it is thus I conceive the will in all its generality; and it is by proceeding from this manner of conceiving it that I will attempt to explain its effects and consequences.

Without doubt the will, thus conceived, is a part of sensibility. The faculty of being affected in a particular manner cannot but be a part of the faculty of being affected in general. But it is a distinct mode of it, and one which may be separated from it in thought. We cannot will without a cause (this is a thing very necessary to be remarked, and never to be forgotten); thus we cannot will without having felt, but we may always feel in such a manner as never to will. We have already said that we can imagine man, or any other animated and sensible being, as feeling in such a manner that every thing would be equal to him; that all his affections, although distinct, would be indifferent to him; and that consequently he could neither desire nor fear any thing; that is to say he could not will, for to desire and to fear is to will: and to will is never but to desire something and to fear the contrary, or reciprocally. On this supposition an animated and sensible being would yet be a feeling being. He could even be discerning and knowing, that is to say judging. It will be sufficient for this that he should feel the difference of his various perceptions, and the different circumstances of each, although incapable of a predilection for any of them, or for any of the combinations of them which he can make; only, and we have before made the remark, the knowledge of the animated being thus constituted would necessarily be very limited. Because his faculty of knowing would have no motive of action; and his faculty of acting, if even it existed, could not exercise itself with intention, since to have an intention he must have a desire, and every desire supposes a preference of some sort.

I will observe, by the way, that this supposition of a perfect indifference in sensibility shows very clearly, in my opinion, that it is erroneously that certain persons have wished to make of what they call our *sentiments* and *affections,* modifications of our being essentially different from those which they name *perceptions* or *ideas,* and refuse to comprehend them under those general denominations of *perceptions* or *ideas:* for the quality of being effective, which certain of our perceptions have, is but a particular circumstance, an accidental quality, with which all our modifications might be endowed; and of which, as we have just seen, all might likewise be deprived. But they would not be the less, as they are in effect *perceptions,* that is to say things perceived or felt. The proof is that some of these modifications, after having possessed the quality of being effective, lose it by the effect of habit, and others which acquire it through reflection, all without ceasing to be perceived, and consequently without ceasing to be *perceptions.* I think therefore that the word *perception* is truly the generic term.

As to the distinction established between the words *perception* and *idea,* I do not think it more legitimate if founded on the pretended property of an idea being an image. For the idea of a *peartree* is no more the image of a tree, than the perception of the relation of three to four is the image of the difference of these two figures, and no one of the modifications of our sensibility is the image of any thing which takes place around us. I think then, that we may regard the words *perception* and *idea* as synonimous in their most extensive signification, and for the same reasons the words *think* and *feel* as equivalent also when taken in all their generality: For all our thoughts are things felt; and if they were not felt they would be nothing; and sensibility is the general phenomenon which constitutes and comprehends the whole existence of an animated being, at least for himself; and inasmuch as he is an *animated being,* it is the only condition which can render him a *thinking being.*

However this may be, none of the animated beings which we know, nor even of those we can imagine, are indifferent to all their perceptions. It is always comprised in their sensibility, in their faculty of being affected, of their being so affected as that certain perceptions appear to them what we call *agreeable,* and certain others *disagreeable.* Now it is this which constitutes the faculty of willing. Now that we have formed to ourselves a perfectly clear idea of it we shall easily be able to see how this faculty produces the ideas of *personality* and *property.*

Section Second.

From the faculty of willing arise the ideas of *personality* and *property.*

Every man who pronounces the word *I* (*myself*) without being a metaphysician understands very well what he means to say, and yet being a metaphysician he often succeeds very badly in giving an account of it, or in explaining it. We will endeavour to accomplish this by the aid of some very simple reflections.

It is not our body such as it is to others, and such as it appears to them which we call our *self.* The proof is that we know very well to say how our body will be when we shall exist no more, that is to say when our *self* shall be no more. There are then two very distinct beings.

It is not moreover any of the particular faculties we possess, which is for us the same thing as *our self.* For we say I have the faculty of walking, of eating, sleeping, of breathing, &c. Thus *I* or my *self,* who possess, am a thing distinct from the thing possessed.

Is it the same with the general faculty of feeling? At the first glance it appears that the answer must be yes, since I say in the same manner I have the faculty of feeling. Notwithstanding, here we find a great difference if we penetrate further. For if I ask myself how I know that I have the faculty of walking? I answer I know it because I feel it, or because I experience it, because I see it, which is still to feel it. But if I ask myself how I know that I feel, I am obliged to answer I know it because I feel it. The faculty of feeling is then that which manifests to us all the others, without which none of them would exist for us, whilst it manifests itself that it is its own principle to itself; that it is that beyond which we are not able to return, and which constitutes our existence; that it is every thing for *us;* that it is the same thing as *ourselves.* I feel because I feel: I feel because I exist; and *I* do not exist but because *I* feel. Then my existence and my sensibility are one and the same thing. Or in other words the existence of *myself* and the sensibility of *myself* are two identical beings.

If we pay attention that in discourse *I* or *myself* signifies always the moral being or *person* who *speaks,* we shall find that (to express ourselves with exactness) instead of saying *I have the faculty of walking* I ought to say the faculty of feeling, which constitutes the moral person who speaks to you has the property of reacting on his legs in such a manner that his body walks. And instead of saying *I have the faculty of feeling,* I ought to say the faculty of feeling which constitutes the moral person who speaks to you exists in the body by which he speaks to you. These modes of expression are odd and unusual I agree, but in my opinion they paint the fact with much truth; for in all our conversations, as in all our relations, it is always one faculty of feeling which addresses itself to another.

The *self* of each of us is therefore for him his proper *sensibility,* whatsoever be the nature of this sensibility; or what he calls his soul, if he has a decided opinion of the nature of the principle of this same sensibility. It is so true that it is this that we all understand by our *self,* that we all regard apparent death as the end of our being, or as a passage to another existence, according as we think that it extinguishes or does not extinguish all sentiment. It is then the sole fact of sensibility which gives us the idea of *personality,* that is to say which makes us perceive that we are a *being,* and which constitutes for us *ourself,* our being.

There is, however, and we have already remarked it,* another of our faculties with which we often identify our *self,* that is our will. We say indifferently it depends on me, or it depends on my will to do such or such a thing; but this observation very far from contradicting the preceding analysis confirms it, for the faculty of willing is but a mode of the faculty of feeling; it is our faculty of feeling so modified as to render it capable to enjoy and to suffer, and to react on our organs. Thus to take the will as the equivalent of *self,* is to take a part for the whole; it is to regard as the equivalent of this *self* the portion of sensibility which constitutes all its energy, that from which we can scarcely conceive it separated, and without which it would be almost null, if it would not even be entirely annihilated. There is then nothing there contrary to what we have just established.

It remains then well understood and admitted that the *self* or the moral *person* of every animated being, conceived as distinct from the organs it causes to move, is either simply the abstract existence which we call the *sensibility* of this individual, which results from his organization or a *monade* without extension; which is supposed eminently to possess this sensibility, and which is also clearly an abstract being (if indeed we comprehend this supposition), or a little body, subtile, etherial, imperceptible, impalpable, endowed with this sensibility and which is still very nearly an abstraction. These three suppositions are indifferent for all which is to follow. In all three *sensibility* is found; and in all three also it alone constitutes the *self,* or the moral person of the individual, whether it be but a phenomenon resulting from his organization, or a property of a spiritual or corporeal mind resident within him.

There remains then but one question, which is to know if this idea of *personality,* this consciousness of *self,* would arise in us from our sensibility in the case in which it would not be followed by *will,* in the case in which it would be deprived of this mode which causes it to enjoy and suffer, and to react on our organs, which in a word renders it capable of *action* and of

---

* See vol. 1st. chap. 13th, page 295, second edition.

passion. This question cannot be resolved by facts, for we know no sensibility of this kind, and if any such existed it could not manifest itself to our means of knowledge. For the same reason the question is more curious than useful; but whatever is curious has an indirect utility, above all in these matters which can never be viewed on too many different sides: we must not then neglect it.

On the point in question we certainly cannot pronounce with assurance that a being which should feel without affection, properly so called, and without reaction on its organs, would not have the idea of *personality,* and that of the existence of its *self.* It even appears to me probable that it would have the idea of the existence of this *self:* for in fact to feel any thing whatever, is to feel its *self* feeling, it is to know its *self* feeling: it is to have the possibility of distinguishing *self* from that which *self* feels; from the modifications of *self.* But at the same time it is beyond doubt that the being which should thus know its own *self* would not know it by opposition with other beings, from which it would be able to distinguish and separate it; since it would know only *itself* and its modes. It would be for itself the true infinite or indefinite, as I have elsewhere remarked,* without term or limit of any kind, not knowing any thing else. It would not then properly know itself in the sense we attach to the word to know, which always imports the idea of circumscription and of speciality; and consequently it would not have the idea of *individuality* and of *personality,* in opposition and distinction from other beings as we have it. We may already assure ourselves that this idea, such as it is in us and for us, is a creation and an effect of our faculty of willing; and this explains very clearly why, although the sole faculty of feeling simply constitutes and establishes our existence, yet we confound and identify by preference our *self* with our *will.* Here I think is a first point elucidated.

A thing still more certain, perhaps, and which will advance us a step further, is that if it is possible that the idea of individuality and personality should exist in the manner we have said, in a being conceived to be endowed with sensibility without will, at least it is impossible it should produce there the idea of property such as we have it. For our idea of property

---

* See vol. 3d, chap. 5, p. 27.

is privative and exclusive: it entails the idea that the thing possessed belongs to a sensible being, and belongs to none but him, to the exclusion of all others. Now it cannot be that it exists thus in the head of a being which knows nothing but itself, which does not know that any other beings besides itself exists. If then we should suppose that this being knows its *self* with sufficient accuracy to distinguish it from its modes, and to regard its different modifications as attributes of this *self*, as things which this *self* possesses, this being would still not have completely our idea of property. For this it is necessary to have the idea of *personality* very completely, and such as we have just seen that we form it when we are susceptible of *passion* and of *action*. It is then proved that this idea of property is an effect, a production of our willing faculty.

But what is very necessary to be remarked, because it has many consequences, is, that if it be certain that the idea of property can arise only in a being endowed with will, it is equally certain that in such a being it arises necessarily and inevitably in all its plenitude; for as soon as this individual knows accurately *itself*, or its moral person, and its capacity to enjoy and to suffer, and to act necessarily, it sees clearly also that this *self* is the exclusive proprietor of the body which it animates, of the organs which it moves, of all their passions and their actions; for all this finishes and commences with this *self*, exists but by it, is not moved but by its acts, and no other moral person can employ the same instruments nor be affected in the same manner by their effects. The idea of property and of exclusive property arises then necessarily in a sensible being from this alone, that it is susceptible of passion and action; and it rises in such a being because nature has endowed it with an inevitable and inalienable property, that of its individuality.

It was necessary there should be a natural and necessary property, as there exists an artificial and conventional one; for there can never be any thing in art which has not its radical principle in nature; we have already made the observation elsewhere.* If our gestures and our cries had not the natural and inevitable effect of denoting the ideas which affect us, they never would have become their artificial and conventional signs. If it were not in

---

* See on this subject, vol. 1st. chap. 16th, page 339, second edition, and different parts of the 2d and 3d volumes.

nature that every solid body sustained above our heads necessarily sheltered us we should never have had houses made expressly for shelter. In the same manner, if there never had been natural and inevitable *property* there never would have been any artificial or conventional. This is universally the case, and we cannot too frequently repeat, man creates nothing, he makes nothing absolutely new or extra-natural (if we may be allowed the expression), he never does any thing but draw consequences and make combinations from that which already is. It is also as impossible for him to create an idea or a relation which has not its source in nature as to give himself a sense which has no relation with his natural senses. From this it also follows that in every research which concerns man it is necessary to arrive at this first type; for as long as we do not see the natural model of an artificial institution which we examine we may be sure we have not discovered its generation, and consequently we do not know it completely.

This observation will meet with many explications. It appears to me that we have not always paid sufficient attention to it, and that it is for this reason we have often discoursed on the subject which now occupies us in a very useless and vague manner. We have brought *property* to a solemn trial at bar and exhibited the reasons for and against it as if it depended on us, whether there should or should not be property in this world. But this is entirely to mistake our nature. It seems were we to listen to certain philosophers and legislators that at a precise instant people have taken into their heads spontaneously, and without cause, to say *thine* and *mine,* and that they could and even should have dispensed with it. But *the thine* and *the mine* were never invented. They were acknowledged the day on which we could say *thee* and *me;* and the idea of *me* and *thee* or rather of *me* and something *other than me,* has arisen, if not the very day on which a feeling being has experienced impressions, at least the one on which, in consequence of these impressions, he has experienced the sentiment of willing, the possibility of acting, which is a consequence thereof, and a resistance to this sentiment and to this act. When afterwards among these resisting beings, consequently other than himself, the feeling and willing being has known that there were some feeling like himself, it has been forced to accord to them a *personality* other than his own, a *self* other than his own and different from his own. And it always has been impossible, as it always will be, that that which is *his* should not for him be different from that which is *theirs*. It was not requisite therefore to discuss at first whether it is well or ill that there exists such or such species of property, the advantages and inconveniences of which we shall see by the sequel; but it was necessary first of all to recognize that there is a property, fundamental, anterior and superior to every institution, from which will always arise all the sentiments and dis-sentiments which are derived from all the others; for there is property, if not precisely every where that there is an individual sentient, at least every where that there is an individual willing in consequence of his sentiment, and acting in consequence of his will. These, or I am greatly mistaken, are eternal truths, against which will fail all the declamations that have nothing for their base but an ignorance of our true existence; and which are indebted to this ignorance for the great credit they have enjoyed at different times, and in different countries.

As no authority can impose on me when it is contrary to evidence, I will say frankly that the same forgetfulness of the true condition of our being is found in this famous precept, so much boasted: *Love thy neighbour as thyself.* It exhorts us to a sentiment which is very good and very useful to propagate, but which is certainly also very badly expressed; for to take this expression in all the rigour of the injunction it is inexecutable; it is as if they should tell us, *with your eyes, such as they are, see your own visage as you see that of others.* This cannot be. Without doubt we are able to love another as much and even more than ourselves, in the sense that we should rather die, bearing with us the hope of preserving his life, than to live and to suffer the grief of losing him. But to love him exactly as ourself, and otherwise than relatively to ourself, once more I say is impossible. It would be necessary for this, to live his life as we do our own.* This has no meaning for beings constituted as we are. It is contrary to the work of our creation, in what manner soever it has been operated.

I am very far from saying the same things of this other precept, which people regard as almost synonimous with the first. *Love ye one another, and*

---

* It is in consequence of a confused notion of this truth that people have never imagined expressions more tender, than to call one *my life, my heart, my soul;* it is as though one should call him *myself.* There is always something hyperbolical in these expressions.

the law is accomplished. This is truly admirable, both for its form and substance. It is also as conformable to our nature as the other is repugnant to it; and it enounces perfectly a very profound truth. Effectively sentiments of benevolence being for us, under every imaginable relation, the source of all our good of every kind, and the universal means of diminishing and remedying all our evils as much as possible, as long as we maintain them amongst ourselves the great law of our happiness is accomplished, in as great a degree as possible.

I shall be accused perhaps of futility for the distinction which I establish between two maxims, to which nearly the same meaning has been commonly attributed; but it will be wrong. It is so different to present to men as a rule of their conduct a general principle, drawn from the recesses of their nature, or one repugnant to it, and it leads to consequences so distant among themselves, that one must never have reflected on it at all not to have perceived all its importance. To myself it appears such, that I cannot conceive that two maxims so dissimilar should have emanated from the same source;*† for the one manifests to me the most profound ignorance, and the other the most profound knowledge of human nature. One would lead us to compose the romance of man, and the other his history. The one consecrates the existence of natural property, resulting from individuality, and the other seems to disregard it. Perhaps it may be wondered that I should treat at the same time the question of the property of all our riches, and that of all our sentiments, and thus mingle economy and morality; but, when we penetrate to their fundamental basis, it does not appear to me possible to separate either these two orders of things or their study. In proportion as we advance, the objects separate and subdivide themselves, and it becomes necessary to examine them separately; but in their principles they are intimately united. We should not have the property of any of our

---

* I conclude from hence that the expression of the one or the other of these precepts, and perhaps of both, has been altered by men, who did not really understand either. I shall often have occasion to make reflections of this kind, because they are applicable to many of these maxims which pass from age to age.

† The first is from Leviticus, chap. xix. The other is from the gospel of St. John, chap. xiii. See the remark in the questions on the miracles, Voltaire vol. 60, page 186. You will be astonished to see that Voltaire considered these two maxims as identical.

goods whatsoever if we had not that of our wants, which is nothing but that of our sentiments; and all these properties are inevitably derived from the sentiment of personality, from the consciousness of our *self.*

It is then quite as useless to the purpose of morality or economy, to discuss whether it would not be better that nothing should appertain *exclusively* to each one of us, as it would be to the purpose of grammar to enquire whether it would not be more advantageous that our actions should not be the *signs* of the ideas and the sentiments which produce them. In every case it would be to ask whether it would not be desirable that we should be quite different from what we are; and indeed it would be to enquire, whether it would not be better that we did not exist at all; for these conditions being changed our existence would not be conceivable. It would not be altered, it would be annihilated.

It remains therefore certain that the *thine* and the *mine* are necessarily established amongst men; from this alone, that they are individuals feeling, willing, and acting distinctly the one from the other, that they have each one the inalienable, incommutable, and inevitable property, in their individuality and its faculties; and that consequently the idea of *property* is the necessary result, if not of the sole phenomenon of pure sensibility, at least of that of sensibility united to the will. Thus we have found how the sentiment of *personality* or the idea of *self,* and that of *property* which flows from it necessarily, are derived from our faculty of willing. Now we may enquire with success, how this same faculty produces all our *wants* and all our *means.*

Section Third.

From the faculty of willing arise all our *wants* and all our *means.*

If we had not the idea of *personality,* and that of *property,* that is to say the consciousness of our *self,* and that of the *possession* of its modifications, we should certainly never have either *wants* or *means;* for to whom would appertain this *suffering* and this *power.* We should not exist for ourselves; but as soon as we recognize ourselves as possessors of our existence, and of its modes, we are necessarily by this alone a compound of weakness and of strength, of wants and means, of suffering and power, of passion and action, and consequently of rights and duties. It is this we are now to explain.

I commence by noticing that, conformably to the idea I have before given of the willing faculty, I will give indifferently the name of *desire* or of *will* to all the acts of this faculty, from the propensity the most instinctive to the determination the most studied; and I request then that it may be recollected that it is solely because we perform such acts that we have the ideas of *personality* and of *property.* Now every desire is a want, and all our wants consist in a desire of some sort; thus the same intellectual acts, emanating from our willing faculty, which cause us to acquire the distinct and complete idea of our *personality,* our *self,* and of the exclusive *property* of all its modes, are also those which render us susceptible of *wants,* and which constitute all our wants. This will appear very clearly.

In the first place every desire is a want. This is not doubtful, since a sensible being, who desires any thing whatsoever, has from this circumstance alone a want to possess the thing desired, or rather, and more generally we may say, that he experiences the want of the cessation of his desire; for every desire is in itself a suffering as long as it continues. It does not become an enjoyment but when it is satisfied, that is to say when it ceases.

It is difficult at first to believe that every desire is a suffering; because there are certain desires, the birth of which in an animated being is always, or almost always, accompanied by a sentiment of well being. The desire of eating for example, that of the physical pleasures of love, are generally in an individual the results of a state of health, of which he has a consciousness that is agreeable to him. Many others are in the same case; but this circumstance must not deceive us. These are the simultaneous manners of being of which we have spoken in our logic,* which mingle themselves with the ideas, come at the same time with them and alter them; but which must not be confounded with them and which consequently it is necessary well to distinguish from desire in itself. For first, they do not always co-exist with it. We have often the want of eating, and even a violent inclination to the act of reproduction, in consequence of sickly dispositions, and without any

---

* See logic, vol. 3d, chap. 6th page 315, and following.

sentiment of well being; and it is the same of other examples which might be chosen. Secondly, were this not to happen, it would not be less true that the sentiment of well being is distinct and different from that of desire; and that that of desire is always in itself a torment, a painful sentiment as long as it continues. The proof is, that it is always the desire of being delivered from that state, whatsoever it is, in which we actually are; which consequently appears actually a state of uneasiness, more or less displeasing. Now in this sense a manner of being is always in effect what it appears to be, since it consists only in what it appears to be to him who experiences it: a desire then is always a suffering either light or profound, according to its force, and consequently a want of some kind. It is not necessary for the truth of this that this desire should be founded on a real want, that is to say on a just sentiment of our true interest; for, whether well or ill founded, while it exists it is a manner of being felt and incommodious, and from which we have consequently a want of being delivered. Thus every desire is a want.

But moreover all our wants, from the most purely mechanical to the most spiritualized, are but the want of satisfying a desire. Hunger is but a desire of eating, or at least of relief from the state of langour which we experience; as the want, the thirst of riches, or that of glory, is but the desire of possessing these advantages, and of avoiding indigence or obscurity.

It is true, however, that if we experience desires without real wants, we have also often real wants without experiencing desires; in this sense that many things are often very necessary to our greater well being, and even to our preservation, without our perceiving it, and consequently without our desiring them. Thus for example, it is certain that I have the greatest interest, or if you please want, that certain combinations, of which I have no suspicion, should not take place within me, and from which it will result that I shall have a fever this evening; but to speak exactly I have not at present the effective want of counteracting these injurious combinations, since I am not aware of their existence; whereas I shall really have the actual want of being delivered from the fever, when I shall suffer the anguish of it, and because I shall suffer the anguish of it; for if the fever were not of a nature to produce in me, for some reason or other, the desire of its cessation, when I should be aware of its proximate or remote effects, I should not have in any manner the want of causing it to cease. We may absolutely say the same things of all the combinations, which take place in the physical or moral order, without our being aware of, or without our foreseeing, the consequences. If then it be true, as we have seen, that every desire is a want, it is not less so that every actual want is a desire. Thus we may lay it down as a general thesis, that *our desires are the source of all our wants,* none of which would exist without them. For we cannot too often repeat it, we should be really impassive if we had no desires; and if we were impassive we should have no wants. I must not be reproached with having taken time for this explication; we cannot proceed too slowly at first: and if I overleap no intermediate proofs, I omit nevertheless, many accessaries, at least all those which are not indispensable.

A first property then of our desires is now well explained; and it is the only one they have, so long as our sensitive system acts and re-acts only on itself. But so soon as it re-acts on our muscular system, the sentiment of willing acquires a second property very different from the first, and which is not less important. It is that of directing all our *actions,* and by this of being the source of all our *means.*

When I say that our desires direct all our actions; it is not that many movements are not operated within us, which the sentiment of willing does not in any manner precede, and which consequently are not the effect of any desire. Of this number are particularly all those which are necessary to the commencement, maintenance and continuation of our life. But first it is permitted to doubt whether at first, and in the origin, they have not taken place in virtue of certain determinations or tendencies really felt by the living molecules, which would make them still the effect of a will more or less obscure; unless it be by the all powerful effect of habit or by the preponderance of certain sentiments more general and predominant, that they become insensible to the animated individual, that is to say, to all results of the combinations which they operate, and finally if it is not for this reason, that they are entirely withdrawn from the empire of perceptible will, or from its sentiment of desiring and willing. These are things of which it is impossible for us to have complete certitude; besides these movements, vulgarly and with reason named *involuntary,* are certainly the cause and the basis of our living existence: but they furnish us no means of modifying, varying, succouring, defending, ameliorating it, &c. They cannot therefore properly be placed in the rank of our means, unless we mean to say that our existence itself is our first mean, which is very true but very insignificant; for it is the datum without which we should have nothing to say, and certainly should say nothing. Thus this first observation does not prevent its being true that our will directs all our actions, which can be regarded as the means of supplying our wants.

The movements of which we have just spoken are not the only ones in us which are involuntary. They are all continued or at least very frequent, and in general regular. But there are others involuntary also, which are more rare, less regular, and which depend more or less on a convulsive and sickly state. The involuntary movements of this second species cannot, any more than the others, be regarded as making part of our individual power. Generally they have no determinate object. Often even they have grievous and pernicious effects for us, and which take place although foreseen, and contrary to our desires. Their independence of our will then does not prevent our general observation from being just. Thus, putting aside these two species of involuntary movements, we may say with truth, that our desires have the effect eminently remarkable of directing all our actions, at least all those that really merit this name, and which are for us the means of procuring enjoyments or knowledge, which knowledge is also an enjoyment; since these are things desired and useful. And we must comprehend in the number of these *actions* our intellectual operations; for they also are for us *means,* and even the most important of all, since they direct the employment of all the others.

Now to complete the proof that the acts of our will are the source of all our means, without exception, it only remains to show that the actions submitted to our will are absolutely the only means we have of supplying our wants, or otherwise satisfying our desires; that is to say, that our physical and moral force, and the use we make of them, compose exactly all our riches.

To recognize this truth in all its details, it would be necessary that we should have already followed all the consequences of the different employments of our faculties, and to have seen their effect in the formation of all that we call our *riches of every kind.* Now it is this we have not yet been able to do, and which we will do in the sequel: it will even be a considerable part of our study. But from this moment we may clearly see that nature, in placing man in a corner of this vast universe, in which he appears but as an imperceptible and ephemeral insect, has given him nothing as his own but his individual and personal faculties, as well physical as intellectual. This is his sole endowment, his only original wealth, and the only source of all which he procures for himself. In effect, if even we should admit that all those beings, by which we are surrounded, have been created for us (and assuredly it needs a great dose of vanity to imagine it, or even to believe it); if, I say, this were so, it would not be less true that we could not appropriate one of those beings, nor convert the smallest parcel of them to our use, but by our action on them and by the employment of our faculties to this effect.

To take examples only from the physical world—

A field is no means of subsistence but as we cultivate it. Game is not useful to us unless we pursue it. A lake, a river, furnish us no nourishment, but because we fish therein. Wood or any other spontaneous production of nature is of no use whatever, until we have fashioned it, or at least gathered it. To put an extreme case, were we to suppose an alimentary matter to have fallen into our mouths ready prepared, still it would be necessary, in order to assimilate it to our substance, that we should masticate, swallow and digest it. Now all these operations are so many employments of our individual force. Certainly if ever man has been doomed to labour, it was from the date of the day in which he was created a sensible being, and having members and organs; for it is not even possible to conceive that any being whatsoever could become useful to him without some action on his part, and we may well say, not only as the good and admirable La Fontaine, that *labour is a treasure;* but even that labour is our only treasure, and this treasure is very great because it surpasses all our wants. The proof is, that like the fortune of a rich man whose revenue surpasses his expenses, the funds of the enjoyment and power of the human species, taken in mass, are always sufficient although often and even always very badly husbanded.

We shall soon see all this with greater developments, and we shall see at the same time that the application of our force to different beings is the sole cause of the value of all those which have a value for us, and consequently is the source of all value; as the property of this same force which necessarily appertains to the individual who is endowed with it, and who directs it by his will, is the source of all property. But from this time I think we may safely conclude, that in the employment of our faculties, in our voluntary actions, consists all the power we have; and that consequently the acts of our will which direct these actions, are the source of all our *means,* as we have seen already that they constitute all our *wants.* Thus this fourth faculty, and last mode of our sensibility, to which we owe the complete ideas of *personality* and *property,* is that which renders us proprietors of *wants* and *means,* of *passion* and of *action,* of *suffering* and of *power.* From these ideas arise those of riches and poverty.

Before proceeding further let us see in what these last consist.

Section Fourth.

From the faculty of willing arise also the ideas of *riches* and *poverty.*

If we had not the distinct consciousness of our *self,* and consequently the ideas of *personality* and of property, we should have no *wants.* All these arise from our desires. And if we had not wants, we should not have the ideas of *riches* and of *poverty;* because to be rich is to possess the means of supplying our wants, and to be poor is to be deprived of these means. An useful or agreeable thing, that is to say a thing of which the possession is an article of riches, is never but a means proximate or remote, of satisfying a want or a desire of some kind; and if we had neither wants nor desires, which are the same things, we should have neither the possession nor the privation of the means of satisfying them.

To take these things in this generality, we perceive plainly that our riches are not composed solely of a precious stone, or of a mass of metal, of an estate in land, or of an utensil, or even of a store of eatables, or a habitation. The knowledge of a law of nature, the habit of a technical process, the use of a language by which to communicate with those of our kind, and to increase our force by theirs, or at least not to be disturbed by theirs in the exercise of our own, the enjoyment of conventions established, and of institutions created in this spirit, are so far the riches of the individual and of the species: for these are so many things useful towards increasing our means, or at least for the free use of them, that is to say, according to our will, and with the least possible obstacle, whether on the part of men or of nature, which is to augment their power, their energy, and their effect.

We call all these *goods;* for by contraction we give the name of *goods* to all those things that contribute to do us *good,* to augment our *well being,* to render our manner of being good or better; that is to say, to all those things, the possession of which is a *good.* Now whence come all those goods? We have already summarily seen, and we shall see it more in detail in the sequel. It is from the just, that is to say from the legitimate, employment, according to the laws of nature, which we make of our faculties. We do not often find a diamond, but because we search for it with intelligence; we have not a mass of metal, but because we have studied the means of procuring it. We do not possess a good field or a good utensil, but because we have well recognised the properties of the first material, and rendered easy the manner of making it useful. We have no provision whatsoever, or even a shelter, but because we have simplified the operations necessary for forming the one, or for constructing the other. It is then always from the employment of our faculties that all these goods arise.

Now all these goods have amongst us, to a certain point, a value determinate and fixed. They even have always two. The one is that of the sacrifices which their acquisition costs us; the other that of the advantages which their possession procures us. When I fabricate an utensil for my use, it has for me the double value of the labour which it costs me in the first place, and of that which it will save me in the sequel. I make a bad employment of my force, if its construction costs me more labour than its possession will save me. It is the same, if instead of making this utensil, I buy it, if the things I give in return have cost me more labor than the utensil would have cost me in making it, or if they would have saved me more labour than this will, I make a bad bargain, I lose more than I gain, I relinquish more than I acquire. This is evident. In the acquisition of any other good than an instrument of labour, the thing is not so clear. However, since it is certain that our physical and moral faculties are our only original riches; that the employment of these faculties, labour of some kind, is our only primitive treasure; and that it is always from this employment that all those things which we call *goods* arise, from the most necessary to the most purely agreeable, it is certain, in like manner, that all these *goods* are but a representation of the labour which has produced them; and that if they have a value, or even two distinct ones, they can only derive these values from that of the labour from which they emanate. Labour itself then has a value; it has then *even* two different ones, for no being can communicate a property which it has not. Yes labour has these two values, the one natural and necessary, the other more or less conventional and eventual. This will be seen very clearly.

An animated being, that is to say sensible and willing, has wants unceasingly reproduced, to the satisfaction of which is attached the continuation of his existence. He cannot provide for them but by the employment of his faculties, of his means; and if this employment (his labour) should cease during a certain time to meet these wants, his existence would end. The mass of these wants, is then the natural and necessary measure of the mass of labour which he can perform whilst they cause themselves to be felt; for if he employs this mass of labour for his direct and immediate use it must suffice for his service. If he consecrates it to another, this other must at least do for him, during this time, what he would have done for himself. If he employs it on objects of an utility less immediate and more remote, this utility, when realised, must at least replace the objects of an urgent utility, which he will have consumed whilst he was occupied with those less necessary. Thus this sum of indispensable wants, or rather that of the value of the objects necessary to supply them, is the natural and necessary measure of the value of the labour performed in the same time. This value is that which the labour inevitably costs. This is the first of the two values, the existence of which we have announced; it is purely natural and necessary.

The second value of our labour, that of what it produces, is from its nature eventual: It is often conventional and always more variable than the first. It is eventual, for no man in commencing any labour whatever, even when it is for his own account, can entirely assure himself of its product; a thousand circumstances, which do not depend on him and which often he cannot foresee, augment or diminish this product. It is often conventional; for when this same man undertakes a labour for another, the quantity of its product, which will result to himself, depends on that which the other shall have agreed to give him in return for his pains, whether the convention were made before the execution of the labour, as with day labourers or wage earners, or does not take place until after the labour has been perfected, as with merchants and manufacturers. Finally this second value of labour is more variable than its natural and necessary value; because it is determined not by the wants of him who performs the labour, but by the wants and means of him who profits from it, and it is influenced by a thousand concurrent causes, which it is not yet time to develop.

But even the natural value of labour is not of an absolute fixture: for first the wants of a man in a given time, even those which may be regarded as the most urgent, are susceptible of a certain latitude; and the flexibility of our nature is such that these wants are restrained or extended considerably by the empire of will and the effect of habit. Secondly, by the influence of favourable circumstances, of a mild climate, of a fertile soil, these wants may be largely satisfied for a given time by the effect of very little labour, while in less happy circumstances, under an inclement sky, on a sterile soil, greater efforts will be requisite to provide for them. Thus, according to the case, the labour of the same man, during the same time, must procure him a greater or smaller number of objects, or of objects more or less difficult to be acquired, solely that he may continue to exist.

By this small number of general reflections we see then, that the ideas of riches and poverty arise from our wants, that is to say from our desires, for riches consist in the possession of means of satisfying our wants, and poverty in their non-possession. We call these means *goods,* because they do us good. They are all the product and the representation of a certain quantity of labour; and they give birth in us to the idea of value, which is but a comparative idea; because they have all two values, that of the goods which they cost and that of the goods which they produce. Since these goods are but the representation of the labour which has produced them, it is then from labour they derive these two values. It has them then itself. In effect labour has necessarily these two values. The second is eventual, most generally conventional, and always very variable. The first is natural and necessary; it is not however of an absolute fixture, but it is always comprehended within certain limits.

Such is the connexion of general ideas, which necessarily follow one another on the first inspection of this subject. It shows us the application and the proof of several great truths previously established. In the first place we see that we never create any thing absolutely new and *extra-natural.* Thus, since we have the idea of value, and since artificial and conventional values exist among us, it was necessary there should be somewhere a natural and necessary value. Thus the labour, from whence all our goods emanate, has a value of this kind, and communicates it to them. This value is that of the objects necessary to the satisfaction of the wants, which inevitably arise in an animated being during the continuance of his labour.

Secondly, we have seen further, that to measure any quantity whatsoever, is always to compare it with a quantity of the same species, and that it is absolutely necessary that this quantity should be of the same species, without which it could not serve as an unit and a term of comparison.* Thus, when we say that the natural and necessary value of the labor which an *animated being* performs during a given time is measured by the indispensable wants which arise in this being during the same time, we give really for the measure of this value the value of a certain quantity of labour; for the goods necessary to the satisfaction of these wants, do not themselves derive their natural and necessary value but from the labour which their acquisition has cost. Thus labour, our only original good, is only valued by itself, and the unit is of the same kind as the quantities calculated.

Thirdly, in fine we have seen that, for a calculation to be just and certain, the unit must be determined in a manner the most rigorous, and absolutely invariable.† Here unhappily we are obliged to acknowledge that our unit of value is subject to variations, although comprehended within certain limits. It is an evil we cannot remedy, since it is derived from the very nature of an animated being, from his flexibility and his suppleness. We must never dissemble this evil. It was essential to recognize it. But it ought not to prevent us from making combinations of the effects of our faculties, in taking the necessary precautions; for since the variations of our sensible nature are comprehended within certain limits, we can always apply to them considerations drawn from the theory of the limits of numbers. But this observation ought to teach us how very delicate and scientific is the calculation of

---

* See vol. 1st, chap. 10th, page 187, and following 2d edition; and vol. 3d, chap. 9th, page 463.

† See vol. 3d, chap. 9th, page 500, and following.

all moral and economical quantities, how much precaution it requires, and how imprudent it is to wish to apply to it indiscreetly the rigorous scale of numbers.

However it be, as this rapid glance on the ideas of riches and poverty, derived from the sentiment of our wants, leads us to speak summarily of all our goods, we ought not to pass in silence the greatest of all, that which comprehends them all, without which none of them would exist, which we may call the only good, of a willing being, *Liberty.* It merits a separate article.

Section Fifth.

From the faculty of willing arise likewise the ideas of *liberty* and *constraint.*

Nothing would be more easy than to inspire some interest in all generous souls, by commencing this chapter with a kind of hymn to this first of all the goods of sensible nature, *Liberty.* But these explosions of sentiment, have no object but to electrize one's self, or to excite the feelings of those whom we address. Now a man who sincerely devotes himself to the search of truth, is sufficiently animated by the end he proposes, and counts on the same disposition in all those by whom he wishes to be read. The love of what is good and true is a real passion. This passion is I believe sufficiently novel, at least it seems to me that it could not exist in all its force, but since it has been proved by reasonings, and by facts, that the happiness of man, is proportionate to the mass of his intelligence, and that the one and the other does and can increase indefinitely. But since these two truths have been demonstrated, this new passion which characterizes the epoch in which we live is not rare, whatever may be said of it, and it is as energetic and more constant than any other. Let us not then seek to excite but to satisfy it, and let us speak of liberty as coolly, as if this word itself did not put in motion all the powers of the soul.

I say that the idea of *liberty* arises from the faculty of willing; for, with Locke, I understand by liberty, the power of executing our will, of acting conformably with our desire. And I maintain, that it is impossible to attach any clear idea to this word when we give it another signification. Thus there would be no liberty were there no will; and liberty cannot exist before the birth of will. It is then real *nonsense,* to pretend that the will is free to exist or not.* And such were almost all the famous decisions, which subjugated the mind before the birth of the true study of the human understanding. Accordingly the consequences which were drawn from these pretended principles, and especially from this one, were for the most part completely absurd. But this is not the time to occupy ourselves with them.

Without doubt, we cannot too often repeat it, a sensible being cannot will without a motive, he cannot will but in virtue of the manner in which he is affected. Thus his will follows from his anterior impressions, quite as necessarily as every effect follows the cause which has the properties necessary for producing it. This necessity is neither a good nor an evil for a sensible being. It is the consequence of his nature; it is the condition of his existence; it is the *datum* which he cannot change, and from which he should always set out in all his speculations.

But when a will is produced in an animated being, when he has conceived any determination whatsoever, this sentiment of willing, which is always a suffering, as long as it is not satisfied, has in recompense the admirable property of reacting on the organs, of regulating the greater part of their movements, of directing the employment of almost all the faculties, and thereby of creating all the means of enjoyment and power of the sensible being, when no extraneous force restrains him, that is to say when the *willing* being is *free.*

Liberty, taken in this its most general sense (and the only reasonable one), signifying the power of executing our will, is then the remedy of all our ills, the accomplishment of all our desires, the satisfaction of all our wants, and consequently the first of all our goods, that which produces and comprehends them all. It is the same thing as our *happiness.* It has the same limits, or rather our happiness cannot have either more or less extension than our liberty; that is to say than our power of satisfying our desires. Constraint on the contrary, whatsoever it be, is the opposite of liberty; it is the cause of all our sufferings, the source of all our ills. It is even rigorously our only evil, for every ill is always the contrariety of a desire. We should

* See vol. 1st, chap. 13th, page 269, 2d edition.

assuredly have none, if we were free to deliver ourselves from it whenever we should wish; it is truely the Oromazis and Orismanes, the good and the evil principle.[2]

The constraint from which we suffer, or rather which we suffer, since it is itself which constitutes all suffering, may be of different natures, and is susceptible of different degrees. It is direct and immediate, or only mediate and indirect. It comes to us from animate or from inanimate beings, it is invincible or may be surmounted. That which is the effect of physical forces, which enchains the action of our faculties, is immediate, while that which is the result of different combinations of our understanding, or of certain moral considerations, is but indirect and mediate, although very real likewise. The one and the other, according to circumstances, may be insurmountable, or may be susceptible of yielding to our efforts.

In all of these different cases, we have different methods of conducting ourselves, to escape from the *suffering of constraint,* to effect the *accomplishment of our desires,* in a word to arrive at *satisfaction, at happiness.* For once again I say these three things are one and the same. Of these different methods of arriving at the only end of all our efforts as of all our desires, of all our wants, as of all our means, we should always take those which are most capable of conducting us to it. This is likewise our only duty, that which comprehends all others. The mean of fulfilling this only duty, is in the first place, if our desires are susceptible of satisfaction, to study the nature of the obstacles opposed, and to do all that depends on us to surmount them; secondly, if our desires cannot be accomplished, but by submitting to other evils, that is to say by renouncing other things, which we desire, to balance the inconveniences, and decide for the least; thirdly, if the success of our desires is entirely impossible, we must renounce them, and withdraw without murmuring within the limits of our power. Thus all is reduced to the employment of our intellectual faculties: First, in properly estimating our wants, then in extending our means, as far as possible; finally in submitting to the necessity of our nature, to the invincible condition of our existence.

But I perceive that I have mentioned the word *duty.* The idea which this word expresses well merits a separate chapter. It is sufficient in this to have

2. The final six words of this paragraph are not found in the French edition.

terminated the examination of all our goods, by showing that since all our means of happiness consist in the voluntary employment of our faculties, *Liberty*, the power of acting according to our will, includes all our goods, is our only good, and that our only duty is to encrease this power, and to use it well, that is to say so to use it as not ultimately to cramp and restrain it.

Would it be desired, before quitting this subject, to apply to this first of all goods, *Liberty*, the idea of value, which we have seen arise necessarily from the idea of *good?* And would it be asked, what is the *value* of liberty? It is evident that the sum of the liberty of a being feeling and willing, being the power of using his faculties according to his will, the entire value of this liberty is equal to the entire value of the employment of the faculties of this being: that if from this sum of liberty a portion only be detracted, the value of the portion detracted is equal to the value of the faculties, from the exercise of which he is debarred, and that the value of that which remains to him is the same with that of the faculties, the use of which he still preserves; and, finally, it is also manifest that, however feeble the faculties of an animated being, the absolute loss of his liberty is for him a loss truly infinite, and one to which he cannot set any price, since it is absolutely every thing for him, it is the extinction of every possibility of happiness; it is the loss of the sum total of his being; it can admit of no compensation, and deprives him of the disposal of what he might receive in return.

These general notions suffice for the moment. I will add but one reflection. It is commonly said that man, entering a state of society, sacrifices a portion of his liberty to secure the remainder. After what we have just said, this expression is not exact. It does not give a just idea either of the cause or of the effect, nor even of the origin of human societies. In the first place, man never lives completely isolated; he cannot exist thus, at least in his first infancy. Thus the state of society does not commence for him on a fixed day, or from premeditated design; it is established insensibly, and by degrees. Secondly, man in associating himself more and more, with his fellow beings, and in daily connecting himself more closely with them, by tacit or express conventions, does not calculate on diminishing his anterior liberty, or on weakening the total power of executing his will, which he previously had. He has always in view its increase. If he renounces certain modes of employing it, it is that he may be assisted, or at least not opposed, in other uses which he may wish to make of it, and which he judges more important to him. He consents that his will should be a little restrained, in certain cases, by that of his fellow beings: but it is that it may be much more powerful over all other beings, and even on these themselves on other occasions, so that the total mass of *power,* or of *liberty,* which he possesses should be thereby augmented. This I think is the idea which should be formed of the effect and the end of the gradual establishment of the social state. Whenever it does not produce this result, it does not attain its destination: but it attains it always in a greater or less degree, notwithstanding its universal and enormous imperfections. We will elsewhere develop the consequences of these observations. Now let us go on to the examination of the idea of duty.

Section Sixth.

Finally, from the faculty of willing arise the ideas of *rights* and of *duties.*

The ideas of *rights* and of *duties* are, by some, said to be correspondent and correlative. I do not deny them to be so, in our social relations; but this truth, if it is one, requires much explanation. Let us examine different cases.

Let us make in the first place a supposition absolutely ideal. Let us imagine a being feeling and willing, but incapable of all action, a simple monad endowed with the faculty of willing, but deprived of a body, and of every organ on which its will can react, and by which it could produce any effect, or have influence on any other being. It is manifest that such a being would have no right, in the sense we often give to this word, that is to say none of those rights which comprehend the idea of a correspondent duty in another sensible being, since it is not in contact with any being whatsoever. But to the eyes of reason and of universal justice, such as the human understanding can conceive them (for we can never speak of other things), this monad has clearly the right to satisfy his desires and to appease his wants; for this violates no law, natural or artificial. It is, on the contrary, to follow the laws of his nature and to obey the conditions of his existence.

At the same time this monad, having no power of action, no means of laboring for the satisfaction of his wants, has no duty: for it could not have the duty of employing in one way rather than another the means which it has not, of performing one action rather than another, since it cannot perform any action.

This supposition then shows us two things; first, as we have already said, that all our rights arise from wants, and all duties from means; secondly, that rights may exist, in the most general sense of this word, without correspondent duties on the part of other beings, nor even on the part of the being possessing these rights: Consequently these two ideas are not as essentially and necessarily correspondent, and correlative, as is commonly believed; for they are not so in their origin. Now let us state another hypothesis.

Let us suppose a being feeling and willing, constituted as we are, that is to say endowed with organs and faculties which his will puts in action, but completely separated from every other sensible being, and in contact only with inanimate beings, if there be such, or at least only with beings which should not manifest to him the phenomenon of sentiment, as there are many such for us. In this state this being still has not those rights, taken in the restrained sense of this word, which embrace the idea of a correspondent duty in another sensible being, since he is not in relation with any being of this kind; yet he has clearly the general right, like the monad of which we have just spoken, of procuring for himself the accomplishment of his desires, or, which is the same thing, of providing for his wants; because this is for him, as for it, to obey the laws of his nature, and to conform himself to the condition of his existence; and this being is such that it cannot be moved by any other impulsion, nor have any other principle of action. This willing being has then, in this case, all imaginable rights. We may even see that his rights are truly infinite, since they are bounded by nothing. At least they have no limits but those of his desires themselves, from which these emanate, and which are their only source.

But here there is something more than in the first hypothesis. This being, endowed like ourselves with organs and faculties which his will puts into motion, is not as the simple monad of which we spoke before. He has means, therefore he has duties; for he has the duty of well employing these means. But every duty supposes a punishment incurred by an infraction of it, a law which pronounces this punishment, a tribunal which applies this law; accordingly in the case in question the punishment of the being of which we speak, for not rightly employing his means, is to see them produce effects less favorable to his satisfaction, or even to see them produce such as are entirely destructive of it. The laws which pronounce this punishment, are those of the organization of this willing and acting being: they are the conditions of his existence. The tribunal which applies these laws is that of necessity itself, against which he cannot guard himself. Thus the being which occupies us has, incontestably, the duty of well employing his means, since he has them; and of observing that this general duty comprehends that of well appreciating, in the first place, the desires or wants which these means are destined to satisfy, of well studying afterwards these means themselves, their extent and their limits, and, finally, of labouring in consequence to restrain the one and extend the other as much as possible: for his unhappiness will never proceed but from the inferiority of means relatively to wants, since if wants were always satisfied there would be no possibility of suffering.

The isolated being in question, has then rights proceeding all from his wants, and duties arising all out of his means; and, in whatever position you place him, he will never have rights or duties of another nature: for all those of which he may become susceptible will arise from these, and will only be their consequences. We may even say that all proceed from his wants, for if he had not wants he would not *need* means to satisfy them; it would not even be possible he should have any means. Thus it would not be conceivable that he could have any duty whatsoever. If you wish to convince yourself of this, try to punish an impassive being. I have then had reason to say, that from the willing faculty arise the ideas of rights and of duties; and I can add, with assurance, that these ideas of rights and duties are not so exactly correspondent, and correlative, the one with the other, as they are commonly said to be: but that that of duties is subordinate to that of rights, as that of means is to that of wants, since we can conceive rights without duties, as in our first hypothesis; and in the second there are duties only because there are wants, and that they consist only in the general duty of satisfying these wants.

The better to convince ourselves of these two truths, let us make a third supposition: let us place this being, organised as we are in relation with other beings, feeling and willing like himself, and acting also in virtue of their will, but which are such that he cannot correspond fully with them, nor perfectly comprehend their ideas and their motives. These animated beings have their rights also, proceeding from their wants: but this operates no change in those of the being whose destiny we investigate. He has the same rights as before, since he has the same wants. He has, moreover, the same general duty of employing his means so as to procure the satisfaction of his wants.

Thus he has the duty of conducting himself with those beings which show themselves to be feeling and willing, otherwise than with those, which appear to him inanimate; for as they act in consequence of their will it is his duty to conciliate or subjugate that will in order to bring them to contribute to the satisfaction of his desires, and as he is supposed incapable of communicating completely with them, and consequently of forming any convention with them, he has no other means of directing their will towards the accomplishment of his desires, and the satisfaction of his wants, than immediate persuasion or direct violence. And he employs, and ought to employ, the one and the other according to circumstances, without any other consideration than of producing the effects he desires.

In truth this being, organized as we are, is such, that a view of sensible nature inspires in him the desire to sympathize with it, that it should enjoy of his enjoyments and suffer of his sufferings. This is a new want which it produces in him, and we shall see in the sequel that it is not one of those of which he ought to endeavour to rid himself, for it is useful for him to be submitted to it. He ought then to satisfy it as the others, and consequently he is under the duty of sparing to himself the pain which the sufferings of sensible beings cause him, so far as his other wants do not oblige him to support this pain. This is still a consequence of the general duty of satisfying all his desires.

The picture which we have just drawn according to theory is the simple exposition of our relations with animals taken in general, which relations are afterwards modified in particular cases according to the degree of knowledge we have of their sentiments, and according to the relations of habit and reciprocal benevolence which take place between us and them, as between us and our fellow beings. I believe this picture to be a very faithful representation of these relations; for it is equally remote from that sentimental exaggeration which would make criminal in us any destruction whatever of these animals, and from the systematic barbarity which would make us consider as legitimate their most useless sufferings, or even persuade us that the pain which a sensible being manifests, is not pain when this sensible being is not made exactly like ourselves.

In fact these two systems are equally false. The first is untenable, because in practice it is absolutely impossible to follow it rigorously. It is evident that we should be violently destroyed, or slowly famished and eaten, by the other animated beings if we never destroyed them; and that even with the most minute attention it is impossible for us to avoid causing a great number of beings, more or less perceptible to our senses, to suffer and die. Now we have incontestably the right to act and to live, since we are born for the one as well as for the other.

The second system is not less erroneous, for in theory it rashly establishes between the different states of sensible nature a line of separation which no phenomenon authorizes us to admit. There is absolutely no one fact which gives us a right to affirm, nor even to suppose that the state of suffering in the animated beings with which we communicate imperfectly, is not exactly the same thing as it is in us or in our fellow beings;* and on this gratuitous supposition, this system condemns us to combat and destroy as a weakness the sentiment, the want the most general and imperious of human nature, that of sympathy and commiseration; a want which we shall soon see is the most happy result of our organization, and without which our existence would become very miserable, and even impossible. Moreover, in practice this system is opposed to the usage the most universal of all times and of all individuals; for there has never been, I believe, an animal in the human form, which has sincerely and originally felt that a sight of suffering, accurately expressed, was a thing of indifference. The indifference which is the fruit of habit, and the pleasure even of cruelty, for cruelty sake, a frightful pleasure, which may have been produced in some *denaturalized* beings by accidental causes, proves that it is the case of a natural inclination surmounted by time, or overcome by effort, and by the pleasure which

---

* Always perhaps with a degree of energy proportionate to the perfection of the organization.

arises in us from every effort followed by success. As to that cruelty which is the product of vengeance, it is a proof the more of the thesis I sustain; for it is because of the profound sentiment that the vindictive being has of suffering, that he wishes to produce it in the one that is odious to him, and he always partakes more or less involuntarily and forcibly of the evil which he causes.

These two opposite systems, but both fruits of a derangement of the imagination, are then equally absurd in theory and practice; this, of itself, is a great presumption in favour of the intermediate opinion which I establish, which moreover is found to be conformable to the usage of all times and all places, and to furnish reason from the conditions of our nature, well observed, for what our manner of being, in respect to the animals, has in it singular and contradictory at the first glance. But what is more forcible, and absolutely convincing, in my opinion, is that the same principle which I have established, *that our rights are always without limits, or at least equal to our wants, and that our duties are never but the general duty of satisfying our wants,* will explain to us all our relations with our fellow beings, and establish them on immoveable bases, and such as will be the same everywhere, and always, in all countries, and in all times, in which our intimate nature shall not have changed.

Let us now make a fourth hypothesis which is that in which we are all placed. Let us suppose the animated being we are now considering in contact with other beings like himself. These beings have wants, and consequently rights, as he has, but this makes no change in his. He has always as many rights as wants, and the general duty of satisfying these wants. If he could not communicate completely with these beings like himself, and make conventions with them, he would be in respect to them in the state in which we all are, and in which as we have just seen we have reason to be in regard to the other animals.

Will any one say this is a state of war? He will be wrong. This would be an exaggeration. The state of war is that in which we incessantly seek the destruction of one another; because we cannot assure ourselves of our own preservation, but by the annihilation of our enemy. We are not in such a relation, but with those animals whose instinct constantly leads them to hurt us. It is not so as to the others; even those which we sacrifice to our wants, we attack only inasmuch as these wants, more or less pressing, force us. There are some of them which live with us in a state of peaceable subjection, others in perfect indifference. With all we wound their will only because it is contrary to ours, and not for the pleasure of wounding it. There is even in regard to all this general necessity of sympathising with sensible nature, which pains us at the sight of their suffering, and which unites us more or less with them. This state then is not essentially a *state of hostility.* It frequently becomes such: but this is by accident. It is essentially the *state of isolation* if we may thus express ourselves. It is that of beings, willing and acting separately, each for his own satisfaction, without being able to explain themselves mutually, or to make conventions for the regulation of the cases in which their wills are opposed.

Such, as we have said, would be the relations of man with his fellow men, if his means of communicating with them were very imperfect. He would not be precisely for them an enemy, but an indifferent stranger. His relations would even then be softened by the necessity of sympathising, which is much stronger in him in the case of animals of his own species; and we must still add to this necessity that of love, which strengthens it extremely in many circumstances, for love has not perfect enjoyment without mutual consent, without a very lively sympathy; and when this sympathy, necessary to the full satisfaction of the desire, has existed, it frequently gives birth to habits of good will, from whence arises the sentiment of fraternity, which produces in its turn ties more durable and more tender.

Nevertheless, in this state quarrels are frequent; and, properly speaking, justice and injustice do not yet exist. The rights of the one do not affect the rights of the other. Every one has as many rights as wants, and the general duty of satisfying these wants without any foreign consideration. There does not begin to be any restrictions on these rights and this duty, or rather on the manner of fulfilling this duty, but at the moment in which means of mutual understanding are established; and consequently conventions tacit or formal. There solely is the birth of justice and injustice, that is to say of the balance between the rights of one and the rights of another, which necessarily were equal till this instant. The Greeks who called Ceres *Legislatrix* were wrong. It is to grammar, to language, they ought to have given this title. They had placed the origin of laws, and of justice, at the moment in which men have amongst them relations more stable, and conventions more numerous. But they ought to have returned to the birth of the first conventions, informal or explicit. In every way the duty of moderns is to penetrate further and more profoundly than the ancients. Hobbes,[3] then, was certainly right in establishing the foundation of all justice on conversations; but he was wrong in saying before, that the anterior state is rigorously and absolutely a state of war, and that this is our true instinct, and the wish of our nature. Were this the case we should never have withdrawn from it.* A false principle has led him to an excellent consequence. It has always appeared to me singularly remarkable, that this philosopher, who of all men who have ever written is perhaps the most recommendable for the rigorous concatenation and close connexion of his ideas, should not however have arrived at this fine conception of the necessity for conventions, the source of all justice, but, by starting from a false or at least an inexact principle (a state of war, the natural state); and that from the just and profound sentiment of the want of peace among men, he has been led to a false idea the necessity of servitude. When we see such examples, how ought we to tremble in enouncing an opinion?†

Yet I cannot help believing that which I have just explained to be true. It seems to me proved, that from our faculty of willing proceed the ideas of *rights* and *duties;* that from our wants proceed all our *rights,* and from our means all our *duties;* that we have always as many *rights* as wants, and the single *duty* of providing for these wants; that the wants and the rights of other sensible beings, whether of our own or a different species, do not

---

* We must however admit that nature, or the order of things, such as they are, in creating the rights of every animated individual, equal and opposed to those of another, has virtually and indirectly created the state of war; and that it is art which has caused it to cease, or at least has frequently suspended it amongst us, by conventions. This still agrees with our general principle, that we create nothing; were there not natural and necessary wars, there never would have been any conventional and artificial ones. The invincibly permanent state of the relations of man with animals of other species, is what disposes him most to treat his fellow beings in an hostile manner.

† This latter error of Hobbes has not, however, been produced in his excellent head, but by the too energetic impression made by the unhappiness of his country; which unhappiness was caused by efforts, the object of which in their origin was resistance to oppression.

3. Thomas Hobbes (1588–1679), English philosopher, author of *Leviathan* (1651).

affect ours; that our rights do not begin to be restrained, but at the moment of the birth of conventions; that our general duty is not changed for this as to its foundation, but only to the manner of fulfilling it; and that it is at this moment alone, that justice and injustice properly so called commence.

It is not yet the time to develop all the consequences of these principles, but it is time to terminate these long preliminaries, by the reflections to which it gives rise.

Section Seventh.

Conclusion.

The general considerations on which we have just dwelt, are those which first present themselves to our understanding when we begin to observe our will. However little we reflect thereon, we see first that it is a mode of our sensibility, which arises from a judgment, clear or confused, formed on what we feel, that if our pure and simple sensibility begins to give us an obscure idea of our *self,* and of the possession of its affections, this admirable mode of our sensibility, which we call *will,* by the resistance it experiences, causes us to know beings different from us, and completes our idea of *individuality,* of *personality,* and *property,* exclusive of whatsoever affects us.* It is not less visible, that this faculty of willing is the source of all our *wants,* and of all our miseries; for an indifferent being would be impassive; and it is equally manifest that this same faculty, by the wonderful power it has of putting our organs into action, and of giving motion to our members, is also the source of all our *means* and of all our resources; for all our power consists in the employment of our physical and intellectual forces. It follows from this, that every animated being, in virtue of the laws of his nature, has the *right* of satisfying all his desires, which are his wants, and the sole *duty* of employing his means in the best possible manner for the attainment of this object; for endowed with *passion,* he cannot be condemned to

---

* This truth has been developed in the first volume in the chapter on *existence,* and in different parts of the two other volumes.

suffer but as little as possible, and endowed with *action,* he ought to avail himself of it to this end. It follows thence, further, that *liberty,* the power of executing his will, is for a willing being the first good, and includes them all, for he would be always happy if he had always the power of satisfying all his desires; and all his ills consist always in *constraint,* that is to say in the inability to satisfy himself. We see moreover that the employment of our force, labour of every kind, is our only primitive riches, the source of all others, the first cause of their value, and that labour itself has always two values. The one is natural and necessary: it is that of all those things which are indispensable to the satisfaction of the wants of the animated being which performs this labour during the time he is performing it. The other is contingent, and often conventional: it consists in the mass of utility that results from this same labour. In fine we see, with equal clearness, that the manner of fulfilling our single duty, that of well employing our means, var-ies according to the circumstances in which we are placed; whether it be when we are in contact with those beings only which do not manifest any sensibility, or when we have to do with animated beings, but to which we can make ourselves but imperfectly understood, or when we are in relation with sensible beings like ourselves, with whom we can perfectly correspond and make conventions. At this point *justice* and *injustice,* properly so called, and true society, commence; the object and motive of which is always to augment the power of every one, by making that of others concur with it, and by preventing them from reciprocally hurting one another.

All these first ideas are good and sound, at least I think so, and begin already to throw some light on the subject with which we are occupied; but they are far from being sufficient. They do not sufficiently inform us what are the numerous results of the employment of our force, of our labour, in a word of our actions, and what new interests their combinations produce among us, nor what are the different sentiments which germinate from our first desires, or what they have useful or injurious to the happiness of all and every one: nor, finally, what is the best possible direction of these actions and sentiments. These are, however, so many subjects necessary to be treated of in order to give a complete history of the *will and its effects;* and it is there we find again the division we announced. It is requisite then to enter into further details, and I will now begin to speak of our actions.

First Part
of the
Treatise on the Will and Its Effects.

Of Our Actions.

☙

CHAPTER I.

Of Society.

❦

The introduction which has been just read is consecrated entirely to an examination of the generation of some very general ideas; the casting of a first glance on the nature of that mode of our *sensibility* which we call the *will,* or the faculty of willing; and to the indication of some of its immediate and universal consequences.

We have therein seen summarily; first, what are inanimate or *insensible* beings, such as many appear to us, which may well exist for the sensible beings, which they affect, but which do not exist for themselves, since they do not percieve it; second, what would be the nature of beings feeling, but *feeling every thing with indifference,* so that from their sensibility no choice, no preference, no desire, in a word no will would result; third, what are those beings *sentient and willing,* such as all the animals with which we are acquainted, and especially as ourselves, but isolated; fourth, and in fine, what beings, *feeling and willing* in our way, become when they are in contact and *in relation with other animals of their species* similar to themselves, and with whom they can fully correspond.

These preliminaries were necessary, that the reader might readily follow the series of ideas, and clearly perceive the connexion, of this second section of the Elements of Ideology with that which precedes it. But it would be inconvenient, in a Treatise on the Will, to say more of beings not endowed with this intellectual faculty; and it would not be less superfluous, having the human species principally in view, to occupy ourselves longer with beings that should be sentient and willing, but living isolated.

Man cannot exist thus; this is proved by the fact, for we have never seen in any corner of the world an animal in the human form, however brutish he might be, which has no kind of relation with any other animal of his own species: that is not less demonstrated by reasoning. For such an individual, strictly speaking, may exist although very miserably, yet certainly he could not reproduce himself. That the species may be perpetuated, it is indispensable that the two sexes should unite; it is even necessary that the infant, produced by their union, should receive for a long time the cares of his parents, or at least those of his mother. Now we are so formed that we have all, more or less, a natural and innate inclination to sympathy; that is to say we all experience pleasure from sharing our impressions, our affections, our sentiments, and those of our fellow creatures. Perhaps this inclination exists amongst all animated beings; perhaps even it is in us from the origin a considerable part of that which so powerfully attracts the two sexes towards each other. What is certain, is that it afterwards augments it prodigiously. It is then impossible that approximations, which our organization renders inevitable, should not develop in us this natural disposition to sympathy, fortify it by exercise, and establish amongst us social and moral relations. Moreover, we are also so organized, that we form judgments of that which we experience, of that which we feel, of that which we see, in a word of all which affects us; we distinguish the parts, circumstances, causes and consequences thereof; and this is to judge of it. It is then impossible that we should not soon be aware of the utility we may derive from the succour of our fellow beings, from their assistance in our wants, from the concurrence of their will, and of their force with ours, a new reason why approximations, fortuitous at first, should become durable and permanent between us; this also is what takes place always, and every where. It is this also which always, and every where, produces the admirable and wise invention of a language more or less perfect, but always as appears, more circumstantial, and more capable of detailed explanations, than that of any other animal. It is then the social state, which is our natural state, and that with which we ought alone to occupy ourselves.

I will not however in this place consider society under a moral relation. I will not examine how it develops, multiplies, and complicates, all our passions and affections; nor what are the numerous duties it imposes on us, nor whence arises for us the fundamental obligation of respecting the conventions on which it rests, and without which it could not subsist. These are researches which will be the object of the second part of this treatise. In this I shall consider the social state only under its economical relation, that is to say relatively to our most direct wants, and to the means we have of satisfying them. It is that which may lead us surely to estimate the value and utility of all our actions, to judge of their merits by their consequences, and consequently of the merit of those sentiments which determine us to one action rather than another.

Now what is society viewed under this aspect? I do not fear to announce it. Society is purely and solely a continual series of exchanges. It is never any thing else, in any epoch of its duration, from its commencement the most unformed, to its greatest perfection. And this is the greatest eulogy we can give to it, for exchange is an admirable transaction, in which the two contracting parties always both gain; consequently society is an uninterrupted succession of advantages, unceasingly renewed for all its members. This demands an explanation.

First, society is nothing but a succession of exchanges. In effect, let us begin with the first conventions on which it is founded. Every man, before entering into the state of society, has as we have seen all rights and no duty, not even that of not hurting others; and others the same in respect to him. It is evident they could not live together, if by a convention formal or tacit they did not promise each other, reciprocally, *surety*. Well! this convention is a real exchange; every one renounces a certain manner of employing his force, and receives in return the same sacrifice on the part of all the others. Security once established by this mean, men have a multitude of mutual relations which all arrange themselves under one of the three following classes: they consist either in rendering a service to receive a salary, or in bartering some article of merchandize against another, or in executing some work in common. In the two first cases the exchange is manifest. In the third it is not less real; for when several men unite, to labour in common, each makes a sacrifice to the others of what he could have done during the same time for his own particular utility; and he receives, for an equivalent, his part of the common utility resulting from the common labour. He exchanges one manner of occupying himself against another, which becomes more advantageous to him than the other would have been. It is true then that society consists only in a continual succession of exchanges.

I do not pretend to say that men never render gratuitous services. Far from me be the idea of denying benevolence, or of banishing it from their hearts; but I say it is not on this that all the progress of society reposes, and even that the happy consequences of this amiable virtue are much more important under a moral relation,* of which we are not at this time speaking, than under the economical relation which now occupies us. I add that if we urge the sense of the word *exchange,* and if we wish, as we ought, to take it in all the extent of its signification, we may say with justice that a benefit is still an exchange, in which one sacrifices a portion of one's property, or of one's time, to procure a moral pleasure, very lively and very sweet, that of obliging, or to exempt oneself from a pain very afflicting, the sight of suffering; exactly as we employ a sum of money to procure an artificial fire work, which diverts, or to free ourselves from something which incommodes us.

It is equally true that an exchange is a transaction in which the two contracting parties both gain. Whenever I make an exchange freely, and without constraint, it is because I desire the thing I receive more than that I give; and, on the contrary, he with whom I bargain desires what I offer more than that which he renders me. When I give my labour for wages it is because I esteem the wages more than what I should have been able to produce by labouring for myself; and he who pays me prizes more the services I render him than what he gives me in return. When I give a measure of wheat for a measure of wine, it is because I have a superabundance of food and nothing to drink, and he with whom I treat is in the contrary case. When several of us agree to execute any labour whatsoever in common, whether to defend ourselves against an enemy, to destroy noxious animals, to preserve ourselves from the ravages of the sea, of an inundation, of a contagion, or even to make a bridge or a road, it is because each of us prefers the particular utility which will result to him from it, to what he would have been able to do for himself during the same time. We are all

---

* In developing and exciting sympathy.

satisfied in all these species of exchanges, every one finds his advantage in the arrangement proposed.

In truth it is possible that, in an exchange, one of the contractors, or even both, may have been wrong to desire the bargain which they conclude. It is possible they may give a thing, which they will soon regret, for a thing which they will soon cease to value. It is possible, also, that one of the two may not have obtained for that which he sacrifices as much as he might have asked, so that he will suffer a relative loss while the other makes an exaggerated gain. But these are particular cases which do not belong to the nature of the transaction. And it is not less true that it is the essence of free exchange to be advantageous to both parties; and that the true utility of society is to render possible amongst us a multitude of similar arrangements.

It is this innumerable crowd of small particular advantages, unceasingly arising, which composes the general good, and which produces at length the wonders of perfected society, and the immense difference we see between it and a society imperfect or almost null, such as exists amongst savages. It is not improper to direct our attention for some time to this picture, which does not sufficiently strike us because we are too much accustomed to it.

What is it in effect which a country anciently civilized offers to our contemplation? The fields are cleared and cleaned, freed from the large vegetables which originally covered them, rid of noxious plants and animals, and in every respect prepared to receive the annual cares of the cultivator. The marshes are drained. The stagnant waters which occupied it have ceased to fill the air with pestilential vapours. Exits have been opened for them, or their extent has been circumscribed; and the lands which they infected have become abundant pastures, or useful reservoirs. The confusion of the mountains has been untangled; their bases have been appropriated to the wants of culture; their parts least accessible, even to the regions of eternal snow, have been destined to the nourishment of numerous flocks. The forests which have been permitted to remain have not continued impenetrable: The wild beasts which retired to them have been pursued and almost destroyed; the wood which they produce has been withdrawn and preserved, the cutting them has even been subjected to periods the most favourable for their reproduction; and the care bestowed on them almost every where is equivalent to a species of culture, and has even been sometimes extended to a most diligent culture. The running waters which traverse all these lands have, likewise, not remained in their primitive state: The great rivers, have been cleared of all the obstacles which obstructed their course; they have been confined by dikes and quays, when this has been necessary; and their banks have been disposed in such a manner as to form commodious ports in convenient situations. The course of streams less considerable has been restrained for working mills and other machines, or diverted to irrigate declivities which needed it, and to render them productive. On the whole surface of the land habitations have been constructed from distance to distance, in favourable positions, for the use of those who cultivate the ground and attend to its produce. These habitations have been surrounded with enclosures and plantations, that render them more agreeable and more useful. Roads have been made to go to them and to take away the produce of the earth. In points where several different interests have concentrated, and where other men have become sufficiently necessary to the service of the cultivators, to be able to subsist on the wages of their labour, habitations have been multiplied and made contiguous, and have formed villages and small towns. On the banks of large rivers, and on the shores of the sea, in points in which the interests of several of these towns have coincided, large cities have been built; which have themselves in time given birth to a still greater one, which has become their capital and their common centre, because it has been found the most favourably situated to unite all the others, and to be provisioned and defended by them. Finally, all these towns communicate with each other, with the neighbouring seas, and with foreign countries, by means of bridges, causeways, canals, in which the whole of human industry is displayed. Such are the objects which strike us at the first aspect of a country where men have exercised all their power, and have appropriated it to themselves for a long time.

If we penetrate the interior of their habitations we there find an immense number of useful animals, raised, nourished, made obsequious, by man, multiplied by him to an inconceivable point; a prodigious quantity of necessaries of every species, commodities, furniture, utensils, instruments, clothing, articles, raw or manufactured, metals, necessary or precious; finally, whatever may sooner or later contribute to the satisfaction of our wants. We admire there above all things, a population really astonishing, all the individuals of which have the use of a perfected language, have a reason developed to a certain point, manners sufficiently softened, and an industry sufficiently intelligent, to live in such great numbers near to one another, and amongst whom in general the poorest are succoured, the weakest defended. We remark, with still more surprise, that many of these men have attained a degree of knowledge very difficult to be acquired, that they possess an infinity of agreeable or useful arts, that they are acquainted with many of the laws of nature, of which they know to calculate the effects, and turn them to their advantage, that they have even had a glimpse of the most difficult of all sciences, since they are able to distinguish, at least in part, the true interests of the species in general, and in particular those of their society, and its members; that in consequence they have conceived laws often just, institutions tolerably wise, and created a number of establishments proper for spreading and still increasing instruction and intelligence; and finally, that not content with having thus insured interior prosperity they have explored the rest of the earth, established relations with foreign nations, and provided for their security from without.

What an immense accumulation of means of well being! What prodigious results from that part of the labours of our predecessors, which has not been immediately necessary to the support of their existence, and which has not been annihilated with them! The imagination even is astonished; and the more so the more it reflects on it, for we should consider that many of these works are little durable, that the most solid have been many times renewed in the course of ages, and that there is scarcely one which does not require continual care and maintenance for its preservation. We must observe that of these wonders that which strikes our attention is not the most astonishing; it is, as we say, the material part. But the intellectual part, if we may so express ourselves, is still more surprising. It has always been much more difficult to learn, and to discover, than to act in consequence of what we know. The first steps, especially in the career of invention, are of extreme difficulty. The labour which man has been obliged to perform on his own intellectual faculties, the immensity of the researches to which he has been forced to have recourse, that of the observations he has been obliged to collect, have cost him much more time and pains than all the works he has been able to execute in consequence of the progress of his understanding. Finally, we must remark that the efforts of men, for the amelioration of their lot, have never been nearly as well directed as they might have been, that always a great portion of the human power has been employed in hindering the progress of the other, that this progress has been troubled and interrupted by all the great disorders of nature and of society; and that many times perhaps all has been lost and destroyed, even the knowledge acquired, even the capacity of re-commencing that which had been already done. These latter considerations might become discouraging. But we shall see elsewhere by how many reasons we ought to be assured against the fear of such misfortunes in future. We will also examine to what point the progress of the species, taken in mass, augments the happiness of individuals, a condition necessary to enable us to rejoice at it. But at this moment let it suffice to have shown the prodigious power which men acquire when united; while separated they can with difficulty sustain their miserable existence.

Smith,[1] if I am not mistaken, is the first who has remarked that *man alone makes exchanges, properly speaking.* See his admirable chapter, 4th of the 1st book of his treatise on the Wealth of Nations. I regret that in re-marking this fact he has not sought its cause with more curiosity. It was not for the author of the Theory of Moral Sentiments to regard as useless a scrutiny of the operations of our understanding. His success and his faults ought to have contributed equally to make him think the contrary. Notwithstanding this negligence his assertion is not the less true. We clearly see certain animals execute labours which concur to a common end, and which to a certain point appear to have been concerted; or fight for the possession of what they desire, or supplicate to obtain it; but nothing announces that they really make formal exchanges. The reason, I think, is that they have not a language sufficiently developed to enable them to make express conventions; and this, I think, proceeds (as I have explained in my second volume, article of interjections, and in my first, on the subject of signs) from their being incapable of sufficiently decomposing their ideas,

---

1. Adam Smith (1723–90), Scottish philosopher and economist, author of *The Wealth of Nations* (1776), where it is suggested that men had a natural propensity to barter.

to generalise, to abstract, and to express them separately in detail, and in the form of a proposition; whence it happens that those of which they are susceptible, are all particular, confused with their attributes, and manifest themselves in mass by interjections, which can explain nothing explicitly. Man, on the contrary, who has the intellectual means which are wanting to them is naturally led to avail himself of them, to make conventions with his fellow beings. They make no exchanges, and he does. Accordingly he alone has a real society; for *commerce is the whole of society,* as labour is the whole of riches.

We can scarcely conceive at first that the great effects, which we have just described, have no other cause than the sole reciprocity of services and the multiplicity of exchanges. However this continual succession of exchanges has three very remarkable advantages.

First, the labour of several men united is more productive than that of the same men acting separately. Is there a question of defence? Ten men will easily resist an enemy, who would have destroyed them all in attacking one after another. Is a burden to be removed? That of which the weight would have opposed an invincible resistance to the efforts of a single individual, yields immediately to those of several acting together. Is some complicated work to be executed? Several things are to be done simultaneously. One does one while another does another, and all contribute to effect what a single man could not have produced. One rows while another steers, and a third casts the net or harpoons the fish; and thus they attain a success impossible without this concurrence.

Secondly, our knowledge is our most precious acquisition, since it is this that directs the employment of our force, and renders it more fruitful, in proportion to its greater soundness and extent. Now no man is in a situation to see every thing, and it is much more easy to learn than to invent. But when several men communicate together, that which one has observed is soon known to all the others, and it is sufficient amongst them that one is found who is very ingenious, in order that precious discoveries should promptly become the property of all. Intelligence then will increase much more rapidly, than in a state of insulation, without calculating that it may be preserved, and consequently accumulated from generation to generation; and still without counting, what is clearly proved by the study of our understanding, that the invention and employment of language and its signs, which would not take place without society, furnish our minds with many new means of combination and action.

Thirdly, and this still merits attention: when several men labour reciprocally for one another every one can devote himself exclusively to the occupation for which he is fittest, whether from his natural dispositions or from fortuitous circumstances; and thus he will succeed better. The hunter, the fisherman, the shepherd, the labourer, the artisan—doing each a single thing—will become more skilful, will lose less time, and have more success. This is what is called the *division of labour,* which in civilised society is sometimes carried to an inconceivable point, and always with advantage. The writers on economics have all attached an extreme importance to the division of labour; and they have made much noise with this observation, which is not ancient; they have been right. Yet this third advantage of society is far from having an interest equally eminent with the two former, the concurrence of force and the communication of knowledge. In all cases, that which is most difficult is to assign to things their true value; for this, we must know them perfectly.

Concurrence of force, increase and preservation of knowledge, and division of labour—these are the three great benefits of society. They cause themselves to be felt from the first by men the most rude; but they augment in an incalculable ratio, in proportion as they are perfected, and every degree of amelioration, in the social order, adds still to the possibility of increasing and better using them. The energy of these three causes of prosperity will show itself still more evidently, when we shall have seen more in detail the manner in which our riches are formed.

CHAPTER II

Of Production, or of the Formation of Our Riches.

ح

It is so true that we cannot reason justly while the sense of words is not well determined, that it is very important in political economy, to know what we ought to understand by the word *production,* in the language of this science. This question, which in itself is not without difficulty, has been still much perplexed by the spirit of system and prejudice. It has been treated of by many able men, at the head of whom we should place Turgot[1] and Smith. But, in my opinion, no one has thrown so much light on it as Mr. Say,[2] the author of the best book I know on these matters, although he leaves still something to be desired.

All the operations of nature and of art resolve into transmutations, into changes, of *form* and of *place.*

Not only we never create any thing, but it is even impossible for us to conceive what it is to create or destroy, if we understand by this word to reduce something to nothing; for we have never seen any being whatsoever arise from nothing, nor return to it. Hence this axiom, admitted by all antiquity, "*nothing comes from nothing, or returns to nothing.*"* What then do

---

* It is very just. I shall believe in the possibility of a creation, when any body shall show me one, or even an annihilation.

  1. Anne-Robert-Jacques Turgot (1721–81), French economist, author of *Reflections on the Formation and Distribution of Wealth* (1766).

  2. Jean-Baptiste Say (1767–1832), French economist, author of *A Treatise on Political Economy, or the Production, Distribution and Consumption of Wealth* (1803).

we do by our labour, by our action on all the bodies which surround us? Never any thing, but operate in these beings changes of form or of place, which render them proper for our use, which make them useful to the satisfaction of our wants. This is what we should understand by *to produce:* It is to give things an utility which they had not. Whatever be our labour, if no utility results from it it is unfruitful. If any results it is *productive.*

It seems at first, and many likewise believe it, that there is a more real production in that labour which has for its object the procurement of first materials, than in that which consists in fashioning and transporting them; but it is an illusion. When I put seed in contact with air, water, earth, and different manures, so that from the combinations of these elements results wheat, hemp, or tobacco, there is no more creation operated, than when I take the grain of this wheat to convert it into flour and bread, the filaments of this hemp to make successively thereof thread, cloth, and clothing; and the leaves of this tobacco to prepare them so as to smoke, chew, or snuff them. In both cases there is a production of utility, for all these labours are equally necessary to accomplish the desired end, the satisfaction of some of our wants.

The man who draws fish from the depths of the sea is no more a creator than those who dry and salt them, who extract the oil, the eggs, &c. &c. or transport these products to me. It is the same with those who dig in mines, who convert the mineral into metal and the metal into utensils, or furniture, and who carry these instruments to those who want them. Each adds a new utility to the utility already produced, consequently each is equally a producer.

All equally study the laws, which govern the different beings to turn them to their profit; all employ, to produce the desired effect, the chemical and mechanical forces of nature. What we call her *vegetative force* is not of another nature, it is but a series of elective attractions, of true chymical affinities with all the circumstances of which we are undoubtedly not acquainted, but yet know how to favor them by our labours, and to direct these in such a manner as to render them useful.

It is then erroneously that they have made agricultural industry a thing essentially different from all the other branches of human industry, and in which the action of nature intervenes in a particular manner; accordingly they have always been greatly embarrassed to know precisely what they should understand by agricultural industry, taken in this sense. They have comprised therein fishing and hunting. But why not likewise comprehend the industry of nomadic shepherds? Is there so great a difference between raising animals to nourish ourselves, and killing or taking them ready raised to nourish ourselves in the same manner. If he who extracts salt from sea water, by exposing it to the action of the rays of the sun, is a producer, why should not he who extracts the same salt from the water of a fountain, by means of the action of fire, and that of the wind, in buildings of graduation, be a producer also? And yet what specific difference is there between his manufacture, and all those which yield other chymical products? If we rank in this productive class him who extracts minerals from the earth, why not also comprehend him who extracts metals from these minerals? If one produces the mineral the other produces the metal, and where shall we stop in the different transformations which this matter undergoes, 'till it becomes a piece of furniture or a jewel? At what point of these successive labours can we say, here we cease to produce, and do nothing but fashion things? We may say as much of those who seek wood in forests, or turf in bogs, or who collect on the shores of the sea or of rivers the useful things which the waters have deposited there. Are they farmers, manufacturers, or carriers? And if they are all these at the same time, why are they more producers under one of these denominations than under the two others? Finally, to speak only of culture, properly so called, I demand that it be precisely determined who is the true producer, the farmer by excellence, he who sows or he who reaps; he who ploughs, or he who fences; he who conveys manure into the fields, or he who leads the flocks to fold in them? For my part I declare that they all appear only as so many different workmen, who concur in the same manufacturing. I stop here, because one might propose to the partisans of the opinion I combat a thousand questions, as insoluble as these, in their system. When we set out from a false principle difficulties arise in crowds: perhaps this is one of the great causes of the obscure, embarrassed, and almost mysterious, language which we remark in the writings of the ancient economists. When ideas are not precise it is impossible that expressions should be clear.

The truth is simply, that all our useful labours are productive, and that those relative to agriculture are so like the others, in the same manner as the others, for the same reason as the others; and have in this nothing particular. A farm is a real manufactory; every thing is operated there in the same way, by the same principles, and for the same causes. A field is a real tool, or, if you please, a store of first materials, which any one may take if it yet belongs to nobody; and which must be bought, rented, or borrowed, if it has already an owner. It does not change its nature, whether I employ it in the raising of grain, in bleaching linen, or for any other purpose. In every case it is an instrument necessary to produce a desired effect, as a furnace, a hammer, or a vessel. The only difference between this instrument and every other, is that to use it, as it cannot be removed, we must go to it, instead of its coming to us.

Once again, agricultural industry is a branch of manufacturing industry, which has no specific character which separates it from all the others. Would you so generalise this term as to extend it to all the labours which have for their object the procurement of first materials? It is then certain that agricultural industry is the first in date and the most necessary of all, because it is necessary that a thing should be procured before it can be applied to use; but it is not for that reason exclusively productive, for most of its productions must yet be further wrought before they become useful to us; and moreover we must then comprehend in agricultural industry, not only that of hunters, fishers, shepherds, miners, &c. but also that of the rudest savages, and even that of all those beasts which live on the spontaneous productions of the earth, since these are first matters which these creatures procure for themselves; in truth, they are immediately consumed, but this does not change the thesis. Certainly these are singular *farmers,* and singular producers.

Will it be insisted that agricultural industry shall be restrained to agriculture, properly so called? Then it is not the first in chronological order, for men are fishers, hunters, shepherds, and mere vagabonds, in the manner of brutes, long before they are farmers. It is not even the only industry productive of primary materials, for we employ many for which we are not indebted to it. Doubtless it is always very important, and is the principal source of our subsistance, if not of our riches; but it cannot be regarded as exclusively productive.

Let us conclude that all useful labour is really productive, and that all the laborious class of society merits equally the name of *productive.* The truly *sterile* class is that of the idle, who do nothing but live, *nobly* as it is termed, on the products of labours executed before their time, whether these products are realised in landed estates which they lease, that is to say which they *hire* to a labourer, or that they consist in money or effects which they lend for a premium, which is still a *wage earner.* These are the true drones of the hive (fruges consumere nati) unless they render themselves deserving by the functions which they discharge or the knowledge which they diffuse; for these are, also, useful and productive labours, although not of an immediate utility in relation to riches; we will speak of them hereafter.

As to the laborious class and that immediately productive of our riches, as its action on all the beings of nature always reduces itself to the change *of form or of place,* it naturally divides itself into two, the manufacturers (including farmers) who fabricate and fashion, and merchants who transport, for this is the real utility of the latter. If they did nothing but buy and sell, without transporting, without retailing, without facilitating any thing, they would be nothing more than incommodious parasites, gamesters, stock-jobbers; of the one and the other of whom we shall shortly speak; and we shall quickly see how much light our manner of considering things throws on the whole progress of society. We must now explain a little more fully in what this utility consists, our only production which results from all labour well understood; and to see how it is appreciated, and how it constitutes the value of whatsoever we call our riches.

CHAPTER III.

Of the Measure of Utility or of Values.

છ૭

This word *utility* has a very extensive signification, for it is very abstract, or rather it is very abstract because it is abstracted from a multitude of different significations. In effect there exist utilities of many different kinds. There are some real, some illusory; if some are solid some are very futile, and we often stupidly deceive ourselves in respect to them. I could cite many examples, but they would not perhaps be to the taste of all readers. It is better that every one should choose those which please him. In general we may say that whatever is capable of procuring any advantage, even a frivolous pleasure, is *useful*. I think this is the real value of this word, for in the end all we desire is to multiply our enjoyments and to diminish our sufferings; and certainly the sentiment of pleasure and of satisfaction is a good. All goods are even nothing more than that differently modified. Whatever, then, procures it is useful.

If it is not easy to say clearly what this utility is of which we speak, it appears still much more difficult to determine its degrees; for the measure of the utility of a thing, real or supposed, is the vivacity with which it is generally desired. Now, how are we to fix the degrees of a thing so inappreciable as the vivacity of our desires? We have, however, a very sure manner of arriving at it. It is to observe the sacrifices to which these desires determine us. If, to obtain any thing whatsoever, I am disposed to give three measures of wheat which belong to me; and if, to obtain another, I am ready to part with twelve like measures, it is evident that I desire the last four times more than the other. In like manner, if I give a man a salary triple of that which

I offer another, it is clear that I value the services of the first three times more than those of the second; or, if I personally do not value them so much, it is however the value generally attached to them, so that I could not procure them at a smaller price; and, since, in fine, I make this sacrifice freely, it is a proof that its object is worth it even to me.

In the state of society which is nothing but a continual succession of exchanges, it is thus that the values of all the products of our industry are determined. This fixation, without doubt, is not always founded on very good reasons; we are often very dear appreciators of the real merit of things. But, in fine, in relation to riches, their value is not the less that which the general opinion assigns to them; whence we see, by the way, that the greatest producer is he who performs that kind of labour most dearly paid for. It matters little whether this labour should be a branch of agricultural, manufacturing, or commercial, industry; and, from hence, we also see that, of two nations, that which has most riches, or most enjoyments, is that whose workmen are the most laborious and the most skillful in every kind, or who devote themselves to the kinds of labour most fruitful; in a word, whose labourers produce the most value in the same time.

This brings us back to the subject of which we had already begun to treat in the introduction (sections three and four): our only original property is our physical and intellectual force. The employment of our force, our labour, is our only primitive riches. All the beings existing in nature, susceptible of becoming useful to us, are not so actually as yet. They only become so by the action which we exercise on them; by the labour, small or great, simple or complicated, which we execute to convert them to our use. They have no value for us, and with us, but by this labour, and in proportion to its success. This is not saying that if they have already become the property of any one, we must not begin by making a sacrifice to him, in order to obtain them, before disposing of them. But they have not become the property of any one, but because he has previously applied to them a labour of some kind, the fruit of which the social conventions assure to him. Thus this sacrifice itself is the price of some labour; and, previous to any labour, these beings had no actual value, and that which they have is never derived but from some employment of our force, of which they are more the object.

This employment of our force, this labour, we have also seen has a natural and necessary value; without which it would never have had an artificial and conventional one. This necessary value is the sum of the indispensable wants, the satisfaction of which is necessary to the existence of him who executes this labour, during the time he is executing it. But here, where we speak of the value which results from the free transactions of society, it is clearly seen that we have in view the conventional and market value; that which general opinion attaches to things, erroneously or reasonably. If it is less than the wants of the labourer, he must devote himself to some other industry, or he must perish. If it is strictly equal to them he subsists with difficulty. If it is greater he grows rich, provided always that he is economical. In every case this conventional and market value is the real one, in relation to riches; it is the true measure of the utility of the production, since it fixes its price.

However, this conventional value, this market price, is not solely the expression of the estimation in which we generally hold a thing. It varies according to the wants and means of the producer and consumer, of the buyer and of the seller; for the product of my labour, even should it have cost me much time and pains, if I am pressed to dispose of it, if there are many similar to be sold, or if there are but small means of paying for it, I must necessarily part with it for a low price. On the contrary, if the buyers are numerous, urgent, rich, I may sell very dear what I have procured very easily.* It is therefore on different circumstances, and on the equilibrium of the resistance between sellers and buyers, that the market price depends; but it is not less true, that it is the measure of the value of things, and of the utility of the labour which produces them.

There is, however, another way of considering the utility of labour, but that is less relative to the individual than to the human species in general. I explain myself by an example. Before the invention of the stocking loom, a man, or a woman, by knitting could make a pair of stockings in a given

---

* Merchants know well that to prosper there is no other mean, but to render the merchandise agreeable, and to be within reach of the rich? Why do not nations think the same? They would rivalise industry only, and would never think of desiring the impoverishment of their neighbours; they would be happy.

time; and received wages proportionate to the degree of interest which was taken in the procurement of the product of that labour, and to the difficulty of this particular labour comparatively with all other kinds. Things thus regulated the stocking loom is invented; and, I suppose that by means of this machine, the same person, without more trouble or more knowledge, can execute precisely three times as much work as before, and of the same quality. It is not doubtful but at first it would be paid three times higher for to those who wear stockings, the manner in which they have been made is indifferent. But this machine, and the small talents necessary for working it, will quickly multiply, since the industry of those who dedicate themselves to this labour is supposed neither to be more painful, nor more difficult, than the industry of those who knit; it is certain they will not have greater wages, although they do three times more work.* Their labour, then, will not be more productive for them; but it will be so for society, taken in mass, for there will be three times as many persons supplied with stockings for the same sum; or rather, to consider only the fabrication of the stockings, every one can have now as many as he could formerly for the third of the money it then required, and consequently will have two-thirds remaining to supply other wants. We may say as much of him who bruised corn between two stones before the invention of mills, with respect to the miller, who does not perhaps gain more; but who grinds an hundred times more, and better. This is the great advantage of civilized and enlightened society: every one finds himself better provided in every way, with fewer sacrifices, because the labourers produce a greater mass of utility in the same time.

It is this also, by the by, which shows the error of those who, to judge of the greater or less degree of ease of the poor classes of society in other times, compare only the price of a day's work with the price of grain; and who, if they find that the first has less increased than the second, conclude that the labourers are more straitened than they were. This is not exact, and probably not true; for, first, we do not eat grain in its natural state; and it may happen that it may have augmented in price, while bread has not, if we now grind and bake more economically. Moreover, although bread is the

---

* I abstract the price of the machine, and the interest it ought to yield.

principal expense of the poor, he has also other wants. If the arts have made progress, he may be better lodged, better clothed, have better drink, for the same price. If the society is better regulated, he may find a more regular employment for his labour, and be more certain of not being troubled in the possession of that which he has gained. In fine, it may very well be, that for the same sum he enjoys more, or at least suffers less. The elements of this calculation are so numerous, that it is very difficult, and perhaps impossible, to make it directly. We shall see in the sequel other means of deciding this question, but at this moment it leads us from the object with which we are occupied. Let us return.

We have seen that the sole and only source of all our enjoyments, of all our riches, is the employment of our force, our labour, our industry, that the true production of this industry is utility; that the measure of this utility is the salary it obtains; and besides that the quantity of utility produced is what composes the sum of our means of existence and enjoyment. Now let us examine the two great branches of this industry, the change of form and the change of place, the fabrication and the transportation, or that which is called *manufacturing* and *commercial industry.*

CHAPTER IV.

Of the Change of Form, or of Manufacturing Industry, Comprising Agriculture.

ↁ

Since the whole of society is but a continual succession of exchanges, we are all more or less merchants. In like manner, since the result of all our labours is never but the production of utility, and since the ultimate effect of all our manufactures is always to produce utility, we are all producers or manufacturers, because there is no person so unfortunate as never to do any thing useful. But by the effect of social combinations, and by the separation of the different kinds of occupation which is its consequence, every one devotes himself to a particular kind of industry. That which has for its object the fashioning and modifying all the beings which surround us, to fit them for our use, we call specifically *manufacturing or fabricating industry;* and, for reasons before given, we comprehend in this that which consists in extracting the primary materials from the elements which contain them, that is to say that which is called *agricultural industry.* Let us examine the processes, and manner of operation, of manufacturing industry in general.

M. Say has well remarked, that in every kind of industry there are three distinct things: First, to know the properties of the bodies which we employ, and the laws of nature which govern them; secondly, to avail ourselves of this knowledge to produce an useful effect; thirdly, to execute the labour necessary to attain this object. That is to say there is in every thing, as he expresses it, theory, application, and execution.

Before the existence of society, or during its infancy, every man is for himself the manufacturer of whatever he wants; and, in every species of fabrication, he is obliged to fulfil alone the three functions of which we have just spoken. But in a more advanced state of society, by the effect of the happy possibility of exchanges, not only every one devotes himself exclusively to the particular industry for which he has the most advantages; but, also, in each kind of industry, the three functions of which we are speaking are separated. Theory is the part of the man of science, application that of the *entrepreneur,* and execution that of the workman.

These three species of labourers must derive a profit from the pains they take, for a man is born naked and destitute. He cannot amass 'till after he has gained; and before having amassed he has nothing, on which to subsist, but his physical and moral faculties; if the use he makes of them produces nothing he must find a different method of employing them, or he will perish. Every one, then, of the labourers of whom we speak must find a salary in the profits resulting from the fabrication in which he co-operates.

But all have more or less need of advances, before they begin to receive this salary, for it is not in an instant, and without preparation, that their service becomes sufficiently fruitful to merit a recompence.

The man of science, or he whom at this moment we consider as such, before he can have discovered or learned truths immediately useful and applicable, has had need of long studies. He has had to make researches and experiments; he has needed books and machines; in a word, he has been obliged to incur charges and expenses, before deriving any advantage from them.

The *entrepreneur* does not less experience the necessity of some preliminary knowledge, and of a preparatory education, more or less extensive. Moreover, before he begins to manufacture, he must obtain a place, an establishment, magazines, machines, first materials, and also the means of paying workmen 'till the moment of the first returns. These are enormous advances.

Finally, the poor workman himself has not certainly great funds; yet there is scarcely a trade in which he is not obliged to have some tools of his own. He has always his clothes and his small collection of moveables. If he has but simply lived 'till the moment in which his labour begins to be worth his bare subsistence, this must always be the fruit of some former labour, that is to say of some riches already acquired, which has provided for it. Whether it be the economy of his parents, or some public establishment, or even the product of alms, which has furnished the expenses, there are always advances which have been made for him, if not by him; and they could not have been made if every one before him had lived from day to day exactly as brute animals, and had not absolutely any thing remaining from the produce of his labour.

What, then, are all these advances, great or small? They are what are commonly called *capitals,* and what I simply name *economies.* They are the surplus of the *production* of all those who have gone before us, beyond their *consumption,* for if the one had always been exactly equal to the other there would be no remainder, not even wherewith to raise children. We have inherited from our ancestors but this surplus; and it is this surplus, long accumulated in every way, always increasing in accelerated progression, which makes all the difference between a civilized nation and a savage horde, a difference, the picture of which we have before sketched.

The economists have entered into many details on the nature and employment of capitals. They have recognized many different kinds. They have distinguished capitals productive and unproductive; capitals fixed, and others circulating, moveable, and immoveable, permanent, and destructible. I see no great use in all these subdivisions. Some are very contestable, others founded on very variable circumstances, and others again entirely superfluous. It seems sufficient for the object we propose to remark, that prior economies are necessary to the commencement of every industrious enterprise, even of small extent; and it is for this reason that in every country the progress of industry is at first so slow, for it is at the commencement above all that economies are difficult; how can it but be difficult to make any accumulations, when a person has scarcely any thing beyond strict necessaries.

However, little by little, with the assistance of time and of some happy circumstances, capitals are formed. They are not all of the same kind; they are not all equal; and this gives birth to three classes of labourers, who cooperate in every manufacture, each raising himself to that to which he has been able to attain, or fixing himself at that which he has not been able to overpass. It is easy to perceive that this is the source of a great diversity in salaries. The man of science, he who can enlighten the labours of manufacturing, and render them less expensive and more fruitful, will necessarily be sought after and well paid. It is true that if his knowledge is not of an immediate utility, or if being useful it begins to diffuse itself and to become common, he will run the risk of seeing himself neglected, and even without employment; but while he is wanted his salary will be large.

The poor workman, who has nothing but his arms to offer, has not this hope: he will always be reduced to the smallest price, which may rise a little if the demand for labour is much greater than that which is offered; but which will fall even below the necessaries of life, if more workmen offer themselves than can be employed. It is in these cases they perish through the effect of their difficulties.

These two kinds of co-operators in manufacturing, the man of science and the workman, will always be in the pay of the *entrepreneur.* Thus decrees the nature of things; for it is not sufficient to know how to aid an enterprize with the head or the hands: there must first be an enterprize; and he who undertakes it, is necessarily the person who chooses, employs, and pays those who co-operate. Now who is he who can undertake it? It is the man who has already funds, with which he can meet the first expenses of establishment and supplies, and pay wages till the moment of the first returns.

What will be the measure of the recompense of this man? It will be solely the quantity of utility which he will have produced and caused to be produced. He can have no other. If having purchased an hundred francs worth of articles, whatsoever, and having expended a hundred more in changing their form, it happens that what goes from his manufactory appears to have sufficient utility to induce a person to give four hundred to procure it, he has gained two hundred francs. If he is offered only two hundred for it, he has lost his time and his pains; if he is offered but one hundred, he has lost the half of his funds; all these chances are possible. He is subject to this incertitude; which cannot affect the wage earner, who always receives the price agreed on, whatever happens.

It is commonly said that the profits of the entrepreneur (improperly called *salaries,* since no one has promised him any thing) ought to represent the price of his labour, the interest of his funds, and indemnification for the risks he has run: it is necessary and just that it should be so. I agree if you please that this is just, although the word *just* is here misapplied; because no one having contracted an obligation with this *entrepreneur,* to furnish him with these profits, there is no injustice committed if he does not receive them. I agree further that this is necessary, for him to continue his enterprize, and not to become disgusted with his profession. But I say that these calculations are not at all the cause of his good or bad success. This depends solely on the quantity of utility he has been able to produce, on the necessity that others are under of procuring it, and finally on the means they have of paying him for it; for that a thing should be demanded it is necessary it should be desired; and to buy it, it is not sufficient to have the desire of possessing it, we must also have another article to give in return.

In this simple exposition, you already find all the mechanism, and the secret springs of that part of production, which consists in manufacturing. You even discover the germ of the opposite interests, which are established between the entrepreneur and those on wages on the one part, and be-tween the entrepreneur and the consumers on the other, amongst those on wages, between themselves, amongst entrepreneurs of the same kind, even amongst entrepreneurs of different kinds, since it is amongst all these that the means of the mass of consumers are more or less unequally divided; and finally amongst consumers themselves, since it is also amongst all of them, that the enjoyment of all the utility produced is divided. You perceive that the wage earners wish there should be few to be hired, and many entre-preneurs, and the entrepreneurs that there should be few entrepreneurs, particularly in the same line as themselves, but many wage earners and also many consumers; and that the consumers, on the contrary, wish for many entrepreneurs and wage earners, and if possible few consumers, for every one fears competition in his own way, and would wish to be alone in order to be master. If you pursue further the complication of these different in-terests, in the progress of society, and the action of the passions which they produce, you will soon see all these men implore the assistance of force in favour of the idea with which they are prepossessed; or, at least, under dif-ferent pretexts, provoke prohibitive laws, to constrain those who obstruct them in this universal contention.

If there be a class which does not follow this direction, it will be that of the consumers; because all the world being consumers, all cannot unite to form a club, and to demand exceptions; for it is the general law, or rather liberty, which is their safe-guard. Thus it is precisely, because their interest is the universal interest, that it has no special representatives, or ravenous *petitioners*. It even happens that illusions divide them, and cause them to lose sight of the principal object; and that they solicit partially, and in different directions, against their real interest; for much knowledge is requisite to know it as it is general; and much justice to respect it, because the world lives on preferences. All those, on the contrary, who have a particular predominating interest, are united by it; form corporations; have active agents; never want pretexts to insist for prevalence; and abound in means, if they are rich, or if they are formidable, as are the poor in a time of troubles, that is to say when the secret of their force is revealed to them, and they are excited to abuse it.

At this moment it is not necessary to follow so far the consequences of the facts which we have established. Let us observe only, that the most necessary labours are the most generally demanded, and the most constantly employed; but, also, that it is in the nature of things, that they should always be the most moderately paid for. This cannot be otherwise. In effect, the things which are necessary to all men, are of an universal and continual use. But, for this reason alone, many occupy themselves constantly in their manufacture, and have soon learnt to produce them, by well known processes, and which require only common understanding; thus they have necessarily become as cheap as possible. Moreover it is indispensable they should not be dear; for almost their whole consumption is always made by people who have but few means, inasmuch as the poor are every where the most numerous, and are every where also the greatest consumers of necessary things, which indeed compose almost their whole expense. If then they were not at a low price they would cease to be consumed, and the poor could not subsist. It is on the lowest price to which they can be brought, that the lowest price of wages is regulated; and the workmen, who labour in their manufacture, are necessarily comprised in this latter class of the lowest wages.

Remark also, that there is nothing in what we have just said of manufacturing industry, which is not as applicable to agriculture as to all other species of manufacture. There are, in like manner, in agriculture, theory, application, and execution; and we find there the three kinds of labourers, relative to these three objects. But what applies eminently to agriculture, is the general truth which we have established, that labours the most necessary are, from this circumstance alone, the worst paid. In effect, the most important and most considerable productions of agriculture, are the cereal plants with which we are nourished. Now I ask to what price corn would rise, if all those employed in its production, were as dearly paid as those who labour in the arts of the most refined luxury? Certainly the poor workmen of all the common trades, could not attain it; they must absolutely die of hunger, or their wages must rise to a level with those of agricultural workmen; but then those of the others would rise likewise in proportion, since they are more sought after; thus the first would not be advanced. They would always be at the lowest possible rate; such is the law of necessity.

What is true of agricultural workmen comparatively with other workmen, is true of agricultural entrepreneurs comparatively with other entrepreneurs. Their processes are well known. It requires but a middling understanding to employ them. Results of a long experience; during the existence of which numerous essays have been made, and, more than is commonly believed, they are in general well enough adapted to the localities; and there are few means of ameliorating them sufficiently, sensibly to augment their profits, whatever may be said by rash speculators who from time to time nearly ruin themselves. Thence it is, that, without extraordinary circumstances,* the profits of agricultural entrepreneurs are very small in proportion to their funds, their risks, and their pains. Moreover, these well known and very simple processes, are nevertheless very embarrassing in practice; they require much care and time, so that in this state, one man can never be sufficient for the employment of large funds. He could not for example direct at the same time five or six farms even if he should have five or six times five or six thousand francs to stock them; and yet this is but

* One of these circumstances, the most extraordinary, is, without contradiction, the discovery of the advantages of the propagation of Spanish sheep, instead of those of the country. This is the immortal glory of M. D'Aubenton, and the fruit of thirty years perseverance. Well! What has happened since this has been established? Even before the cultivator could procure these animals, and before he well knew the manner of deriving advantage from them, he gives already a much higher rent for lands on which he hoped to be able to raise them: That is to say, a part of the profits is taken from him in advance; the remainder will not fail to be taken from him at the next lease.

a moderate sum, in comparison with certain lines of commerce. Thus this man, who cannot make great profits in proportion to his funds, is at the same time unable to employ considerable funds. It is then impossible that he should ever make a real fortune. This is the reason why there always are and ever will be few capitals employed in agriculture, in comparison with the quantity of those which exist in society. Let us prove this truth by facts; they will show us at the same time why agricultural operations often take different forms, which have not, or do not appear to have any thing analagous in the other arts. It is an interesting subject, which I have not yet seen well explained in any of our books on agriculture, or of economy.

You never see, or at least very rarely, a man having funds, activity, and a desire of augmenting his fortune, employ his money in buying a large extent of land, to cultivate it, and make of it his profession for life. If he buys it, it is to sell again; or to find resources necessary to some other enterprize; or to take from it a cutting of wood; or for some other speculation, more or less transitory. In a word, it is an affair of commerce, and not of agriculture. On the contrary, you often see a man possessed of a good landed estate sell it, to employ the price in some enterprize, or to procure for himself some lucrative situation. It is because culture is not really the road to fortune.

Accordingly, almost all the rich who purchase lands, if they are in business, do it because they have greater funds than they can employ in their speculations; or because they wish to place a part beyond the reach of hazard. If they occupy public functions, or if they do nothing but live at their ease, it is to place their funds in a solid and agreeable manner. But neither the one nor the other propose to occupy themselves the land which they buy. Be it pleasure or business, they always have something which interests them more. They hope never to have any further trouble with them, than to rent them to entrepreneurs of culture, as they would rent* the money

---

* It will be matter of astonishment to hear me say *rent* money, as we say rent lands, or a house; but I am more justly surprised, that when they say lend money, they do not also say to lend land—for it is the same thing. The truth is, we ought not to say lend but in cases of gratuitous loans.

When we have a property whatsoever, there are but six ways of using it. To preserve or destroy it, to give or sell it, to lend or rent it. They do not precisely destroy lands, but they keep them or give them, or sell them, or lend them, or rent them, as they do every thing else. There is the same difference between a lending and renting, as between giving and selling.

which has served to purchase them, and receive the interest, without troubling themselves whether its employment has produced loss or profit to the borrower, who makes use of it.

It is perhaps fortunate that the rich thus purchase lands to rent them; for agriculture being a laborious and little profitable profession, those who devote themselves to it have generally small means, as we have just observed. If they were obliged to begin by buying the land they wish to cultivate, all their funds would be absorbed; there would nothing remain for the other advances necessary to culture, and still they could undertake but small enterprizes. It is then more convenient for them to find lands to be rented, than to be forced to buy them; but this is not more convenient to them than it is convenient to other entrepreneurs, and to themselves, to find money to borrow, when they need it to give a greater extent to their enterprizes; and this is only advantageous to them under the same restrictions, that is to say it lessens their profits and renders their situation more precarious; for it is well known that a merchant, who does not carry on at least the greater part of his business on his own funds, is in a very dangerous situation, and rarely has great success. However, such is the situation even of those whom we call great farmers.

In a word, proprietors who let lands are lenders, and nothing more. It is very singular that we have almost always confounded and identified their interest with that of agriculture, to which it is as foreign as that of the lenders of money is to all the enterprizes undertaken by those to whom they lend. We cannot sufficiently wonder to see that almost all men, and particularly farmers, speak of great proprietors of land with a love and respect truly superstitious; regard them as the pillars of the state, the soul of society;* the foster fathers of agriculture, while they most frequently lavish horror and contempt on the lenders of money, who perform exactly the same office as the others.† A rich incumbent who has just let a farm exorbitantly high considers himself as a very clever, and what is more, as a very useful man; he

---

* If it is in considering them as men in general, enlightened and independent, it is just; but if in their quality of proprietors of land, it is absurd.

† The lenders of land have even a great advantage over the others, because when they have found a mean of obtaining a higher rent, they have by this circumstance augmented their capital: land is sold according to its rents. This does not happen to the lenders of money.

has not the least doubt of his scrupulous probity, and he does not perceive that he is exactly the same thing as the most pinching usurer, whom he condemns without hesitation, and without pity. Perhaps even his farmer, whom he ruins, does not any more than himself see this perfect similitude; so much are men the dupes of words. It is true that so long as they are so, they understand things badly; and, reciprocally, so long as they understand badly the things of which they speak, they but imperfectly comprehend the words which they use. I cannot help returning frequently to this fact, for it is a great inconvenience to just reasoning; which, however, we must endeavour to attain in every matter.

However it be, much land being in the hands of the rich, there is much to be rented; and this, as we have said, is the reason why there may be a great number of enterprizes of agriculture, although there is not a proportionate mass of funds in the hands of the men who consecrate themselves to this state. In time these rented lands arrange and distribute themselves in the manner the most favourable to the conveniencies of those who intend to work them. Hence arise to great proprietors different kinds of rural work, which are not the effect of caprice or of hazard, as is believed without reflection, but which have their causes in the nature of things, as we shall see.

In fertile countries the fecundity of the soil does not turn directly to the profit of him who cultivates it, for the proprietor does not fail to demand a rent as much higher as they are more productive. But this land yielding a great deal, the quantity which a man can employ furnishes a considerable mass of production. Now all things being otherwise equal, as the profits of every entrepreneur are always proportioned to the extent of his manufacture, here the profits may be sufficiently great to attract the attention of men possessed of a certain degree of care and capacity. Once again, it is not the fecundity of the soil which has enriched and enlightened them; but it is this fecundity which attracts them, and prevents them from transferring their means to other speculations. These men wish to make a profit from all their means; they would not be satisfied with a small work, which would leave useless a part of their funds and personal activity, and would yield them, but small profits. For their convenience great properties are distributed into large masses of land, of commonly from three to five hundred acres, with a good habitation near them. They desire nothing else.

They bring the gear, teams, cattle, provisions, sufficient to enable them to wait; they do not fear being long without receiving, to receive yet more in the end. They make tests, they sometimes discover new means of production, or of sale. In a word they manufacture, they trade, and hold their rank amongst the entrepreneurs of industry. These are our *great farmers,* and this *our great culture.* Notwithstanding these fine names, a great farm is yet without doubt a sufficiently small manufactory; but if it is almost the *minimum of manufacturing* industry in general, it is the *maximum* of agricultural industry in particular.

When the soil is less fertile, this industry cannot raise itself to this point. Put the same number of acres in a farm, and the productions will be insufficient. Put therein the double, and one man will not be sufficient by himself to work it;* besides the expenses and risks augment in a greater proportion, the enterprize is no longer worth the pains. You cannot then find the same kind of men to undertake it. And if there be capitals somewhat considerable, and intelligence in those cantons, they will be carried elsewhere. What then happens? These lands, which already yield less, the proprietors divide into still smaller portions, to place them within the competence of more persons of those of slender means, and who often even do not make the cultivation of these lands their sole occupation. It is in these places that you often see small farms, or simply houses with very little land, or even lands without any buildings. Yet these grounds are rented. Those who take them, even bring to them the instruments and animals indispensable. In short they make a profit from them, by their own labour; but it is not to be expected that they should display there the same physical and moral means, as the great farmers of whom we have just spoken. They are generally small rural proprietors who are found in these places, who join this work to their former occupations, and are contented if the whole together furnishes them with the means of living and rearing a family, without pretending much to augment their ease, and without the possibility of it, but by extraordinary chances. This is what many writers call *small culture,* in opposition to that

---

* If he takes it, it will be to under-rent and divide it. Then he will be a parasite being a speculator and not a cultivator. This is done by the principal farmers of large farms where they are let on half-stocks. Their object is traffic.

of which we have just spoken. Yet we shall see that there are several cultures still smaller, or, if you please, more miserable than this. Observe always that this kind of small culture and even that by hand, of which we shall soon speak, ordinarily pay a higher rent to proprietors than the great, in proportion to the quantity and quality of the land, by the effect of the concurrence of those who present themselves in great numbers to work it, because they have no other industry within their reach; but it is precisely this high rent which irrevocably fixes these cultivators in that state of mediocrity, or penury, which renders their culture so indifferent.

When the soil is still more ungrateful, or when by the effect of different circumstances the small rural proprietors are rare, the great proprietors of land have not this resource of forming small farms; they would not be worth the trouble of working them and there would be no body applying for them. They adopt then another plan: They form what are commonly called *domains* or sharecroppings; and they frequently attach thereto as much or more land than is contained in the great farms, particularly if they do not disdain to take into account the waste lands, which commonly are not rare in these places, and which are not entirely without utility, since they are employed for pasture, and even now and then are sown with corn to give rest to the fields more habitually cultivated. These tenant farms, as we have seen, are sufficiently large as to extent, and very small as to product; that is to say they require great pains and yield little profit. Accordingly none can be found having funds who are willing to occupy them, and to bring to them domestics, moveables, teams of horses and herds. They will not incur such expenses to gain nothing. It is as much as these tenant farms would be worth, were they abandoned for nothing, without demand of any rent. The proprietor is himself then obliged to stock them with beasts, utensils and every thing necessary for working them; and to establish thereon a family of peasants, who have nothing but their hands; and with whom he commonly agrees, instead of giving them wages, to yield them half of the product, as a recompense for their pains. Thence they are called *sharecroppers,* workers on half-shares.

If the land is too bad, this half of the produce is manifestly insufficient to subsist, even miserably, the number of men necessary to work it. They quickly run in debt, and are necessarily turned away. Yet others are always found to replace them, because these are always wretched people who know not what to do. Even those go elsewhere, often to experience the same fortune. I know some of these tenant farms which, in the memory of man, have never supported their labourers on the half of their fruits. If the tenant farm is somewhat better, the sharecroppers vegetate better or worse; and sometimes even make some small economies, but never enough to raise them to the state of real entrepreneurs. However, in those times and cantons in which the country people are somewhat less miserable, we find in this class of men some individuals who have some small matter in advance; as for example, so much as will nourish them during a year in expectation of the first crop, and who prefer taking a tenant farm on lease, at a fixed rent, rather than to divide the produce of it. They hope by very hard labour to derive a little more profit from it. These are in general more active, and gain something if the ground permits, if they are fortunate, if their family is not too numerous, if they have not given too great a rent for the land; that is to say if a number of circumstances rather improbable have united in their favour. Yet we cannot regard them as true farmers, as real entrepreneurs; since it is always the proprietor who furnishes the gear, the beasts, &c. and they contribute only their labour. Thus it is still proper to range them in the class of sharecroppers.

The mass of beasts, which the proprietor delivers and confides to the sharecropper, is called leasing. It increases every year by breeding, in places where they raise the young, and the *sharecropper* divides the increase as he divides the harvest; but on quitting he must return a *leased livestock* of equal value with that he received on entering; and, as he has nothing to answer, the proprietor or his agent keeps an active watch over him, to prevent him from encroaching on the funds by too great a sale. In some places, the proprietors not being willing or able to furnish the stock of *leased livestock,* there are cattle merchants, or other capitalists, who furnish them, who watch over the *sharecropper* in like manner, and take half the *increase* as the interest of their funds; on the whole, it is very indifferent to the sharecropper, whether they or the proprietor do it. In every case we can only see in him a miserable entrepreneur, without means, weighed down by two lenders at high premiums (he who furnishes the land and he who furnishes the cattle), who take from him all his profits, and leave him but a bare and sometimes insufficient subsistence. It is for this reason that this kind of cultivation is also justly called *small culture,* although it is exercised on sufficiently large masses of property.

There exists still another species of work to which the name of *small culture* is also given. It is that of small rural proprietors, who labour their lands themselves. Almost all the nations of modern Europe have set out from an order of things, wherein the totality of the soil was the exclusive property of a small number of great proprietors; and all the rest of the population laboured solely for them as domestics, as serfs, or as wage earners. But by the effect of industry always acting, and of successive alienations, there has been found in almost every country a greater or less number of these small proprietors of land, who all have this in common, that they live on their land, and their trade is to cultivate it. However, with respect to culture, it is wrong to arrange them all in the same class; for amongst them are some who have a somewhat considerable extent of ground; and it is particularly on poor lands we find them, because it is these that the rich have alienated in preference, not being able often to draw any thing from them themselves. These certainly do not incur the same expenses in their culture as the rich farmers of great farms; but they labour with draught animals of a better or worse quality, and they have some flocks. In a word, their work is absolutely similar to that of the small farmers, of whom we have spoken before.* There are others again who possess a very small extent of ground, and who work it with their hands alone, whether in vegetables, or in grain, or vines. These even positively require this manner of working, which, as we see, is very different from the preceding one: besides the greater part of those who thus employ themselves cannot live solely on the produce of their soil, and undertake day labour a part of the year. We must assimilate to these latter all those who hold on leases from rich persons small habitations, with spots

---

* See what is the difference of the employment of funds. This man, who cultivates on a small scale, has perhaps an estate on which he could raise thirty thousand francs. If he would sell it he would have wherewithal to take a large farm in a good country; he would be much better, and would gain more: But perhaps he does not know that this possibility exists far from him. Were he to know it he would fear the risks and his own inexperience: and, besides, man holds to his habits, and to the pleasure of property.

of ground attached to them; and who are known by the name of *tenants, labourers, cottagers,* &c. &c. Their industry is absolutely the same, and their existence quite similar; except that the small rent they pay represents the interest of the capital which the others possess: Here, then, is a third thing which is also called *small culture;* and which comprehends two kinds of it, very different from each other.

This is not all: there are many writers who call *great culture* that which is done with horses, and *small culture* that which is done with oxen; and who believe that this division answers exactly to that of farmers and sharecroppers. But these two designations are far from being equivalent, for on one side the labourers work with their hands: nothing prevents the cultivators of small farms, and the small proprietors of the first of the two species which we have distinguished, from labouring sometimes with horses or mules; and these cultures do not the less deserve the name of *small.* Moreover it may well be if such should be the local conveniences, that the great farmers may work with oxen; and I believe this is seen in several countries. On the other side, it is true that in general the sharecroppers work with oxen: 1st. Because this method being less expensive, the greater part of proprietors prefer it. 2d. Because commonly the poor countries, which are those where we see sharecroppers, produce bad hay, little or no oats, and are not susceptible of artificial meadows. 3d. Because these sharecroppers being negligent and unskilful, it is difficult to confide to them animals so delicate as horses. But it is not this which constitutes them sharecroppers, and which distinguishes between them and farmers. Their specific character is that of being wretched, without means, and unable to make any advances. It is that which reduces them to be sharecroppers, and makes their culture really *small;* although by reason of the extent of their tenant farms, which commonly occupy a great deal of ground, there are some who still call it *great culture,* in opposition to that of small farmers or small labourers, or in opposition only to culture by hand.

Finally, that nothing may be wanting to the confusion of ideas, there are some anglophile authors (as Arthur Young) who amuse themselves by calling *small culture* that of our greatest farmers, because they there see lands fallow, reserving exclusively the name of *great culture* for that system of rotation which themselves approved, without reflecting that in the smallest of all cultures, that by hand, we most frequently see land that is never suffered to rest.

Thus we see by fair statement five or six different manners of employing the same words, of which two or three at least separate things absolutely similar, and unite others totally different; and these words are continually used without explaining in which sense they are taken. Proceeding thus, it would be a great miracle if they should understand one another.

I think if it is wished to write with some precision on agriculture, we must banish the expressions *great* and *small* culture as too equivocal; but distinguish carefully four sorts of culture, which have very distinct characters, because they are essentially different; and under which we can arrange all imaginable cultures.* These are first the *large farms,* or the culture of rich and intelligent entrepreneurs, who make largely all the necessary advances. We see them only in places worth the trouble. 2dly. The *small farms,* or the culture of entrepreneurs who likewise employ draught animals of their own, but whose means of all kinds are less extensive. They are generally found on poorer soils. (This class includes the small farmers, and the small proprietors, of the first of the two species which I have distinguished.) 3dly The tenant farms, or the culture by sharecroppers, who also employ draught animals, but which do not belong to them. This is peculiar to bad soils. 4thly. *Day labourers,* or the culture by hand, as well that of proprietors as of tenants. We find these everywhere, and especially in wine regions. But they are in general less numerous in very good or in very bad countries: In the first because the rich have kept almost all the land, in the others because the land would not compensate them, and they prefer going to seek their livelihood by day labour elsewhere. This division appears to me clearer and more instructive than all the others, because it shows the causes of the effects. Let us therefore use it as to what remains for us to say.

---

* If I dare to affirm this, it is not because I have travelled much; but I have had property for about forty years, in a country of great farms, a country of vineyards, and of bad tenant farms. I have always followed their progress with attention; and more with a view to the general effect than to any particular interest. I have effected sensible ameliorations in the two latter, and I am persuaded that when we have thus a sufficient field of observation we gain more by thoroughly examining than by multiplying them.

I think I have proved that the proprietors of lands, who do not work them themselves, have absolutely nothing in common with agriculture, nor with the laws which govern it, nor with the interests which direct it; that they are purely and solely rentiers and lenders of a particular kind; and, consequently, that having to give an account of the fabrication of the products, I ought to put them aside, and consider only the entrepreneurs of culture.

Then I have shown that it is indispensable that the entrepreneurs of the most necessary manufactures should be, of all others, those who make the most slender profits, in proportion to the quantity of their advances and productions; and further, that agricultural undertakings have this particular inconvenience, that one man is not sufficient to give them so great an extent as to compensate for the smallness of his profits by the greatness of his business.

I have shown afterwards that the most fertile countries are those alone, in which the products of the quantity of land which one man can manage are sufficiently considerable to make the lot of the entrepreneur tolerable; that it is for these reasons that those countries are also the only ones in which we see entrepreneurs of culture having sufficient means and capacity; and that they moreover seldom act on their own funds, but on those of others, which is always a disadvantageous situation for manufacturers. We call them, however, *great farmers.*

2dly. That when the lands are less good, the profits become so very slender, that we can no longer find but indifferent and insufficient entrepreneurs. These are the *small farmers.*

3dly. That when the soil is still worse, the profits becoming absolutely null, the owner is reduced to the necessity of having no entrepreneur; for sharecroppers are really but receivers of wages, since they make no advances and furnish only their labour.

4thly. and finally, That other circumstances render the enterprize so small that the entrepreneur and labourer are necessarily one and the same person, who employ no machine but their hands, and employ even them often elsewhere. Such are the *day labourers.* Such a business can scarcely tempt a capitalist.

There is, however, an exception to these general truths. It is in favour of the culture of very precious productions: such as certain drugs for dying, or wines highly esteemed. There great profits may be made. Accordingly we sometimes see great capitalists buy lands suitable to these productions, cultivate them themselves, draw from them all their profits, and make of them immense and fortunate speculations. But this exception itself confirms the rule; for these productions have the merit and the price of rarities. They are a real merchandise of luxury. Thus these speculations, although agricultural, are not in the class of manufactures of things of the first necessity.

If this picture is exact, if it is a faithful representation of facts, if it is true that agriculture, even under the most favourable circumstances, is not and cannot be but a laborious and not very profitable profession, we must not be astonished that it does not hold the first rank in society, and that capitals do not seek it. We should perceive that they are not and never will be so employed but by those who cannot or know not how to employ them otherwise. The only mean of causing numerous capitals to be employed in agriculture is, then, to cause them to superabound elsewhere. This evil, if it be one, is incurable; and it is very useful to know it. For however we may say that agriculture is the first of arts; that it is the foster mother of man; that it is his natural destination; that we are wrong in not honouring it more; that the emperor of China ploughs a furrow every year, and a thousand similar fine things; all this will amount to nothing, and will change nothing in the march of society. These are vain declamations which do not merit our attention. Let us make only some short reflections on the first of these phrases, because it conceals an error. To bring it to light is to refute it.

Certainly agriculture is the first of arts in relation to necessity; for before all things we must eat in order to live. If they mean to say this only, they say what is incontestible but very insignificant.

If they understand by these words that agriculture is the only art absolutely necessary, the assertion is very inexact; for we have other very pressing wants besides that of eating, as for example that of being clothed and lodged. Moreover culture itself, in order to be in a small degree developed, needs the succour of many other arts, such as that of melting metals and fashioning wood; and its products, to be completely appropriated to our use, still require at least that of the miller and baker. Here then we see many other indispensable arts.

Finally, if they have pretended to affirm, as many will have it, that agriculture is the first of arts in relation to riches, the pretended axiom is completely false. In the first place we have seen, in respect to individuals, that those who devote themselves to agriculture are inevitably of the number of those who make the smallest profits: thus they cannot be of the richest. Now what is true of every individual cannot be false of nations, which are but collections of individuals. If you doubt the strength of this demonstration place on one side twenty thousand men occupied in the cultivation of wheat for sale, and on the other an equal number occupied in making watches. Suppose that both find a market for their produce, and see which will be the richest: Such are Geneva and Poland.

One of the things which has most contributed to the mistake of so manifest a truth is also an equivocal expression. We take very frequently our means of *subsistence* for our means of *existence.* These are two very different things. Our means of subsistence are without contradiction alimentary matters; and the quantity of these that can be procured in a country is the necessary limit of the number of men who can live therein. But our means of existence is the sum of the profits we can make by our labour, and with which we can procure for ourselves both subsistence and other enjoyments. It is in vain that the Pole raises a great quantity of wheat: the overplus of what he consumes, which he is obliged to sell to foreigners at a low price, with difficulty supplies his other wants. He does not live the better on it, nor multiply more. The Genevan, on the contrary, who does not gather even a potato, but makes great profit on the watches he manufactures, has that with which he can buy grain and all other things necessary for him; on which he can bring up his children, and likewise economise. The first, notwithstanding the great quantity of his means of subsistence, has very few of the means of existence: The second, having great means of existence, procures abundantly the articles of subsistence which he has not, and whatever else he wants. It is therefore true that these are two things, which it is very wrong not to distinguish carefully. This fault shows itself in many otherwise excellent works, (particularly in that of Mr. Malthus[1] on population) in which it casts an ambiguity over some explications, valuable in all respects. It is therefore a point which it was well to elucidate.

1. Thomas Malthus (1766–1834), English political economist, author of *An Essay on the Principle of Population* (1798), in which he argued that population growth would inevitably outgrow natural resources.

Let me not, however, be accused of mistaking the importance of agriculture, and of wishing that it should be neglected. In the first place I know very well that, although useful in itself, it is not the only thing to be desired either for individuals or for societies; and that a nation, notwithstanding great means, has but a precarious existence if it depends on strangers for its subsistence. I know, moreover, that although each single enterprize of culture cannot be regarded but as a very small manufactory, as in a large country their number is immense in comparison with that of all other works, they compose a very great portion of the industry and wealth of a nation. The great details into which I have gone to analyse the operation of all the springs of agricultural industry, prove sufficiently the importance I attach to it; and certainly to show clearly that a profession is at the same time very necessary, and very unprofitable, is the best method of proving that it should be favoured. But we have not yet reached this point. The only object at present is to establish facts. We will afterwards draw their conclusions; and if the first of these operations has been well performed the second will not be difficult. Let us confine ourselves then to these generalities on manufacturing industry, and speak of commercial industry.

CHAPTER V.

Of the Change of Place,
or of Commercial Industry.

❧

The isolated man would manufacture to a certain point, because he would labour for himself; but he would not trade, for with whom could he have trade? Commerce and society are one and the same thing. Accordingly we have seen in the first chapter, that society from its origin is essentially nothing but a continual commerce, a perpetual series of exchanges of every kind, of which we have rapidly indicated the principal advantages and the prodigious effects. Commerce then exists long before there are merchants, properly so called. These are agents who facilitate it, and who serve it, but who do not constitute it. We may even say that the exchanges which they make in their commercial capacity are but preparatory exchanges; for the exchange for use is not completed, has not fully attained its end, until the merchandise has passed from him who manufactured to him who wants it, whether to consume it or to make it the subject of a new manufacture; and the latter ought at this moment to be regarded as a consumer. The merchant, properly so called, interposes between these two persons, the producer and the consumer; but it is not to injure them. He is neither a parasite nor an inconvenient person: On the contrary, he facilitates relations, commerce, society; for, once again I repeat, all these are one and the same thing between this producer and this consumer. He is useful then, and consequently a producer also; for we have seen (Chapter II.) that whosoever is useful is a producer, and that there is no other way of being so. It is now to be shown how the merchant is a producer of utility. But previously let us give some preparatory explanations, which will be of service to us in the sequel. We have in the first chapter only shown the general advantages of exchange, and those of the commerce between man and man. Let us render sensible those of the commerce between canton and canton, and country and country; and for this purpose let us take France for example, because it is a very large and well known country.

Let us suppose the French nation the only one in the world, or surrounded with deserts impossible to be traversed. It has portions of its territory very fertile in grain; others more humid, which are good only for pasturage; others formed of arid hills, which are only proper for the cultivation of vines; finally others more mountainous, which can produce little else than wood. If each of those portions should be reduced within itself what would happen? It is clear that in the corn districts a tolerably numerous population could still be subsisted; because it would at least have the mean of amply satisfying the first of all wants, that of nourishment: however this is not the only want. Clothing, shelter, &c. &c. are also necessary. These people then will be obliged to sacrifice in woods, pasturage, and bad vines, much of this good land; of which a much smaller quantity would have sufficed to procure for them what they wanted by way of exchange, the remainder of which would still have nourished many other men, or served to provide better for those who live there. Thus this people would not be so numerous as if they enjoyed commerce, and yet they will want many things. This is still more true of those who inhabit the hills suitable to vines. If they are even industrious they will only make wine for their own use, not being able to sell it. They will exhaust themselves in unfruitful labours to produce on their arid hills some grain of inferior quality, not knowing where to purchase; they will want every thing else. The population, although agricultural, will be miserable and thin. In districts of marshes and meadows, too humid for corn, too cold for rice, it will be much worse. They must necessarily cease to cultivate, and be reduced to be graziers, and even to nourish as many animals only as they can eat. It is very true that in this situation, having beasts of burden, of draught, and for the saddle, to render themselves formidable, they will soon become brigands, as all nomadic people are; but this will be an evil the more. As for the country of woods there would be no mean of living but hunting, in proportion and so far as they would be able to find wild animals, without even thinking to preserve their skins; for what use could they make of them? This however is the state of France: if you suppress all correspondence between its parts, one half is savage the other badly provided.

Let us suppose, on the contrary, this correspondence active and easy, but always without exterior relations. Then the production proper to each canton would no longer be arrested for want of outlets, nor by the necessity of pursuing in spite of localities, labours very unfruitful but necessary for want of exchanges, in order themselves to provide either well or ill for all their wants, or at least for the most pressing. The country of good land will produce as much corn as possible; and will send it to the country of vineyards, which will produce as much wine as can be sold. Both will supply the country of pasturage, in which the animals will multiply in proportion to the market, and the men in proportion to the means of existence which this market would procure for them. And these three countries united would feed in the mountains the most rugged industrious inhabitants, by whom they will be furnished with wood and metals. They would increase the quantity of flax and hemp in the north to send linen cloth into the south; which last would increase their silks and oils to pay for them. The smallest local advantages would be turned to profit. A district of flint would furnish gun-flints to all the others which have none, and its inhabitants would live on the produce of this supply. Another of rocks alone will send mill-stones into several provinces. A little spot of sand will produce madder dye for all the diers. Some fields of a certain kind of clay will furnish earth for all the potteries. The inhabitants of the coast will set no bounds to their fishing, being able to send their salted fish into the interior; it will be the same with sea salt, with alkalies from marine plants, with the gums of resinous trees. New kinds of industry will be seen arising every where, not only for the exchange of merchandise, but also by the communication of knowledge; for if no country produces all things, none invents all things. When there is communication, what is known in one place is known every where; and it is much readier to learn, or even to perfect, than to invent; besides it is commerce itself which inspires the desire of inventing, it is even its great extension which alone renders possible many different kinds of industry.

Yet these new arts occupy a multitude of men, who do not live on their labour, because that of their neighbours having become more fruitful suffices to pay them. Here then is the same France, lately so indigent and uninhabited, filled with a numerous and well provided population. All this is solely owing to the better employment of every local advantage and of the faculties of every individual, without a necessity for the French nation to have made the smallest profit at the expense of any other nation, without even a possibility of its so doing, since our hypothesis supposes it alone in the world. We will see elsewhere what we should think of those pretended profits which one people makes at the expense of another, and how we ought to appreciate them. But we may affirm in advance, that they are illusory or very small; and that the true utility of exterior commerce, that in comparison with which all others are nothing, is to establish between different nations the same relations which interior commerce establishes between different parts of the same nation, to constitute them, if we may thus speak, in a state of society with one another; to enlarge thus the extent of market for all, and by this mean increase likewise the advantages of the interior commerce of every one.

This commerce, without doubt, can and does exist, to a certain point, before there are merchants, properly so called; that is to say men who make commerce their sole occupation; but it could not be much developed without their assistance. When a man has manufactured, or is in possession of some useful thing, he may, it is true, exchange it himself, without an intermediary, for another useful thing which some other man possesses; but this is not often either easy or commodious. This other man may not have a desire of selling when we wish to buy; he may be unwilling to sell but a great deal at a time; he may not care for that which is offered in exchange; he may be very distant; we may even not know that he has that which we desire. In fine, in the course of life one has need of an almost infinite multitude of different things. If it were necessary to draw directly each of them from its immediate producer, one would pass their whole time in going backward and forward, and even in distant journeys; the inconveniences of which would greatly surpass the utility of the things which would be their object; it would therefore be necessary to do without them.

The merchant comes: He draws from all places the things which superabound therein, and carries thither those which they want. He is always ready to buy when any one wishes to sell, and to sell when any body wishes to buy. He keeps his merchandise till the moment it is wanted, and retails it if necessary. In short, he takes it off the hands of the producer, who is encumbered with it, places it within reach of the consumer who desires it; and all their relations have become easy and commodious: Yet what has he done? In his commercial capacity he has operated no change of form, but he has operated changes of place, and a great utility is produced. In effect, since values are the measure of degrees of utility (see chapter 3d), it is manifest that a thing carried from a place where it is at a low price and brought to one in which it bears a high one, has acquired by its transportation a degree of utility which it had not before.

I know that this explication is so simple that it appears foolish, and that all this appears written for children; for men are not supposed to be ignorant of facts so common and truths so trivial. But these trivial truths demonstrate another very much contested, which is, that whoever produces utility is a producer, and that the merchant is quite as much one as those to whom they have wished exclusively to give this title. Now let us search what is his recompense for the utility he has produced.

If we examine commercial industry it presents us the same aspect as manufacturing industry. Here also, there is theory, application and execution; and consequently three kinds of labourers, the man of science, the entrepreneur, and the workman. Also, it is true that those whose labour is applied to the most necessary things are inevitably the worst paid; but it is not as in the enterprizes of agriculture. The entrepreneur can augment his speculations indefinitely as far as the market permits, and thus compensate the smallness of his profits by the extent of his business. Hence the proverb, there is no small trade in a large city. The head of a commercial enterprize also gives salaries to those he employs: He makes all the advances; and he is recompensed for his pains, his expenses, and his risks, by the augmentation of value which his labour has given to things, an augmentation which causes his *sales to surpass his purchases.* It is true that as a manufacturing entrepreneur he loses, instead of gaining, if being deceived in his speculations his labour is unfruitful. Like him, also, he labours sometimes on his own funds, sometimes on those he borrows. In short, the similarity is complete, and this dispenses me from entering into more details. It is not yet time to discuss delicate questions, nor to appreciate the merit of certain very complicated combinations. As yet we have had occasion to give a general glance of the eye only on the march of society and the train of affairs. If we have formed a just idea of them we shall soon see that many things which are thought very mysterious are merely perplexed by prejudice and quackery, and that mere common sense is sufficient to resolve difficulties which appear very embarrassing when we have not returned to principles. To complete the laying our foundation let us say a word of money.

CHAPTER VI

Of Money.

I have already spoken of the development of industry, and even of that of commerce; and I have not yet said a word of *money.* It is because in effect it is not more indispensable to commerce than merchants. Those are its agents, this its instrument. But it can and does exist, to a certain point, before and without these two helps, although they are very useful to it.

We have seen in the third paragraph of the introduction, and in the third chapter, which treats of *values,* that all useful things have a determinate value. They have even two; but at this moment I speak only of the conventional value, or market price. All these values are measured the one by the other. When, to procure any thing whatsoever, one is disposed to give a double quantity of any other thing whatsoever, it is evident that the first is twice as much esteemed as the second. Thus the relation of their value is fixed; and one can exchange or negotiate these two things at this rate, without recourse to any thing intermediate. We can give hay for corn, or corn for wood; a cartload of potters clay, or of brick earth, for some plates or tiles, &c.; but it is evident that this is very inconvenient, that it occasions removals so troublesome as to render most affairs impracticable; that many of these merchandises are not divisible, so as to correspond well with the others; that many amongst them cannot be indefinitely preserved until the moment of finding employment for them, and that were they preserved we are still greatly embarrassed if, as must continually happen, what we have is not precisely that which suits him who possesses what we desire; or if he wishes but a very small quantity of ours, when we want a large quantity of his. In the midst of all these difficulties commerce then ought to be very languishing, and consequently industry also. It is proper to dwell a little on these inconveniencies, for we are always but little affected by those which we have never experienced. We do not even imagine them. Having never seen such an order of things, we have no lively idea of it; it appears to us almost chimerical. But it has existed, and probably for a very long time before that of which we still complain; and even with reason, although it is much better.

Happily amongst all useful things there is one kind which is distinguished, that of the precious metals. These like others are a merchandise, inasmuch as they have the necessary value which results from the labour their extraction and transportation have cost, and the market value given them, by the possibility of making them into vases, ornaments, or different conveniencies and instruments. But they have moreover the property of being easily refined; so that we know very exactly what quantity we have of them, and that all their parts are similar, which renders them very comparable, and leaves no fear of their being of different qualities. Besides they are inalterable, and susceptible of being divided into portions as great or small as we wish. Finally, they are easily transported. These qualities must cause every one to prefer these metals to every other useful thing, whenever we only wish to preserve the value we possess for an indefinite time until the moment of want. For every one who has any merchandise subject to damage, the quality of which may be uncertain or changeable, which is of great incumbrance, or little susceptible of being retailed on occasion, is naturally disposed to exchange it for another which has none of those inconveniencies. From this general disposition, it will naturally result, that the merchandise, which possesses so many advantages in this respect, should become by degrees the common measure of all others. This is also what has happened every where. This appears singular when the reason is unknown, but inevitable when known. It is the same in all cases. So soon as a thing is, be assured there are victorious reasons why it should be, which however does not mean that stronger reasons may not afterwards be discovered why it should no longer be. But here it is not the case. The precious metals once become the common and general measure, the universal type of all exchanges, acquire still an advantage which they had not before. It is first to have a greater market value, as they have acquired a new kind of utility (but this would not affect the object which now occupies us); and next their market value, their price becomes more constant than that of any other merchandise. Being in constant demand in all places, and on every occasion, they are not subject to the variations experienced by a thing sometimes sought sometimes refused: Besides they do not depend on the inconstancy of the seasons, and very little on that of events. Their total quantity does not change, but from causes slow and rare. They are then every day more confirmed in their character of being the common measure of exchanges. However they are not yet *money*. As yet they are transmitted only in bars and ingots, and at every change of hands they must be assayed and weighed; this is troublesome.

When society is a little more perfected, the competent authority intervenes to give to this mean of exchanges a greater degree of commodiousness. It divides these metals into portions adapted to the most ordinary uses. It impresses on them a mark which indicates the total weight; and in this weight the quantity of foreign matter which it has been convenient to leave therein for the facility of manufacture, but which is not to be counted for real value. This is what is called the *weight* and *standard*. In this state the metals have become completely money; and authority has done a benefit in giving them this character. We shall see hereafter that it has but too often done evil by other acts of its power in this way.

This short explanation of the nature of money shows us, first, that there can only be one metal which can really be *money*, that is to say to the value of which we refer all other values; for in every calculation there can be but one kind of unit which serves as a basis. This metal is silver, because it is this which is best adapted to the greatest number of subdivisions, of which there is need in exchanges. Gold is too rare, the other metals too common.

Gold, however, comes in aid of silver in the payment of very great sums; as would, also, the precious stones if they were divisible without a loss of value. But it is only as a subsidiary that it is employed, and only by referring the value of gold to that of silver. The proportion in Europe is nearly as fifteen or sixteen to one; but it varies, as every other proportion of value according to the demand. In China it is commonly as twelve or thirteen to one; whilst in Indostan, on the contrary, we are told it is about as eighteen or twenty to one. Thus there is a profit in carrying silver to China, because for twelve ounces of silver you have there one ounce of gold, which on return into Europe is worth fifteen ounces of silver, whereby you have gained three ounces; and, on the contrary, there is a profit in carrying gold into Indostan, because for one ounce of gold you there have eighteen of silver, and thus you have gained three ounces of the latter metal. Political authorities may however very well coin money of gold and fix its proportion with that of silver, that is to say, determine that, whenever there are no stipulations to the contrary, one ounce of gold or fifteen or sixteen ounces of silver shall be received indifferently. It is as in judicial actions, they establish that when there are sums of money that ought to bear an interest which has not been stipulated by the parties, that interest shall be so much per cent. But they cannot, or at least ought not to prevent individuals from regulating between themselves the quantity of gold which they wish to give, or receive, for a certain quantity of silver, any more than from determining by agreement the rate of interest of the sum they lend or borrow. Accordingly, it is thus these two things are always arranged in the great operations of commerce, even in spite of all laws to the contrary; because without it business would not be done at all.

As to copper money, or that of billion,* wherever there is one of silver it is not real money. It is a false one. If it contained a sufficient quantity of copper to be really worth the quantity of silver to which it is made to correspond, it would be five or six times as heavy as it is, which would render it very inconvenient. Still this proportion would vary as that of gold, and more frequently, because of the more numerous uses for which copper is employed. Thus copper money is worth but the quantity of silver agreed to be given in barter for it. Accordingly it ought only to serve for the facilitation of small fractions, in which this exaggeration of its value would be of no importance; because the moment after it is paid away at the same rate, in making it fulfill the same function. But when, as has happened sometimes, the payment of large sums of money with copper is authorized, it

---

* Billion is a mixture of a great deal of copper, and so little silver, that the extraction of the latter would not be worth the expense.

greatly wrongs him who receives it; as he can never find an opportunity of realising by agreement such large masses at their nominal value; but only at their real value, which is five or six times less. Let us conclude, then, that there can never be but one metal which may be the common term of comparison, to which may be referred all values; and that this metal is silver.

Since the utility of the impression, which makes of a piece of metal, a coin of money, consists in the establishment of its standard and weight, we see further that it was very superfluous to invent, for the keeping of accounts, imaginary monies, such as livres, sous, and deniers, and others of this kind, which however are called *money of account*.* It would have been much clearer to say a coin of one ounce, of half an ounce, of an eighth of an ounce, or a grain of silver, than a piece of six livres, of three livres; of twelve or of fifteen sous. We should have always known the quantity of silver of which we wished to speak. This idea presents itself so naturally, that I am induced to believe it would have prevailed, if all monies had been of the same standard: But, as their degree of purity has always been very different, the wish perhaps has been to have a mean of expressing that such an ounce of silver was worth a sixth more than such another, in saying that the one is worth six livres, and the other five. Perhaps, also, the expression of which I speak has been rejected precisely because it was too clear: For those who have participated in these matters, have always wished that others should understand nothing of them, and they have their good reasons for it. We shall see many proofs of it.

However this may be, these arbitrary denominations being once admitted and employed in all the obligations contracted, we should take great care to make no change of them; for when I have received thirty thousand livres and have promised to repay them at a certain time, if, in the interval, the government says that the quantity of silver which was called three livres shall be called six, or which is the same thing, if it makes crowns of six livres, which do not contain more silver than was contained in the crowns of three, I who pay with these new crowns do not really return but the half of what I had received. This is merely an accommodation of which

* Several of these denominations have been originally names of real monies, a Louis, Crowns and Ducats.

an indebted legislator wishes to avail himself with his numerous creditors; and it is to veil and disguise it that he gives me such an advantage with mine, and even with himself, if by chance I am his debtor. It is true that he knows well that he has none; but it has an air of generality and reciprocity which resembles equity and dazzles. In spite of this deception, let us speak plainly, this is permitting every one to rob so as to rob himself; and it is, as we must acknowledge, what almost all governments have so frequently done with so much audacity and so little moderation, that, for example, what is now called in France a *livre,* and which formerly really was a pound of silver of twelve ounces, is scarcely one out of eighty-one parts thereof at present, when the mark is worth fifty-four livres; government, then at different times has stolen eighty parts out of eighty-one which it owed; and if there still exists a perpetual annuity of *one livre,* established in those ancient times in consideration of *twenty livres* received, it is paid at present with one part out of eighty-one of what was originally promised, and of what is honestly due. If at this time none of these annuities remain, it is because they have been successively reimbursed in the same manner as interests are at present. What is more frightful in such legal iniquity, is that it is not merely to permit injustice, it is to enjoin it, to enforce it. For, except in rare circumstances, an individual of the greatest probity is obliged to avail himself of the odious permission given him, since, every one using it against him, he would soon be ruined, and even insolvent. Thus he has but a choice between two bankruptcies, and he ought to decide in favour of that which the law authorises.

We will follow no farther the moral effects of such laws; this is not the place; and, besides, they are sufficiently sensible, their economical effects are these: First, all the creditors, who are reimbursed, are suddenly impoverished; and all the debtors, including the government, are enriched by their losses. Thus it is an extraordinary levy of money on a single class of citizens; which is even very unequally apportioned amongst them, and is further augmented uselessly by the whole portion which goes to the profit of other citizens, who find themselves in a position like that of the government, whose apparent interests are the motives of the measure.

Secondly, all the creditors who are not actually reimbursed their capitals are impoverished in like manner; because their rent is discharged with the same nominal value, but with a less real one. Here the thesis changes for the government. It is of the number of those creditors frustrated in the whole of what it receives in annual imposts; for they are paid with the same quantity of money, but with one-half less of effective silver, if it has diminished the value of money by an half. In truth, as it has the power in its hands, it soon doubles the existing imposts, and thus thinks itself at par; and that it has a clear gain of what it has avoided paying.

However, it is not so; for the third effect of this fine operation is to cause a fear that at every moment it may recommence, and that no further reliance can be had in plighted faith; to excite by this mean inquietude in all relations, and eventually to diminish all industrious and commercial speculations. Thus the public suffers, national riches diminish, and a great part of the imposts become ineffectual; for the labour which paid them is decreased, and he who gains nothing can contribute nothing. Moreover, the government has always need of being furnished with many supplies and advances; which it cannot exact by force. The price is doubled, if the value of the money is diminished one-half. This is quite plain. But, besides, every thing has become dear and scarce; and, what is more, in bargaining it is made likewise to pay for the fear it has created of its being a second time wanting in good faith. Thus its expenses are augmented in a greater proportion than its revenues, even after it has doubled the imposts.

In last result it has committed a robbery, which has caused to itself much more evil than it has produced good. Yet it is this which for a long time was very generally regarded as a wise operation of finance. It is here, then, we may well wonder how men are the dupes of words. To the shame of the human understanding, it would perhaps have been sufficient to preserve it from such an illusion, that the pieces of money should have been, as we have said, designated solely by their weight, instead of bearing insignificant names. It is very probable that then they would have seen, that half an ounce could never become an ounce.

Yet in truth, this becomes doubtful, when we see illusions, more gross and injurious than these, still succeed with many men, or at least be only imperfectly distinguished. This reflection leads us directly to paper money, with which Europe is inundated at the moment in which we are speaking

(1810); and to which recourse is always had, in spite of the constant experience of its inevitable effects.

To defend an injustice it is always necessary to rest it on an error. This is an universal rule. Those who have wished to defraud their creditors of a part of the money they owed them, by diminishing the quantity of silver contained in the money with which they expected to pay them, have all pretended that silver has no value in itself, as we cannot drink or eat it; that it is but the sign of real values; that it is the impression of the monarch which gives it the quality of a sign, and that it is indifferent whether it be put on a greater or smaller quantity of metal. One might answer them, if silver has no value, why do you retain that which you owe? You have no occasion for it. Give it to us first, then you may put your impression on pieces of wood if you please, and you will see the effect it will produce. It does not seem necessary to be very sharp sighted to devise this overwhelming answer. Yet it has not been made because it was not so easy to prove directly that silver, as all useful things, has a proper and necessary value: indeed, to demonstrate this incontestably, it was necessary to return, as we have done, and perhaps as has never been done before, to the first and only cause of all value, labour.

This foolish notion (we must call things by their names) that money is but a *sign* is then maintained, and still repeated every day. Many writers give no other name to money; and persons who think themselves historians and politicians gravely give you an account of the system of Law and discuss it at full length, without perceiving, after a hundred years of reflection, that it is solely on this notion it was founded, and that all the rest consists but in accessories, imagined to mask this foundation.* The notable principle, then, of which we are speaking is neither abandoned nor proscribed. If they no longer avail themselves of it to degrade the coins, it is not because they are ashamed of it; it is because they have found a way of making a more complete application of it. For, in fact, in the most false of coins, there remains always a little silver. In that which is now substituted for it

---

* It is for this reason that Law himself, when the abbé Terrasson proposed to him to reimburse the Catholic Church with his paper, answered: the Roman Clergy are not such fools.

there is not any; this is still better. They have not followed the counsel we just now gave, of putting the stamp of the prince on pieces of wood; they put it on paper, and this amounts to the same. The multiplied relations of perfected society have suggested this idea and likewise serve to mask the fraud. Let us explain this.

Paper, like every thing else, has no necessary value, but that which it has cost to manufacture it; and no market value, but its price in the shop as paper. When I hold a note, or an obligation of any kind, of a solvent person, to pay me at sight an hundred ounces of silver, this paper has only the real value of a piece of paper. It has not that of the hundred ounces of silver which it promises me. It is for me only the sign that I shall receive these hundred ounces of silver when I wish; in truth, when this sign is of an indubitable certainty, I am not anxious about realizing it. I may even, without taking this trouble, pass it by agreement to another person, who will be equally tranquil with myself, and who may even prefer the sign to the thing signified; because it is lighter and more portable. We have not yet either the one or the other any real value (I count for nothing that of the piece of paper), but we are as sure of having it when we wish, as with the money we are sure of having a dinner when we shall be hungry. It is this that induces us both to say, that this paper is the same thing as the silver. But this is not exact; for the paper only promises, and the silver alone is the value itself.

Proceeding from this ambiguity, the government comes and says, you all agree that the paper of a rich man is equal to silver. Mine, for much stronger reasons, should have the same property, for I am richer than any individual; and moreover, you agree that it is my impression alone which gives to silver the quality of being the sign of all values; my signature communicates to this paper the same virtue. Thus it is in all respects a real money. By a surplus of precaution, they do not want inventions to prove that the paper about to be emitted really represents immense values. It is hypothecated, sometimes on a considerable quantity of national domains, sometimes on the profits of a commercial company, which are to have prodigious success; sometimes on a sinking fund, which cannot fail to produce marvellous effects; sometimes on all these together. Urged by arguments so solid, all who hope that this operation will enable government to grant them gifts, and all its actual creditors, who fear that without this expedient they will not be paid at all, who hope to have this paper among the first, and to pass it away very soon, before it is discredited; and who moreover, calculating that if they lose something by it, they may amply indemnify themselves by subsequent affairs, do not fail to say they are fully convinced that the paper is excellent; that it is an admirable invention, which will secure the safety of the state; that they are all ready to take it; that they like it as well as silver; that their only embarrassment would be if they should meet with persons stubborn and distrustful, as there will always be, who would not be willing to receive it; that to prevent this inconvenience it will be necessary to compel every body to do as they do, and that then all difficulties will have vanished. The public itself, prejudiced by so many sophisms, which have such numerous supporters, at first relishes the measure, then desires it, and persuades itself that one must be absurd or evil intentioned not to approve it. Thus they make a real *paper money,* that is to say a paper which every one has a right to give and is obliged to take as good money; and it is not perceived that it is precisely the force they employ to render this paper better, which radically vitiates it.

In effect the government, which has only created it to liberate itself, makes in the first place enough to extinguish all its debts. It is commanded to be received, people are disposed to do it; it circulates with facility, it is in every one's hands concurrently with silver. It appears even at first to increase the activity of commerce, by multiplying capitals. Moreover it is only employed in large payments, and in the placing of funds. Thus the daily service and that infinite multitude of small exchanges which constitute the habitual march of society, continue as usual, and every body is satisfied.

Afterwards the same authority uses the same mean for its ordinary expenses. It observes necessarily less economy, conscious of resources always ready. It embarks in enterprizes, either of war, politics or administration, of which it would not have dared to think, knowing well that without this facility they would surpass its abilities. The paper is then greatly multiplied. The contractors for the government are the first to say that all things have grown very dear, that they must have much higher prices. They are careful not to avow, that it is because a promise is not silver, and that the promise begins to appear doubtful. They attribute this fact, at which they appear surprised, to a momentary encumbrance, which it will be easy to remove by slackening all payments except their own; to the intrigues of a party of mal-contents, which should be suppressed; to the jealousy of foreigners, who will only deal with them for ready money, for the objects they are obliged to draw from them. It is impossible not to yield to such good reasons; and, above all, to necessity. The expenses are therefore augmented considerably, and the paper likewise.

People receive it still because they are forced; but every one demands much more of it for the same thing. Soon an acknowledged and known proportion is established between paper and silver. It becomes so disad-vantageous to the paper, that those who live on salaries, rentiers, and the proprietors of leased estates, who are paid with this money are greatly ag-grieved. Salaries are augmented, particularly those of the officers of govern-ment; which is by so much the more burthened; the others suffer horribly. At this epoch, of the depreciation of paper, government already experiences the same loss in its imposts that individuals do on their annuities and rents. This embarrasses it, but this is not the moment to augment the public burthens. It is easy to create paper to supply the deficiency it experiences. It prefers this mean; hence a new cause of emission and depreciation.

The difference between paper and silver encreasing progressively, no one ventures to give any credit, or to make any loan; they do not even venture to buy in order to sell again; because they know not at what price they may be able to resell; all commerce languishes. The proportion or rather the disproportion continually increases; it arrives to that point that the daily transactions for things of the first necessity, and which require only small sums paid in silver, become impossible, for an hundred francs in paper would be given rather than twenty-five in silver; and, for the same reason, if you owe twelve francs nobody will give you the change on a note of an hundred. There is universal outcry and complaint. Disputes are indeterminable, because both parties are right. The evil is supposed to be remedied by making notes for the smallest sums, and they are made,* but nothing is gained by this, for from this moment we no longer see a crown; and so soon as the most usual things are paid for with paper, they rise to a

---

* We have seen them even for five sous. You may judge whether it be possible to superintend them, and if three-fourths of them were not false.

price proportioned to the discredit of the paper, that is to say, to such that nobody can afford them. The public authority is then inevitably forced to regulate the necessaries of life.

Then society ceases and universal brigandage begins. All is fraud or punishment. The government lays requisitions every where, and the people plunder; for nothing but force can oblige a sale at loss, or to part with things which they fear soon to want themselves. In fact a general want takes place; for no one makes new provisions, or new products, for fear of suffering new spoliations. All trades are abandoned. There is no longer possibility of living on the produce of regular industry: every one subsists on what he can conceal, or on what he can lay his hands, as in an enemy's country. The poorest die in crowds. We may say in the strictest sense, that society is dissolved; for there are no longer any free exchanges.

There is no longer any necessity for small notes, for the largest hardly suffice for the smallest sums. We have seen three thousand livres paid for a pair of shoes, and been very happy to obtain them in secret at this price; for force may well oblige a thing which exists to be given for nothing, but it cannot oblige it to be made. Having reached this point, the government on the contrary must give a very high nominal value to every piece of its paper, not merely that it may be of some use, but that, even to itself it may represent a little more real value than its fabrication has cost. This is the reason that in France, towards the last of the existence of paper money, government thought proper to make mandates, which were nothing but assignats of a new form;[1] but to which was attributed a value an hundred times greater than that of the others, without which they would not have paid the cost of making them. Thus the process reached that pass that a note of a hundred francs in assignats, for example, had not effectively the real value of the piece of paper on which it was written; and it would have been worth more for him who received it if blank, or rather if he had received the price which it had cost.*

---

* It is true that these mandates were the end of all; that they lasted but a few days; and that they never had a real currency: for no fear of punishment could determine any one to take them at any price.

1. Assignats were a form of paper currency issued during the period of the French Revolution. They were subject to hyperinflation and quickly became worthless.

Such a fact appears incredible; yet we have all witnessed it, and it clearly proves two important truths: The one, that when we endeavor to go contrary to the nature of things, we are inevitably pushed to the most monstrous extremities; the other, that it is as impossible to give to things a real value which they have not, as to take from them the natural and necessary value which they have, which consists (we cannot too often repeat it) in the labour which their production has cost.

In vain would it be said that *paper money*, may be used, without being abused to this excess. Constant experience proves the contrary; and, independently of experience, reason demonstrates, that once abused, we are forced to abuse it more; and that it is not made *money*, that is to say having a forced circulation, but on purpose to be abused. For when you leave it to a free course, the moment in which a fear that you cannot fulfill your engagements occasions an unwillingness to receive it, indicates the moment in which effectively you begin to form engagements beyond your resources, that is to say to abuse it; when you give it a forced currency, it is because you are unwilling to be warned of that moment, and are determined to go beyond it, that is to say to enter into engagements which you cannot fulfill. In a word when your paper is good, it is useless to oblige people to receive it; when bad, it is iniquitous and absurd to force it to be received as good. No solid answer can ever be given to this dilemma. Mirabeau had therefore great reason to utter the celebrated phrase, which he too much forgot afterwards: *All paper money is a frenzy of despotism run mad.*[2]

We have seen that the consequences of the madness are still more fatal than those of the debasement of coins. The reason is simple. This debasement when not repeated, has but a momentary effect, by which many suffer as by a hail storm, and others profit as by a windfall; but all things resume quickly their ordinary course. On the contrary, the gradual depreciation of paper money, during all the time of its existence, produces the effect of an infinite number of successive debasements continued to total annihilation; and during all this time, no one knowing on what to calculate, the progress

2. Probable reference to Victor de Riqueti, marquis de Mirabeau (1715–89), French economist of the physiocratic school. However, it is more likely a reference to his son, Honoré-Gabriel Riqueti (1749–91), one of the early leaders of the French Revolution.

of society is completely interverted. Add to this, that paper is made to much larger amounts than even bad money is coined. Thus the evil is still much greater.

Let us conclude, that *paper money* is the most culpable and most fatal of all fraudulent bankruptcies; that the adulteration of *metallic monies* comes next; and that when a government is sufficiently unfortunate to be no longer able to pay its debts, it can do nothing better than declare frankly its insolvency, and come to terms faithfully with its creditors, as an imprudent but honest merchant. The evil is much less; reputation remains, and confidence is soon renewed: three inestimable advantages. Wherever there is candour, and probity, there is remedy for misfortune. This is one of the numerous points at which *economy* and *morality* are joined; and which render them but different parts of the same subject, the case of that one of our intellectual faculties which we call *the will.*

After having thus spoken of silver, its uses, its real value, of the danger of pretending to replace it by fictitious values, it is proper to turn our thoughts for a moment to what is called the *interest of money.* This subject like many others would be very simple, if endeavours had not often been used to obscure it; and if it had never been treated on, but after the preliminaries with which we have preceded it.

Since we rent horses, coaches, furniture, houses, lands, in a word whatever is useful and has a value, we may well rent money also, which is likewise useful, has a value, and is exchanged every day for all these things. This rent of money is what is called *interest.* It is as legitimate as every other rent. It ought to be equally free. There is no more reason why public authority should determine its rate, than that of the lease of a house or a farm. This principle is so evident, that it ought never to have met with any difficulty.

There is nevertheless what is called *legal interest;* it is that which tribunals adjudge in judiciary cases, in cases in which the parties have not been able to agree, but in which it is still just that the debtor should pay some interest. It is very proper that the law should have determined it beforehand. It should neither be too high nor too low; not too high, that the debtor of good faith, who wished to pay his debts, but has been prevented by circumstances not depending on himself, should not be aggrieved for having been obliged to detain his money. Not too low, that the debtor of bad faith, who has had recourse to chicanery to defer payment, may not gain by having retained the disposition of his funds. In a word, it should be such that neither the creditor nor the debtor should be injured. For this purpose, the law should fix it as it is to be presumed that the parties would have agreed on, that is to say conformably to the most ordinary rate in analogous circumstances. But once again I repeat it, this *legal interest* should be of no consideration, whenever the parties have themselves been able to make their agreements. The public authority should never intervene in particular transactions, but to ensure their execution, and to lend its support to the fidelity of engagements.

It is true however, that it is the interest of society in general, that the interest of money should be low. First, because all the rents, paid by industrious men to capitalists, are so far funds taken from the laborious class for the profit of the idle. Secondly, because, when these rents are high, they absorb so large a part of the profits of industrious enterprises that many become impossible. Thirdly, because the higher these rents are, the greater the number of those who live without doing any thing. But all this is not a reason for government to fix the rate of interest; for we have already seen that society has absolutely the same motives for desiring that the rents of land should be at a low rate;* and yet no one has ever proposed to declare

---

* Agriculture is no where so flourishing and advancing as in those countries where the rents of land are as yet nothing; because there are still lands belonging to nobody; for then all the produce of these lands is for him who cultivates them. See the western part of the United States of America.

This should teach us to appreciate the sagacity of those profound politicians, who pretend that it is highly advantageous to a nation that its landed property should sell very high; because, say they, it follows that its soil, which is a large part of its capital, has a great value. They have no doubts on the subject.

However there are two ways of understanding the expression, very dear. Do they wish to say, that it is desirable that land should be sold high, in proportion to the rent which may be drawn from it? that is true; for this proves that the interest of money is low, and that the idle take but little from the laborer.

But do they wish to say that it is good that an acre of land should sell dear in proportion to what it will produce? that is false; for this price is so much taken from him who is going to work this acre, thus it is to say, that it is advantageous to take from this useful man a part of his means, and often to render his enterprize impossible by augmenting its expenses. Experience and reason declare equally against this mistake.

usurious and illicit the rents of farms which exceed a certain price. More-over, to fix the rate of interest is not a mean of diminishing it; on the con-trary, it is only in some manner to invite to dissimulation: for the lender will always require the most he can get for the enjoyment of his capital; and he will also be indemnified for the risk he runs in eluding an imprudent and even an unjust law. The only mean of diminishing the price of the interest of money is to make the mass of a nation rich, that thus there may be large sums to be lent, and that industrious men nevertheless have little need of borrowing.

Instead of fixing the rate of interest, we might perhaps extend to this kind of convention the principle of *damage for more than the half,* which, in certain cases, authorises the annulment of engagements; but the applica-tion of this principle would often be very embarrassing in matters of loan: it would require attention to many circumstances of difficult estimate, and especially to the degree of risk run by the lender in parting with his funds. At least, I would wish in this supposition for still stronger reasons, that the rents of land should be comprised under the same rule; for there is no risk of the funds being carried off. But I would always prefer that individuals should be left entirely free in their conventions.

To finish this chapter on money, and all that has relation to it, it remains for us to say a word on *exchange* and on *banks.* These are two very distinct things which are often confounded; let us examine them separately.

Exchange, or the service of an exchanger, is an operation the most sim-ple. It is to barter money for money when it is required. It is only necessary to know how much pure gold or silver is contained by each of the two to render the same quantity he receives, and to take a stipulated reward for the small service he performs; or it is to barter ingots for money. This is still exactly the same thing. It is only necessary further to take into account the small increase of value which is given to the metal by the quality of money, impressed on it by the effigy or seal of the sovereign. If the standard value of metals were as easy to be established as their weights, the personal inter-est, the most inventive in fishing in troubled water, could not throw the least obscurity on a similar transaction; and, notwithstanding this small difficulty of the assay, it is still sufficiently clear when nothing else is min-gled with it, because the two things to be exchanged are present. It is only requisite to value both and to barter. But the operation of the exchanger is often complicated with that of the banker. Let us now explain this.

The function of the banker is to enable you to receive in another town, the money which you deliver him in this in which you are. In this he renders you a service, for if you have need of your money in that other town, either to pay debts or to expend there, you must send or carry it thither; and this occasions expense and risk. The banker, who has a correspondent there, gives you a note called a *bill of exchange,* in virtue of which the correspondent remits you your amount. On an inverse occasion, the same correspondent gives to another person a like bill of exchange on your banker; thus they are quits, and they have obliged two persons; and, as every service merits a reward, they have retained at each time for their recompense a stipulated portion of the money transported. Such is the service and the profit of a banker.

I have always been astonished that writers, who have given long dissertations on this negociation, who know its utility, who have exaggerated its importance, have mistaken the increase of value, which a merchandise receives by a change of place; and have refused the quality of producer to the merchant, who transports it: for in this case, which is the most simple, it is very clear that when you, who live in Paris, owe an hundred francs at Marseilles, you would rather give your banker an hundred and one francs, than to carry yourself or send your hundred francs to Marseilles: and, reciprocally, if you had there an hundred francs, you would rather receive ninety-nine of them at Paris of the same banker, than go to Marseilles and receive the whole amount. Merchandise delivered at its destination has then really a value which it had not before; it is this which engages you to give your banker a recompence, although it costs him nothing to render you this service.

To this first profit he commonly adds another. You give him your money to day, the bill which he gives you in return will only be payable in fifteen or twenty days, more or less; time must be allowed for its arrival; the correspondent must be apprized; he might not have the funds; pretexts are never wanting to lengthen the delay. However it is not till the day of payment that the banker credits the sum to his associate. Thus, during all the interval, he enjoys your money gratuitously and can put it to use; and as money bears an interest it is a profit sufficiently considerable: for it is plain, that if he has successively eighteen or twenty similar commissions; he has gained the interest of the sum for a whole year.

To these calculations must be added a third. When many Marseillese are indebted to the Parisians, they all demand bills payable at Paris. These become scarce; the bankers may be embarrassed in furnishing them, their correspondents being already in advance with them. They take occasion hence to demand of you, independent of their commission, an hundred and two or three ounces of silver for procuring an hundred to your order at Paris; and you, who are under a necessity of acquitting yourself, will give it, not being able to do it for less. For a contrary reason, if Parisians have at the same time need of bills on Marseilles, the bankers of Paris might for an hundred ounces of silver give them a bill for an hundred and two or three ounces, since this is the price put on them at Marseilles. But as they alone are well acquainted with these fluctuations, they always combine to prevent the individuals from the whole profit, and to throw on them more than a necessary loss; and this is a new source of profit for them.

This is what is called, not very properly, in my opinion, the *course of exchange;* and what ought rather, as I think, to be called the *course of banking:* for these two cities being in the same country, and employing the same money, there is no exchange, but merely a transportation of specie, which is the proper office of the bank. This course is said to be at par, when an hundred ounces of silver in one place are paid with an hundred in another; and that it is high or low, when it requires more or less,* always independently of the banker's commission.

---

* When less than a hundred francs are sufficient to pay an hundred elsewhere, it is said that the exchange is *low.* This is the case with the city which, compensation being made, still remains creditor, because apparently it has sent to the other more merchandise than it has received. This low exchange gives it an advantage in importation, for it can pay for the same things with less silver. But for the same reason it is disadvantageous if it continues to export, for it will require more money to pay them for the same quantity of merchandise. This is equivalent to a rise of price, and diminishes the demand.

This sole consideration, independently of many others, shows how ridiculous it is to believe that a country can always and constantly export more than it imports. It would be quickly arrested merely by the course of exchange. But we are not yet come to the examination of the reveries on the pretended balance of commerce; it suffices to have made this observation.

The operation of exchange, on the contrary, mingles itself with that of banking, and complicates it when funds are to be transported from one country to another: for the sum which is received at Paris, and for which a bill is given on London, has been deposited in French money and will be paid in English money. We must ascertain then the concordance of these two monies, and determine how much pure metal is contained in each, according to the known laws of their manufacture. We must estimate too, at least approximately, what the pieces of money in the two countries may have lost since they have been in circulation. Hence it is that all other things being equal, less is demanded to pay the same sum in any country, when the money is ancient, and has consequently suffered much waste by use, and by the fraud of clippers, than when it is quite new and untouched: for in the latter case it contains really more metal, and the bearer of the bill will receive more for the same sum. This exchange is yet another source of profit for the bankers.

To this all the operations of exchange and banking are reduced, which as we see are very simple, and would be very clear if all coins bore the name of their weight and the mark of their standard value; and if pedantry and charlatanism had not concealed and disguised notions so common, under a multitude of barbarous names and cant terms, such as the initiated alone can understand.

Bankers render yet another kind of service. When the bearer of a bill of exchange, not yet due, has need of money, they advance it to him, retaining the interest of the sum for the time remaining before the day of payment. This is called *discount*. Sometimes they receive from an individual effects not demandable other than bills of exchange; as bills of credit of long terms, title papers of property, and hypothecations on land; and guaranteed by these securities they advance money to him, making him pay an interest higher or lower. At other times, knowing a man to be solvent, they give him for a retribution a credit on them for a determinate sum; and they make themselves the agents of all his business, undertake to collect all his credits and to pay all his debts. These are so many ways of being useful; but in all these cases they are essentially *lenders* and *agents for business,* and not properly *bankers,* although bank services are mingled with these operations. All this, nevertheless, is ordinarily comprehended under the names of banks of discount, accommodation, credit, circulation, &c.

All these bankers, exchangers, agents, lenders, discounters, at least the richest and most accredited amongst them, have a strong tendency to unite themselves into large companies. Their ordinary pretext is, that transacting thus much more business they may be content with a smaller profit on each, and perform all the services on much better terms; but this pretext is illusory—for if they transact more business they employ more funds, and surely it is not their intention that every part of their funds should yield them a smaller profit. The truth is, that, on the contrary, they wish, by getting almost all the business into their own hands, to avoid competition, and make greater profits without any obstacle. Government, on their part, are much disposed to favor the establishment of these large companies, and to give them privileges to the detriment of their rivals, and of the public, with the expectation of receiving from them loans, either gratuitous or at a low rate which these never refuse. It is thus that the one sells its protection and the other buys it; and this is already a very great evil.

But these companies are of a much greater inconvenience. They emit bills payable at sight, bearing no interest, which they give for ready money. All those who depend on them, or are connected with them (and they are very numerous), take their notes with eagerness and offer them to others. The public even which has great confidence in their solvency receives them willingly as very convenient. Thus they spread with facility, and are multiplied extremely. The company reaps in this an enormous gain, because the whole sum represented by these bills has cost it nothing but the manufacture of its paper, and yield it a profit as ready money. However this is not yet an inconvenience, because these bills are always realized the moment they are demanded.

But soon the government, which has created it but for this purpose, asks of this company enormous loans; it dares not and cannot refuse them, because it depends on government to overthrow it by withdrawing its support for a moment. To satisfy this demand, it is obliged to create an excessive quantity of new notes; it delivers them to the government, which employs them very quickly; the circulation is overdone with them; inquietude follows, every one wishes to realise them. It is evidently impossible, unless government repays that which it has borrowed; and this it does not do. The company can then but invoke its support. It asks to be authorized not to pay its notes, and to give them a forced circulation. It obtains its request, and society finds itself in the full state of *paper money,* of which we have seen the consequences. It is thus that the *caisse d'escompte** produced the *assignats* in France. It is thus that the bank of London has brought England to the same state in which it is at this moment. It is thus all privileged companies end: to the extent that they are privileged they are radically vicious; and every thing essentially bad always terminates badly, notwithstanding its transient successes; all things hang together, and necessity is invincible.

It would be easy to show that were these great machines so sophisticated not to produce the horrible danger which we have just described, the advantages promised by them would be illusory or very inconsiderable, and could add but very little to the mass of national industry and wealth. But it is not necessary to enter now into details; it suffices for us to have seen in a general manner the progression of affairs. Before going further, let us look back on the road over which we have travelled. It is the mean of not going wrong as we advance.

* A bank existing at Paris at the commencement of the Revolution.

CHAPTER VII.

Reflections on What Precedes.

ഏ

Many readers will perhaps imagine that, so far, I have followed rather a whimsical course; that I have often ascended very high to establish truths very common; that I have disposed my chapters in an order which does not appear methodical; and, above all, that I have abandoned the subjects which I have treated without giving them all the developements of which they are susceptible. But I pray them to remark, that this is not a mere treatise on political economy. It is the second section of a treatise on our intellectual faculties. It is a treatise on the will, forming a sequel to a treatise on the understanding. My intention is much less to exhaust all the details of the moral sciences, than to see how they are derived from our nature, and from the conditions of our existence, in order to detect with certainty the errors which may have slidden into them by not ascending to this source of all we are and all we know. Now to execute such a design it is not the abundance of ideas we are to seek, but their severe enchainment, and a course uninterrupted and without chasms. Still however I am persuaded that, without perceiving it, we are already much further advanced than we are aware.

In fact, we have seen that the faculty of willing, the property of being endowed with will, by giving us a distinct knowledge of our individuality, gives us thereby and necessarily the idea of property; and that thus property, with all its consequences, is an inevitable result of our nature. Here then is already a great source of rambling disquisition and of declamation totally drained.

We have afterwards seen that this same will, which constitutes all our wants, is the cause of all our means of providing for them; that the employment of our force, which it directs, is the only primitive riches and the sole principle of the value of whatever has one for us.

Before drawing any consequences from this second observation, we have likewise seen that the state of society is not only very advantageous to us, but is also so natural to us that we could not otherwise exist. Here then is another subject of common place notions, very false, exhausted.

Uniting these two points, the examination of the effect of the employment of our force, and of that of the increase of efficacy given to it by a state of society, has enabled us to discover what it is to *produce* for beings like ourselves, and what we ought to understand by this word. This, also, annihilates a great subject of ambiguity.

Strengthened by these premises, after some elucidations of the measure of utility of things, it was easy for us to conclude that all our industry reduces itself to a change of form and of place, and consequently that culture is a form of manufacturing like every other; which dissipates many clouds obscuring this subject; and has enabled us to see very clearly the progress of every kind of industry, its interests, and the obstacles opposed to them. This likewise leads us to appreciate both men and things very differently from what is commonly done.

Finally, amongst all the things which have a value, we have remarked those which possess the qualities proper for becoming *money;* and we have easily recognised the advantages and the utility of this good and real money, and the danger of debasing it and of replacing it by another entirely fictitious and false in continuation; we have even cast a rapid glance on the small operations, commonly regarded as very great, to which the *exchange* of these monies and their *economical transportation,* under the name of *banking,* give place.

From whence it follows, if I am not mistaken, that we have acquired clear and certain ideas on all the important circumstances in the *formation* of our riches. Nothing then remains but to see in what manner their *distribution* amongst individuals is effected, and in what manner their *consumption* is effected, that is to say the use we make of them. We shall then have an abridged but complete treatise on all the results of the employment of our means of existence.

This second part, the distribution of riches in society, is perhaps that one of the three which gives place to the most delicate considerations, and in which we meet with phenomena the most complicated. However, if we have well elucidated the first, we shall see the obscurity of this fly before us, and all dissipate with facility. Let us endeavour to follow constantly the clue that guides us.

CHAPTER VIII.

Of the Distribution of Our Riches amongst Individuals.

❦

Hitherto we have considered man *collectively;* it remains to examine him *distributively.* Under this second point of view he presents an aspect very different from the first. The human species, taken in mass, is rich and powerful, and sees a daily increase of its resources and its means of existence; but it is not so with individuals. All in their quality of animated beings are condemned to suffer and to die: All, after a short period of increase, should they even live through it, and after some momentary successes, should they obtain them, relapse and decline; and the most fortunate amongst them can do little more than diminish their sufferings and retard their term. Beyond this their industry cannot go. It is not useless to have this gloomy but true picture of our condition present to our minds. It will teach us not to desire impossibilities, and not to consider as a consequence of our faults what is a necessary result of our nature. It brings us back from romance to history.

There is more. These resources, these riches, so insufficient for happiness, are also very unequally divided amongst us; and this is inevitable. We have seen that *property* exists in nature: for it is impossible that every one should not be the proprietor of his individuality and of his faculties. The *inequality* in these is not less: for it is impossible that all individuals should be alike, and have the same degree of force, intelligence and happiness. This natural inequality is extended and manifested in proportion as our means are developed and diversified. While they are very limited it is less striking, but it exists. It is an error not to have recognised this among savage nations. With them particularly it is very grievous: for it is that of force without restraint.

If, to banish from society this natural inequality, we undertake to disregard natural property, and oppose ourselves to its necessary consequences, it would be in vain: for nothing which has its existence in nature can be destroyed by art. Such conventions, if they were practicable, would be a slavery too much against nature, and consequently too insupportable to be durable; and they would not accomplish their purposes. During their continuance, we should see as many quarrels for a greater share of the common goods, or a smaller part of the common trouble, as can exist among us for the defence of the property of individuals; and the only effect of such an order of things would be to establish an equality of misery and deprivation, by extinguishing the activity of personal industry. I know all they tell us of the community of property with the Spartans; but I reply boldly it is not true because it is impossible. I know well that at Sparta the rights of individuals were very little respected by the laws, and totally violated in respect to slaves. But a proof that nevertheless they still had property, is that there were thefts. Oh! tutors, what contradictory things you have said, without being aware of it!

The frequent opposition of interest among us, and the inequality of means, are then conditions of our nature, as are sufferings and death. I do not conceive that there can be men sufficiently barbarous to say that it is a good; nor can I any more conceive, that there should be any sufficiently blind, to believe that it is an evitable evil. I think this evil a necessary one, and that we must submit to it. The conclusion which I should draw from it (but it is as yet premature) is, that the laws should always endeavour to protect weakness; while too frequently they incline to favour power. The reason is easily perceived.

After these data, society should have for its basis, the free disposition of the faculties of the individual, and the guarantee of whatever he may acquire by their means; then every one exerts himself. One possesses himself of a field by cultivating it, another builds a house, a third invents some useful process, another manufactures, another transports; all make exchanges;

the most skilful gain, the most economical amass. One of the consequences of individual property is, if not that the possessor may dispose of it according to his will after death, that is to say at a time when he shall no longer have any will, yet at least that the law determines in a general manner to whom it shall pass after him; and it is natural that it should be to his nearest kindred. Then inheritance becomes a new mean of acquiring; and what is more, or rather what is worse, of acquiring without labour. However, so long as society has not occupied all the space of which it may dispose, all still prosper with care; for those who have nothing but their hands, and who do not find a sufficiently advantageous employment for their labour, can go and possess themselves of some of those lands which have no owners, and derive from them a profit so much the more considerable, as they are not obliged to lease or buy them. Accordingly care is general in new and industrious nations. But when once all the country is filled, when there no longer remains a field, which belongs to nobody, it is then that overcrowding begins. Then those who have nothing in advance, or who have too little, can do no otherwise than put themselves in the pay of those who have a sufficiency.* They offer their labour every where, it falls in price. This does not yet prevent them from begetting children and multiplying imprudently; they quickly become too numerous. Then it is only the most skilful and the most fortunate among them who can succeed. All those whose services are in the least demand, can no longer procure for themselves but a subsistence the most strict, always uncertain, and often insufficient. They become almost as unhappy as if they were still savages.

It is this class, destitute of the favours of fortune that many writers on economy call *non-proprietors;* this expression is vicious in several respects. First, there are no non-proprietors, if by that we understand men entirely without the right of property. Those of whom we speak are more or less poor; but they all possess something, and have a need of preserving it. Were they but proprietors of their individuality, of their labour, and of the wages of this labour, they would have a great interest that this property should be respected. It is but too often violated, in many of the regulations made by

---

* Once more I repeat, that hired labourers are not solely in the pay of the proprietors of land, but in that of all those who have capitals with which to pay their wages.

men who speak of nothing but property and justice. When a thing exists in nature, no one is without interest in it. This is so true of the right of property, that the felon, even, who is about to be punished for having violated it, if he is not entirely cut off from society, has an interest that this right should be respected: For the day after he had undergone his punishment, he could not be sure of any thing that remained to him, if property were not protected.

Secondly, the same writers, in opposition to the pretended *non-proprietors,* call by the name of *proprietors* those only who possess estates in land. This division is entirely false, and presents no meaning; for we have seen that a landed estate is but a capital like another, like the sum of money which it has cost, like every other effect of the same value. One may be very poor, possessing a small field, and very rich without possessing an inch of land. It is therefore ridiculous to call the possessor of a poor inclosure a proprietor, and to refuse this title to a millionaire. It would be more reasonable to divide society into poor and rich, if we knew where to place the line of demarcation. But if this division were less arbitrary, it would not be less illusory in relation to property. For, once again I repeat, the poor man has as much interest in the preservation of what he has, as the most opulent.

A distinction more real in respect to the difference of interests, would be between the wage earners on the one part, and those who employ them on the other, whether consumers or entrepreneurs. The latter, under this point of view, may be regarded as the consumers of labour. This classification would, without doubt, have the inconvenience of uniting together things very different; as, for example, of classing among the hired, a minister of state, with a day-labourer, and of placing amongst consumers the smallest master workman with the richest idler. But in fine, it is true that all the wage earners have an interest in being paid high, and that all those who employ them have an interest in paying them low. It is true, however, that the entrepreneur who has an interest in paying little to the hired, has the moment after an interest in being paid high by the definitive consumer; and, above all, it is true, that we are all more or less consumers: for the poorest day labourer consumes articles produced by other hired persons; on which I make two reflections.

First, the interest of the hired being that of a very great number, and the interest of the consumers being that of all, it is singular enough that modern governments should be always ready to sacrifice first the hired to the entrepreneurs, in shackling those by apprenticeships, corporation privileges, and other regulations; and afterwards to sacrifice the consumers to these same entrepreneurs, by granting to these privileges, and sometimes even monopolies.

Secondly, I remark, that although each of us has particular interests, we change so frequently our parts in society, that often we have under one aspect an interest contrary to that which we have under another, so that we find ourselves connected with those to whom we were opposed the moment before; which fortunately prevents us from forming groups who are constantly enemies. But, above all, I observe that in the midst of all these momentary conflicts, we are all and always united by the common and immutable interests of proprietors and consumers, that is to say, that we have all and always an interest, first, that property be respected; secondly, that industry should be perfected; or, in other words, that manufacturing and transportation should be in the best state possible. These truths are useful, to comprehend perfectly the workings of society, and to be sensible of all its advantages. It was a desire of rendering them evident which induced me to enter into these details. Let us return to the subject of the distribution of riches, from which they have drawn us, although they are not foreign to it.

I have a little hastened above the moment in which distress begins to make itself felt in the bosom of new societies, by fixing it at the instant in which all land has a master, and at which it can no longer be procured, without being bought or rented. Certainly at this epoch a great mean of care is exhausted, labour loses an opportunity of employing itself in a manner extremely advantageous, and the mass of subsistence ceases to increase as rapidly; because there can no longer be a question of establishing new cultures, but only of perfecting the old, a thing always more difficult and less productive than is generally believed. However immense resources still remain. All the arts offer them in competition, especially if the race of men who form the new society have sprung from an industrious and enlightened nation, and if it has relations with other civilized countries: for then there is no question about inventing and discovering, which is always very slow; but of profiting and practising what is known, which is always very easy.

In fact, so long as agriculture offered such great advantages, all men unemployed, or not profitably enough employed to their liking, have turned themselves to that. They have only thought of extracting productions from the earth, and exporting them. Observe that without a facility of exportation, the progress of agriculture would have been much less rapid, but with this circumstance, it has employed all hands. Wages excessively high have scarcely been able to determine a sufficient number of individuals to remain attached to the profession of the other arts the most necessary. But for all those things, the manufacture of which has not been indispensable within the country itself in which they are consumed, it has been more economical to draw them even from a great distance, and they have not failed to do it! Accordingly the commerce of these infant nations consists at first solely in exporting raw products, and importing manufactured articles.

Now what happens at the epoch of which we are speaking, when all the territory is occupied? Agriculture no longer offering the means of rapid fortune, the men who have been devoted to it spread into the other professions; they offer their labour; they obstruct one another; wages lower in truth: But long before they have become as low as in the countries anciently civilized from whence manufactured articles are drawn, there begins to be a profit in manufacturing within the country itself the greater part of these articles: for it is a great advantage for the manufacturer to be within reach of the consumer, and not to fear for his merchandise either the expenses or dangers of a long voyage, nor the inconveniences which result either from the slowness or difficulty of the communications; and this advantage is more than sufficient to counterbalance a certain degree of dearness in the manufactory. Manufactories then of every kind are established. Several of them, with the aid of some favourable circumstances, open to themselves foreign markets after having supplied the internal consumption, and give birth to new branches of commerce. All this occupies a numerous population, who live on the produce of the soil, which then is no longer exported in as great quantities, because it has not augmented in the same proportion. This new industry is for a long time increasing, as was agricultural industry, which was the first developed, and so long as it increases, it affords, if not riches, at least ease to the lower classes of people.* It is not until it becomes stationary or retrograde that misery begins, because all lucrative employments being filled, without a possibility of creating new ones, there is every where more labour offered than demanded. Then it is inevitable that the least skilful and least fortunate among the labourers should find no employment, or receive but insufficient wages for what they do. Many of them necessarily languish, and even perish, and a great number of wretched must constantly exist. Such is the sad state of old nations. We shall soon see from what causes they arrive at it sooner than they ought, and by what means it might to a certain point be remedied. But previously some explanations are still necessary.

In fact, I am so bold as to believe that the picture which I have just traced, of the progress of societies from their birth, presents striking truths. There is in it neither a system made at pleasure, nor a theory established beforehand. It is a simple exposition of facts. Every one may look and see, if it is not thus they present themselves to the unprejudiced eye. It may even be observed that I have represented a nation, happily situated, enjoying all kinds of advantages, and making good use of them, and yet we come to this painful conclusion, that its state of full prosperity is necessarily transient. To account for a phenomenon so afflicting, it is not possible to stop at these vague words, of degeneration, of corruption, of the old age of nations (as if an abstract being could be really old or young like a living individual), all metaphorical expressions, which have been strangely abused, with which we have often been satisfied for want of better, but which in truth explain nothing, and which if they had a prevalence, would express effects rather than causes. We must then penetrate further. Every inevitable event has its cause in nature. The cause of this is the fecundity of the human species. Thus it is necessary to consider population; and afterwards we will resume the examination of the distribution of our riches.

---

* How very desirable it would be in such a case, that the superior class of society should be sufficiently enlightened to give to the inferior ideas completely sound of the social order, during this happy and necessarily transient period, in which it is the most susceptible of instruction. If the United States of America do not profit of it, their tranquility and even safety will be much exposed, when interior and exterior obstacles, and inconveniences, shall have multiplied. This will be called their decline and corruption. It will be the slow but necessary effect of their anterior improvidence and carelessness.

CHAPTER IX.

Of the Multiplication of Individuals, or of Population.

Love is a passion which so violently affects our heads, that it is not astonishing we should often be mistaken on all its effects. I acknowledge I no more partake of the zeal of the moralists, to diminish and constrain our pleasures, than of that of the politicians, to increase our fecundity and accelerate our multiplication. Each appears to me equally contrary to reason. At a proper time I may develope my opinions on the first point, at present the second is under consideration. Let us begin by establishing facts, by taking a view of all which surrounds us.

Under this relation, as under every other, we see nature occupied solely with the species, and not at all with the individual. Its fecundity is such in every kind, that if almost the totality of germs which it produces were not abortive, and if much the greater part of the beings brought forth did not perish almost immediately for want of aliment, in a very short time a single species of plants would suffice to cover the whole earth, and one single species of animals to people it entirely. The human species is subjected to the common law, though perhaps in a smaller degree than many others. Man is led to reproduction, by the most violent and imperious of his inclinations. A man and a woman, having attained ripe age, well constituted, and surrounded with the means of providing abundantly for all their wants, are able to raise many more children than are necessary to replace themselves on the scene of the world; and, if their career is not shortened by some unforeseen accident, they die surrounded with a numerous family, which continues always increasing. Accordingly the human race, when circumstances are favourable, multiplies very rapidly. The United States of North America furnish a proof of this, their whole population doubling in twenty years, and in some places in fifteen, and even in twelve years; and, that too where the emigration is almost nothing, and without the fecundity of women being greater there than elsewhere. And it is also to be remarked, on the contrary that, whatever be the cause, cases of longevity are rare in that country, so that the mean duration of life would be shorter there than in the greater part of Europe, without the great number of infants who perish from want in this same Europe. Here is an incontestable datum, on which we can rest.

If this be so, why then is population stationary, and sometimes retrograde, in so many places, even very healthy ones? Here we must recollect the distinction we have already established, in the 4th Chapter, between our means of existence and our means of subsistence. The latter are the alimentary matters with which we are nourished; they are the most necessary part of our means of existence, but they are only a part. By these last we are to understand, all which contributes to defend us against all the dangers and all the sufferings of every kind; thus they consist in all the resources, whatever, with which we are furnished by the arts and sciences, that is to say by the entire mass of our knowledge. This distinction, well understood, we may establish as a general thesis, that *population is always proportioned to the means of existence;* and this single principle will give us an explanation of all the facts, and all their circumstances.

Amongst savages population is not only stationary, but little numerous, because their means of existence are very slender. Independently of their frequent want of subsistence, they have neither the conveniences sufficient, nor the attentions necessary for raising their children; accordingly the greater part perish. They neither know how to defend themselves against the severity of the seasons, nor the insalubrity of the climate; nor against the epidemics which frequently carry off three-fourths of a population. Having no sound ideas of the social state, wars are continual and destructive, vengeance atrocious; their women and old men are often abandoned. Thus it is misfortune and suffering, amongst them, which render the fecundity of the human species useless, and perhaps diminishes it.

Civilized people have all the resources which are wanting to the others; accordingly their population becomes numerous sooner or later; but we see it stops every where, when it has attained to that point, that many men can no longer procure by their labour sufficient wages to raise their children, and conveniently take care of themselves. If in general it is yet a little progressive, although very slowly in the actual state of our old societies, it is because the arts and sciences, and particularly the social science, being constantly cultivated there more or less perfectly, their progress is always adding from time to time some little facilities to the means of living, and open some new vents to commerce and industry. It is true that things proceed thus, that when from some causes, natural or political, great sources of profit are diminished in a country, population immediately becomes retrograde; and, on the contrary, when it has been suddenly diminished by great epidemics, or cruel wars, without knowledge having suffered, it quickly regains its level; because labour being more in demand, and better paid, the poor have more means of preserving their children and themselves.

If from these general observations we pass to particular facts, we shall find the reason for them with the same ease. Let us take Russia for the first example. I do not pretend to make either eulogy or satire on this nation, which I know not: But we may safely affirm that it is not more skillful than other European nations, yet it is proved that its population increases more rapidly than that of other states of Europe. It is because it has a great extent of land; which as yet, having no masters, offers large means of existence to those who go or are carried thither: and if this immense advantage does not there produce a multiplication of men as rapid as in the United States, it is because its social organization and its industry are far from being as perfect. Fertile countries, all things otherwise equal, are more peopled than the others, and easily repair their disasters, because their land furnishes great means, that is to say the labour applied to the land is there fruitful. Accordingly, Lombardy and Belgium, so often ravaged, are always flourishing. Poland however, which is very fertile, has a small population, and that stationary; because its inhabitants being serfs, and wretched, have in the midst of abundance very slender means of existence. But suppose for a moment the small number of men, to whom these serfs belong, and who devour their substance, driven from the country, and the land become the property of those who cultivate it, you would see them quickly become industrious, and multiply rapidly. Two other countries, in general tolerably good, Westphalia and even Switzerland, notwithstanding the latter has wiser laws, have small population through want of industry; while Geneva, Hamburgh, and all Holland have it in excess. On the contrary, Spain, which is a delicious country, has few inhabitants relatively to its extent. However it has been proved, that for the forty or fifty years, which preceded the present unhappy war, its population sensibly increased; because they had been able to free its industry from some of its fetters, and in some degree to increase their information. It is then well proved, that *population is always proportioned to the means of existence.*

This truth has been already avowed by many political writers; but we see in their works, that they have not perceived all its extent. M. Say, whom I have already cited, and whom I may frequently cite, is I think the first who has clearly said, in his first book, chap. 46, "That nothing can increase population but what favours production; and that nothing can diminish it, at least permanently, but what attacks the sources of production." And observe that by production M. Say understands *production of utility.* It is even after him that I have given this idea of it. Now to *produce* in this sense, is clearly to add to our means of existence, for whatever is useful to us is a mean of providing for our wants; and indeed nothing merits the name of *useful,* but for this reason. Thus the principle of M. Say is exactly the same with that which I have established. Accordingly he draws from it this very just conclusion, that it is absurd to attempt to influence population by direct encouragements, by laws concerning marriages, by premiums granted to numerous families, &c. &c. He justly laughs on this subject at the famous ordinances of Augustus, of Louis XIV and of so many other legislators, so much boasted of. These are in effect very false measures, which could in no way augment population; and he added, very justly, in my opinion, that the smallest regulation hurtful to industry, made by these princes could and must have diminished the number of men. I think absolutely the same.

M. Malthus goes much further still. He is, at least as far as I am acquainted, of all the authors who have written on population, the one who
has treated the subject the most profoundly, and has developed all its consequences. His work, singularly remarkable, should be regarded as the last
state of science on this important object, and he leaves almost nothing to
be desired. M. Malthus does not limit himself to prove, that though population is arrested at different degrees in different countries, and according
to different circumstances, it is always and every where as great as it can be,
having regard to the means of existence. He shows that always in civilised
nations it is too great for the happiness of man; because that men, and
above all the poor, who every where constitute the great number, urged by
the stimulus so imperious to reproduction, always multiply imprudently
and without foresight; and plunge themselves into inevitable misery by a
multiplication of the men, who demand occupation, and to whom none
can be given. All he advances is founded not only on convincing reasoning, but on tables of deaths, births, marriages, of the mean duration of life,
and of the total population collected in different countries and discussed
with care.

I add this latter point as very necessary: for it is to be observed first that
all these data not only are often inexact, but that even when exact, they
require to be examined attentively, and compared the one with the other,
with much sagacity, before consequences are drawn from them; without
which they would lead to serious errors. Secondly, that however imperfect
these documents may be, they exist but in few countries, and within a
short time only; so that in political economy, as in astronomy, we should
calculate very little on ancient and distant observations. Even in France the
simple registers of mortality deserve scarcely any confidence before the year
1700; and none of the other circumstances have been collected. Also, in the
examples of population which I have above cited, I have made no mention
of what is told respecting certain eastern countries, and of some nations
ancient or of the middle age. If China, if Spain, in the time of the Romans,
are or were as populous as we are told, there must certainly have been local
reasons for the fact. But we have no means of knowing it sufficiently to see
the causes clearly, and to venture to draw consequences. It is the same case
with all the parts of the political and domestic economy of the ancients,

founded almost solely on the practice of slavery, and the profits or losses of war, and very little on the free and peaceful developement of industry. It is an order of things entirely different from our modern societies. As to the prodigious number of men which some authors pretend to have existed in France—for example under Charles V or under Charles the IX in the fourteenth and sixteenth centuries, that is to say at times in which industry was as unskilful and the social order as bad as we have seen it in Poland in the eighteenth century—I believe the only answer to be made to these assertions is that which I have opposed to the marvellous union, which is said to have reigned at Sparta. That is, that it is not true because it is not possible.

However it may be, all those who have reflected on these matters agree, that *population is always proportioned to the means of existence.* M. Say concludes therefrom, with reason, that *it is absurd to think it possible to augment population otherwise than by an augmentation of these means;* and Mr. Malthus proves further, that it is *barbarous to endeavour to augment this population always too great,* and the excess of which is the source of all miseries; and that, even in relation to power, the chiefs of nations lose by it: for since they cannot continue in life a greater number of men than they can at the same time subsist, by multiplying births they only multiply premature deaths, and augment the number of children in proportion to that of adults; which produces a weaker population, numbers being equal. *The interest of men, under every consideration, then is to diminish the effects of their fecundity.*

I will say no more on the subject, which is but too clear of itself; and which nevertheless has given occasion to such false opinions, before it was thoroughly explained. We leave them for time to destroy.

CHAPTER X.

Consequences and Developments of the Two Preceding Chapters.

ↂ

Let us always return to the point of departure. An animated being, and especially man, is endowed with sensibility and activity,* with passion and action, that is to say with wants and means. While we were considering the manner in which our riches are formed, we might be charmed with our power and the extent of our means; in fact these are sufficient to render the species prosperous, and give it a great augmentation, both in number and in force. A man and woman, inept and scarcely formed, might end by covering the whole earth with a numerous and industrious population. This picture is very satisfactory; but it changes essentially its colour, when, from the examination of the formation of our riches, we pass to that of their distribution amongst the different individuals. There we every where find the superiority of wants over means; the weakness of the individual, and his inevitable sufferings. But this second aspect of the same object ought neither to disgust nor discourage us. We are thus formed. Such is our nature; we must submit, and make the most we can of it by a skilful use of all our means, and by avoiding the faults which aggravate our evils.

The two chapters which we have just read, although very short, embrace important facts; and, joined to prior explanations, give notions sufficiently certain on our true interests. It only remains to profit of them.

* We might say with nerves and muscles, for it goes to that.

We have seen, that we must be satisfied to permit an opposition of interests, and an inequality of means to exist among us; and that the best we can do is to leave to every one the freest employment of his faculties, and to favour their entire development.

We have moreover seen that this employment and development of faculties, although profiting unequally the different individuals, succeeded in conducting all to the highest state of well-being possible, so long as space, the greatest of all resources, was not wanting; and that when all the land is occupied, other subsidiary resources sufficed to support for a long time a high state of general prosperity.

We have also seen that, having once arrived to the period of being crouded and constrained, it is inevitable that those who have the smallest means will be able to procure by the employment of these means, but a bare satisfaction of their most urgent wants.

We have finally seen that, the multiplication of men continuing in all the classes of society, the superfluity of the first has been successively cast into the inferior classes; and that that of the last having no longer any resource, has been necessarily destroyed by wretchedness. It is this which causes the stationary and even retrograde state of population, wherever it is found, in spite of the great fecundity of the species.

This latter fact, population nearly stationary in all nations arrived to a certain degree of development, was for a long time scarcely remarked; because it is but lately, that we have begun to occupy ourselves with some success on social economy. It has ever been concealed by political commotions, which have produced disturbers of it; and has been disguised by the unfaithful or insufficient monuments of history, which have authorized mistakes. Finally, when it has been sufficiently observed and established, it has been with difficulty attributed to the real cause; because they had not an idea sufficiently clear of the progress of society, and of the manner in which its riches and power are formed. Today, it appears to me we are able to put all this beyond a doubt.

Let us recollect that society is divided into two great classes, that of men, who, without having any thing in advance, work for wages, and that of men who employ them. This granted, it is evident that the first—taken in mass—live, daily and yearly, only on what the totality of the second has to distribute to them every day and every year. Now this latter class is of two kinds: the one lives on their revenue, without labour. These are the lenders of money, the lessors of lands and houses, and in a word the rentiers of every kind. It is very clear that these men, in the long run, cannot give more in a year to those they employ than the amount of their revenue, or they would encroach on their funds. There is always a certain number who use them thus, and who ruin themselves. Their consumption diminishes or ceases; but it is replaced by those who become enriched, and the total continues the same. This is but a change of hands, of which even the ordinary quantity may be nearly estimated in the different countries. These men, taken in mass, make no profit; thus the sum total of their revenue, which is devided amongst the hired, is a constant quantity. If it makes some insensible progress, it can only be by the slow improvement in agriculture; which, by rendering land a little more productive, furnishes ground for a small augmentation of rents. For as to the hire of their money lent, it does not vary. If ever it did augment by a rise in the rate of interest, it would be an evil which, injuring many enterprises, would diminish much more the faculties of the second class, who feed those who work for wages.

This second kind of persons is composed of those who join to the product of their capital, that of their personal activity, that is to say the entrepreneurs of any kind of industry whatsoever. It will be said that these make profits, and augment their means annually; but, first, this is not true of all. Many of them manage their affairs badly, and go to decay instead of thriving. Secondly, those who prosper, cease to labour after a certain time, and go to fill the void which is daily produced in the class of those who live without doing any thing, by the fall of spendthrifts withdrawing from it in consequence of having badly managed their fortunes. Thirdly, in fine, and this is decisive, this class of *industrial entrepreneurs* has necessary limits, beyond which it cannot go. To form any enterprize whatever, it is not sufficient to have the desire and means: it is necessary to be able to dispose of the products in an advantageous manner, which more than defrays the expenses they cost. When once all profitable employments are filled, no new ones can be created, unless others fall, at least unless some new outlets are opened. This second fund for the support of the hired class is also, then, in our ancient societies, a quantity nearly constant like the first.

Things being thus, we see clearly why the number of hired does not augment, when the funds which might provide for their support, cease to increase. It is because all who are born beyond the requisite number perish through want of the means of existence. This is very easy to be conceived. We even comprehend that it is impossible for it to be otherwise, for every one knows that if four persons are daily to divide a loaf of bread, barely sufficient for two, the weaker will perish, and the stronger will subsist only because they quickly inherit the portion of the others.

If we further observe, that when the men who live solely on their revenues multiply so much that this revenue suffices for them no longer, they return into the class of those who join their labour to the product of their funds; that is to say of those whom we have called *industrial entrepreneurs,* and that when these, in their turn, become too numerous, many are received and link into the class of wage earners, we shall see that this latter class receives as we may say the too great plenitude of all the others; and that, consequently, the limits beyond which it cannot go are those of the total production.

This single point, well elucidated, gives us an explanation of all the phenomena relative to population. It shows why it is retrograde in one country, stationary in another, while it is rapidly progressive in a third; why it is arrested sometimes sooner sometimes later, according to the degree of intelligence and of activity of different people, and the nature of their governments; why it is quickly re-established after great calamities of a transient nature, when the means of existence have not been destroyed; why, on the contrary, without any violent shock, it sometimes languishes and perishes gradually, from causes difficult to be perceived, from the single change of a circumstance little remarkable. In a word, it gives us the solution of all the questions of this kind, and moreover furnishes us with the means of drawing therefrom an infinity of important consequences. I am only embarrassed with their number, and the choice of those which I ought to notice.

I will commence by remarking, with satisfaction, that humanity, justice and policy, equally require that of all interests, those of the poor should always be the most consulted, and the most constantly respected; and by the poor I mean simple wage earners, and every where those whose labour is worst paid.

First, humanity: for we should observe, that when it respects the poor, the word *interest* has quite a different degree of energy, from what it has when men are spoken of whose wants are less urgent, and sometimes even imaginary. We every day say, that the interests of one minister are contrary to those of another; that such a body has interests opposed to those of another body; that it is the interest of certain entrepreneurs, that the raw material should sell high; and the interest of some others to buy them low. And we often espouse these motives with warmth as if they were worth the trouble. Yet this means no more than that some men believe, and often erroneously, that they have a little more or a little less enjoyment under some circumstances than under others. The poor, in his small sphere, has, assuredly, also interests of this kind; but they disappear before greater ones; we only do not perceive them, and, when we attend to him, the question is almost always on the possibility of his existence or the necessity of his destruction, that is to say of his life or his death. Humanity does not permit interests of this kind to be placed in the balance with simple conveniences.

Justice is equally opposed to it; and, moreover, it obliges us to take into consideration the number of those interested. Now, as the lowest class of society is every where much the most numerous, it follows, that whenever it is in opposition with others, what is useful to it, ought always to be preferred.

Policy leads us to the same result: for it is well agreed, that it is useful to a nation to be numerous and powerful. Now it has just been proved, that the extent to which the lower class can go, is that which determines the limits of the total population; and it is not less so by the experience of all ages and countries, that wherever this lowest class is too wretched, there is neither activity, nor industry, nor knowledge, nor real national force, and we may even say, nor interior tranquillity well established.

This granted, let us examine what are the real interests of the poor; and we shall find that, effectually, they are always conformable to reason and the general interest. If they had always been studied in this spirit, we should have acquired sounder ideas of social order, and we would not have eternized war, sometimes secret, sometimes declared, which has always existed between the poor and the rich. Prejudices produce difficulties, reason resolves them.

We have already seen, that the poor are as much interested in the maintenance of the right of property as the most opulent: for the little they possess is every thing for them, and of consequence infinitely precious in their eyes; and they are sure of nothing, but so far as property is respected. They have still another reason for wishing it; it is that the funds on which they live, the sum of the capitals of those who employ them, is considerably diminished when property is not assured. Thus they have a direct interest, not only in the preservation of what they possess, but also in the preservation of what is possessed by others. Accordingly, notwithstanding that from the fatal effects of misery, of bad education, of the want of delicacy, and of a sense of injustice, it would perhaps be true to say, that it is in the lowest class that most crimes are committed* it is, however, also true, that it is this class which has the highest idea of the right of property, and in which the name of thief is the most odious. But when you speak of property, comprehend under this term, as the poor do, personal property, as well as that which is moveable and immoveable. The first is even the most sacred, since it is the source of the others. Respect that, in them, as you wish they should respect, in you, those which are derived from it; leave to him the free disposition of his faculties, and of their employment, as you wish him to leave to you that of your lands and capitals. This rule is as politic, as it is just and unattended to.

After the free disposition of his labour, the greatest interest of the poor man is that this labour should be dearly paid. Against this I hear violent outcries. All the superior classes of society, and in this view I even comprehend the smallest chief of a workshop, desire that the wages should be very low, in order that they may procure more labour for the same sum of money; and they desire it with so much fury, that when they can, and the laws permit them, they employ even violence to attain this end, and they prefer the labour of slaves, or serfs, because it is still at a lower rate. These men do not fail to say, and persuade, that what they think is their interest, is the general interest; and that the low price of wages is absolutely necessary to the development of industry, to the extension of manufactures and

---

* This is very doubtful, if we take into consideration the difference in the number of individuals.

commerce, in a word, to the property of the state. Let us see how much truth there is in these observations.

I know it would be disagreeable that the price of workmanship should be so dear as to render it economical to draw from abroad all transportable things: for then those engaged in their fabrication would suffer, and would become extinct; it would be a foreign population which the consumers would pay, and support, instead of a national one. But, first, this degree of dearness would be no longer for the interest of the poor, since, instead of being well paid, they would want employment; and, moreover, it is impossible, or at least it could not continue; because, on one part, the wage earners would lower their pretentions so soon as they found themselves out of employ; and, on the other, if the price of a days's work still remained so high as to afford them a great degree of ease, they would soon multiply sufficiently to be obliged to offer their labour at a lower rate. I add that if nevertheless the price of workmanship should still remain too high, it would no longer be to the scarcity of workmen that it ought to be attributed, but to unskilfulness and bad workmanship; and then it would be the unskilfulness, ignorance, and laziness, of men which ought to be combated. These are effectually the true causes of the languor of industry, wherever it is remarked.

But where are these sad causes met with? Is it not always and uniformly there where the lowest class of the people is most miserable? This furnishes me new arms against those who believe it to be so useful, that labour should be badly paid. I maintain that their avidity blinds them. Do you wish to assure yourselves of it? Compare the two extremes, St. Domingo and the United States; or, rather, if you wish objects nearer together, compare in the United States the northern with those of the south. The first furnish only very common articles; workmanship is there at a rate that may be called excessive, yet they are full of vigour and prosperity, while the others remain in langour and stagnation, although they are adapted to productions the most precious, and that they employ the species of labourers the worst paid, namely slaves.

What this example particularly demonstrates we see in all times, and in all places; wherever the lowest class of society is too wretched, its extreme misery, and its abjectness, which is a consequence of it, is the death of industry, and the principle of infinite evils, even to its oppressors. The existence of slavery among ancient nations should be regarded as the source of their principal errors in economy, morality and politics, and the first cause of their continual fluctuation between anarchy, turbulent, and often ferocious or an atrocious tyranny. The slavery of the blacks, or aborigines in our colonies, which had so many means of prosperity, is equally the cause of their languor, their weakness, and the gross vices of their inhabitants. The slavery of serfs of the soil, wherever it has existed, has equally prevented the development of all industry, of all sociability, and of all political strength; and even in our own days, it has reduced Poland to such a state of weakness, that an immense nation existed for a long time only through the jealousy of its neighbors, and has ended by seeing its territory divided as easily as a private patrimony, so soon as the pretenders to it have come to an agreement among themselves. If from these extreme cases, without attending to the fury of the rabble in France, or to the excesses of John of Leyden and his peasants in Germany, we come to the calamities caused by the populace of Holland, excited by the house of Orange; to the disquietudes arriving from the lazzarone of Naples, the trans-tiberians of Rome; and, in fine, to the embarrassments which even at this moment are caused in England, by the enormity of the poor tax, and the immensity of its wretched population, which nothing but punishments can restrain; I think all mankind will agree that when a considerable portion of society is in a state of too great suffering, and consequently too much brutalized, there is neither repose nor safety, nor liberty, possible even for the powerful and rich; and that, on the contrary, these first citizens of a state are really much greater, and happier, when they are at the head of a people enjoying honest ease, which develops in them all their intellectual and moral faculties.

On the whole, I do not pretend to conclude, that the poor ought to employ violence, to fix the price which they may demand for their labour. We have seen that their first interest is a respect for property; but I repeat that the rich ought no more to fix this price authoritatively, that it ought to leave to them the most free and entire disposition of their slender means. And here justice also pronounces in their favour; and I add, that they ought to rejoice if the employment of their means procure them an honest ease, for policy proves that it is the general good.

Observe, also, that if it is just and useful to allow every man to dispose of his labour, it is equally so, and for the same reasons, to allow him to choose his residence. The one is a consequence of the other. I know nothing more odious, than to prevent a man from emigrating from his country, who is there so wretched as to wish to quit it, in spite of all the sentiments of nature, and the whole force of habits, which bind him to it. It is moreover absurd: for since it is clearly proved, there are always in every country as many men as can exist in it under the given circumstances, he who goes away only yields his place to another who would have perished if he had remained. To wish that he should remain, is as if two men being inclosed in a box, with air but for one, it should be wished that one or both should be smothered, rather than suffer either one or the other to go out. Emigration, far from being an evil, is never a sufficient succour; it is always too painful to resolve on it for it to become in any degree considerable, the vexations must be frightful; and even then the void it operates, is quickly filled, as that which results from great epidemics. In these unhappy cases, it is the sufferings of men that ought to be regretted; and not the diminution of their number.

As to immigration I say nothing. It is always useless, and even hurtful, unless it be that of some men who bring new knowledge. But then it is their knowledge, and not their persons, that is precious; and such are never very numerous. We may without injustice prohibit immigration; and it is this precisely of which governments have never thought. It is true they have still more rarely furnished many motives for desiring it.

After sufficient wages, which is of first importance to the poor, the next is, that these wages should be constant. In fact it is not a momentary augmentation, or accidental increase, of his profits which can ameliorate his situation. Improvidence is one and perhaps the greatest of his evils. An extravagant consumption always destroys quickly this extraordinary surplus of means, or an indiscrete multiplication divides it among too many. When then this surplus ceases, those who lived on it perish, or those who enjoyed it must restrict themselves; and in the latter case it is never the consumptions least useful which cease first, because these are the most seducing. Then misery recommences in all its horrors, with a greater degree of intensity. Thus we may say, in general terms, that nothing which is transient is really useful to the poor; in this also he has the same interests as the social body.

This truth excludes many false political combinations, particularly if we join with it this other maxim equally true: that nothing forced is durable. It teaches us, also, that it is essential to the happiness of the mass of a nation, that the price of provisions of the first necessity should vary the least possible: for it is not the price of wages in itself that is important; it is their price compared with that of the things necessary for life. If for two sous I can buy bread sufficient for the day, I am better nourished than if I were to receive ten sous, when twelve would be necessary to complete my daily ration. Now we have before shown (Chap. 4th and elsewhere) that the rate of the lowest wages is regulated, and cannot fail of being regulated in the long run, by the price of the things necessary to existence. If the price of necessaries suddenly abates, wage earners without doubt profit momentarily; but without durable utility to them, as we have just said. This, then, is not desirable. If, on the contrary, this price augments, it is much worse; and the evils which result aggravate each other. First, he who has nothing more than what is necessary, has nothing to spare, thus all the poor are in distress: but, moreover, in consequence of this distress, they make extraordinary efforts; they are more urgent to be employed; or in other words, they offer more labour. Other persons who lived without labour, have need of this resource. There is no employment for them. They are hurtful to one another by this competition. This occasion is taken to pay them less, when they have need of being better paid. Accordingly, constant experience proves that in times of want wages fall, because there are more workmen than can be employed; and this continues till a return of abundance, or till they perish.

It is then desirable that the price of commodities, and above all that of the most important, should be invariable. When we shall come to speak of legislation, we shall see that the mean of making this price as little variable as possible, is to leave the most entire liberty to commerce; because the activity of speculators, and their competition, makes them eager to take advantage of the smallest fall to buy, and the smallest rise to sell again; and thus they prevent either the one or the other from becoming excessive. This method is also the most conformable with a respect for property, for the just and the useful are always united. For the present let us limit ourselves to our conclusion, and extend it to other objects.

Sudden variations, in certain parts of industry and commerce, occasion, though in a manner less general, the same effect as variations in the price of commodities. When any branch of industry whatever takes suddenly a rapid increase, there is a greater demand for labour than is ordinary: a profit here results to the labourers; and they use it as all other momentary profits, that is to say badly. But afterwards should this industry be slowed down or extinguished, distress arrives; every one must seek resources. In truth there are many more in this case than in that of a dearness, which is a universal misfortune. The unoccupied workmen here may go elsewhere. But men are not abstract and insensible beings. Their removals are not made without sufferings, without anguish, without breaking up imperious habits. A workman is never so adapted to the business he seeks as to that which he is forced to quit. Besides he is there superfluous—he produces a glut, and consequently a depression of the ordinary wages. Thus every one suffers. This is the great unhappiness of nations predominating in commerce, and the inconvenience of an exaggerated development of industry, a development which from being exaggerated is subject to vicissitudes. It is what at least should prove, that it is very imprudent for a political society to seek to procure a factitious prosperity by forced means. It can but be fragile, it is enjoyed without happiness, and is never lost without extreme evils.

It has been remarked that nations essentially agricultural are less subject to suffer from these sudden revolutions of industry and commerce, in consequence, the stability of their prosperity has been greatly vaunted, and to a certain point with reason. But I think it has not been sufficiently remarked, that they are more exposed than commercial nations to the most cruel of all variations, that of the price of grain: it seems that this ought not to be, and yet it is, it is even easy to find the reason. A people devoted to agriculture are spread over a vast territory. This territory is either entirely inland, or if it borders on some sides on the sea, it has necessarily a great portion of its extent deeply inland. When the crops fail their succours can only be carried by land, or by ascending rivers, a kind of navigation, always very expensive and often impossible. Now as grain and other alimentary matters, are articles of great burthen, it happens that when they are brought to the place in which they are wanted, their price from the expenses of transportation, is so high, that scarcely any one can purchase. Accordingly it is known from experience that all importations of this kind in times of calamity, have merely served to console and calm the imagination; but have never been real resources: the poor then must absolutely restrict their consumption to the point of suffering greatly, and the most destitute must perish. There is no other mean of preventing the whole from perishing, when the dearth is very great. It is in this case that in a besieged town, all the useless mouths if possible are sent away. It is the same calculation. The defence would still be prolonged, if they dared to rid themselves of all the defenders who are not indispensable; but the consumption of war operates their destruction: and it is perhaps this cruel, but wise combination, which determines the otherwise useless sorties, made by certain governors near the end of a seige—sorties very different from those made at its commencement, in mere bravado.

Men would greatly augment the security of their existence, and the possibility of their occupying certain countries, if they could reduce alimentary matters to small bulk, and consequently to easy transportion. In truth, they would immediately abuse this faculty, to injure themselves, as shepherd tribes avail themselves of the facility of transportation produced by the celerity of their beasts of burden, to become brigands: for nothing is so dangerous as a transportable man. We have only to observe the enormous advantage which temperance gives to armies in invasions. This is the power of the species badly employed; but in short it is its power—and it is this power which, in case of dearth, is wanting to agricultural and peaceful nations, spread over a vast territory.

Commercial nations, on the contrary, are either insular, or extended along the coasts of the sea. Accessible every where, they may receive succour from all countries. For prices to become excessive among them, the crops must have failed in all the habitable globe. Even then it would only rise to the mean rate of general dearness, and never to the extreme rate of the local dearness of the inland countries most destitute. These nations, then, are exempt from the greatest of disasters; and, as to the less general evils resulting from the revolutions which take place in some branches of industry and commerce; I observe that they are rarely exposed to them if they have left to this industry and to this commerce their natural course—and if they have not employed violent means to give them an exaggerated extension. I conclude, not only that their condition is better, but also that their misfortunes are produced by their faults, whilst those of the others proceed from their position; and that thus they have more means of avoiding these misfortunes. We were necessarily led to this result, and ought to have seen it in advance: for since society, which is a continual commerce, is the cause of our power and of our own resources; it would be contradictory, that where this commerce is the most perfect, and most active, we should be more accessible to misfortune.

If, therefore, it were proved that the prosperity of commercial nations was less solid, and less durable (a fact I do not believe true, at least amongst moderns),* it would be necessary, first, to distinguish between happiness and power, and to remark, that in the calamities of which we have just spoken, the happiness of individuals in agricultural nations is much at hazard, but their power subsists; because the loss of men, who perish in dearth, is quickly repaired by new births when it ceases, the habitual means of existence, not having been destroyed; whereas in a commercial nation, when a branch of industry is annihilated, it is sometimes annihilated without return, and without a possibility of being replaced by another; so that that part of the population which it brings to ruin cannot be again restored. But, as we have said, this latter case is rare, when not provoked by faults. If, independently of this, it were proved that the prosperity of commercial nations is frail, in proportion to the internal vices to which they are subject, it would not be proper to impute it to commerce itself, but to accidental causes, and principally to the manner in which riches are frequently introduced into these states, which favours extremely their very unequal distribution; and this is the greatest and most general of evils. On examination, we should find there, as every where, the human race happy from the development and increase of its means; but ready to become unhappy

---

* The examples of the ancients prove nothing, because their political economy was entirely founded on force. The inland people were brigands, the maritime people pirates. All wished to be conquerors. Then chance determines the destiny of a nation.

from the bad use it makes of them. The discussion of this question, in all its extent, will find its place elsewhere.

However, it may be, it is then certain that the poor are proprietors as well as the rich; that in their quality as proprietors of their persons, of their faculties, and of their product, they have an interest in being allowed the free disposition of their persons and labour; that this labour should produce them sufficient wages; and that these wages should vary as little as possible, that is to say they have an interest that their capital should be respected, that this capital should produce the revenue necessary for existence, and that this revenue if possible should be always the same; and in all these points their interests conform to the general interest.

But the poor is not only a proprietor, he is also a consumer: for all men are both the one and the other. In this latter quality he has the same interest as all consumers, that of being provisioned in the best and cheapest manner possible. It is necessary then for him, that manufacture should be very expert, communications easy, and relations multiplied: for no one has a greater need of being supplied on good terms than he who has few means.

What must be thought then of those who maintain that ameliorations of the methods and the invention of machines, which simplify and abridge the processes of art, are an evil for the poor? My answer is that they have no idea of their real interest, nor of those of society: For one must be blind not to see that when a thing which required four days labour can be made in one, every one for the same sum can procure four times as much; or, consuming only the same quantity, may have three-fourths of his money remaining to be employed in procuring other enjoyments, and certainly this advantage is still more precious to the poor than to the rich. But, say they, the poor gained these four days labour, and now he will gain but one. But, say I, in my turn, you forget then that the funds on which all the wage earners live are the sum of the means of those who employ them; that this sum is a quantity nearly constant; that it is always employed annually; that if a particular object absorbs a smaller part of it, the surplus, which is economised, seeks other destinations; and that thus, while it is not diminished, it hires an equal number of labourers; and that moreover, if there is a mean of augmenting it, it is by rendering fabrication more economical; because this is the mean of opening new outlets, and of giving possibility to new enterprises of industry, which are as we have seen, the only sources of the increase of our riches. These reasons appear to me decisive. If the contrary reasons were valid, we should have to conclude that nothing is more beneficial, than the execution of useless labour, because there is always the same number of persons occupied; and that there would not remain fewer for the execution of the same quantity of necessary labour. I grant this second point. But, first, this useless labour would be paid with funds which would otherwise have paid for useful labour and which will not pay it—thus nothing is gained on this side. Secondly, from this unfruitful labour nothing remains; and, if it had been fruitful, there would have remained from it useful things for procuring enjoyments, or capable, by being exported, to augment the mass of acquired riches. It appears to me that nothing can be answered to this, when we have once clearly seen on what funds wage earners live. This series of combinations will occur when we shall speak of the employment of our riches. It is for this I have developed it: For so much reasoning appears unnecessary to prove that labour acknowledged useless is useless, and that it is more useful to execute useful labour. Now to this single truth is reduced the apology for machines and other improvements.

They have made against the construction of roads and canals, and generally against the facility of communications, and the multiplicity of commercial relations the same objections as those I have just refuted. I give them the same answer. It has moreover been pretended that all this is in another way hurtful to the poor, by raising the price of provisions. The truth is, that it raises their price at times when they are too low from the difficulty of exporting them; but it reduces their price, when too high from the difficulty of importing them. Thus it renders the prices more constantly equal; and I conclude, on the principles we have established, that it is a great benefit to the poor and to society in general.

I admit, however, that all these innovations, advantageous in themselves, may sometimes produce at first a momentary and partial restraint—it is the effect of all sudden changes; but, as the utility of these is general and durable, this consideration ought not to retard them. It is only requisite that society should give succour to those who suffer for the moment; and this it can easily do, when it is prospering in the mass.

It is then true that notwithstanding the necessary opposition of our particular interests, we are all united by the common interests of proprietors and consumers; and, consequently, it is wrong to regard the poor and the rich, or the wage earners and those who employ them, as two classes essentially enemies. It is particularly true, that the real interests of the poor are always the same as those of the society taken in mass. I do not pretend to say that the poor always know their real interests. Who is he that always has just ideas on these matters, even amongst the enlightened? But, in fine, it is much that things are thus; and it is a good thing to know it. The greatest difficulty, in impressing this, is, perhaps, to be able clearly to point out the cause. This I think we have now done. Arriving at this result, we have examined by the way several questions, which, without diverting us from our road, have retarded our march. Yet I have not thought it right to pass them by without notice, because, in things of this kind, all the objects are so intimately linked together that there is no one which, being well cleared up, does not throw great light on all the others.

But we are not only opposed in interests, we are also unequal in means. This second condition of our nature deserves also to be studied in its consequences, without which we cannot completely know the effects of the distribution of our riches among different individuals; and we shall but imperfectly know what we ought to think of the advantages and inconveniences of the increase of these same riches, by the effect of society. Let us at first establish some general truths.

Declaimers have maintained that *inequality* in general is useful, and that it is a benefit for which we ought to thank Providence. I have but one word to answer. Amongst sensible beings, frequently with opposite interests, justice is the greatest good: for that alone can so conciliate them, that none may have cause of complaint. Then inequality is an evil not because it is in itself injustice, but because it is a powerful prop to injustice wherever justice is in favour of the weak.

Every inequality of means, and of faculties, is at bottom an inequality of power. However, when we enter into detail, we can and ought to distinguish between the inequality of power, properly so called, and the inequality of riches.

The first is the most grevious; it submits the person itself. It exists in all its horror among brutal and savage men; with them it places the weak at the mercy of the strong. It is the cause why among them there are the fewest relations possible, for it would become insupportable. If it has not been always remarked among them, it is because scarcely ever accompanied by an inequality of riches; which is what strikes us most forcibly, having it always under our eyes.

The object of the social organization is to combat the inequality of power; and most frequently it causes it to cease, or at least diminishes it. Men shocked with the abuses still prevalent in society, have pretended that, on the contrary, it augments this inequality; and it must be confessed, that when it totally loses sight of its destination it justifies the reproaches of its bitterest detractors. For example wheresoever it continues slavery, properly so called, it is certain that savage independence, with all its dangers is still preferable. But it must be admitted nevertheless that this is not the object of society; and that it tends, most frequently with success, to diminish the inequality of power.

By diminishing the inequality of power, and thus establishing security, society produces the development of all our faculties, and increases our riches, that is to say our means of existence and enjoyment. But the more our faculties are developed, the more their inequality appears and augments; and this soon introduces the inequality of riches, which brings with it that of instruction, capacity and of influence. Here, in a word, as appears to me, are the advantages and inconveniences of society. This view shows us what we have a right to expect from it, and what we ought to do to perfect it.

Since the object of society is to diminish the inequality of power, it ought to aim at its accomplishment, and since its inconvenience is to favour the inequality of riches, it ought constantly to endeavour to lessen it, always by gentle, and never by violent, means: for it should always be remembered, that the fundamental base of society is a respect for property, and its guarantee against all violence.

But it will be asked, when inequality is reduced entirely to an inequality of riches, is it still so great an evil? I answer, boldly, yes: For, first, bringing with it an inequality of instruction, of capacity, and of influence, it tends to re-establish the inequality of power and consequently to subvert society.

Again, considering it only under an economical relation, we have seen that the funds on which wage earners live are the revenues of all those who have capitals; and among these it is only entrepreneurs of industry who augment their riches, and consequently the riches of the nation. Now it is precisely the possessors of great fortunes who are idle, and who pay no labour but for their pleasure. Thus the more there are of great fortunes, the more national riches tend to decay and population to diminish. The example of all times, and all places, supports this theory: For wherever you see exaggerated fortunes,* you there see the greatest misery and the greatest stagnation of industry.

The perfection of society, then, would be to increase our riches greatly, avoiding their extreme inequality. But this is much more difficult at certain times, and in certain places, than in others. An inland agricultural people having few relations, living on a sterile soil, unable to increase their means of enjoyment but by the slow progress of its culture, and the still slower progress of their manufactures, will easily, and for a long time, avoid the establishment of great inequality among their citizens. If the soil is more rich, and especially, if in some places it produces articles in great demand, large fortunes will be more easily acquired: If it has mines of precious metals, many individuals will certainly ruin themselves by working them; but some will acquire immense riches: or, if the government reserves to itself this profit, it will soon be enabled to procure for its creatures an exaggerated opulence; and it is very probable it will not fail to do it. Too many causes concur to produce this effect. Finally, if you suppose this people, still poor, to become conquerors, to seize on a rich country, and to establish themselves in it as conquerors, here is at once the greatest inequality introduced: First between the victorious and the conquered nation, and afterwards among the conquerors themselves: for where force decides it is very difficult to have equitable partitions. The lots of the different individuals are as different, as their degrees of authority in the army or of favour with the chief. Moreover, they are exposed to frequent usurpations.

---

* To judge of the exaggeration of certain fortunes, consider their proportions: for there may be Englishmen near as rich, or richer than the greatest Russian or Polish lords; but they live in the midst of a people generally in much more easy circumstances—consequently the disproportion, though real, is much less.

The fortune of maritime nations is generally more rapid. Yet there we remark the same varieties. Navigators may be reduced to small profits, to carrying, to fishing, to commerce with nations from which great profits cannot be made. Then it is easy for them to remain long nearly equal amongst themselves. They may, on the contrary, penetrate into unknown regions; have in profusion the most rare articles; establish relations with people from whom they can derive immense profits; take to themselves great monopolies; found rich colonies, over which they hold a tyranical empire; or even became conquerors, and import into their country the productions of countries very extensive subjected by their arms, as the English in India, and the Spaniards in South America. In all these cases, there is more or less of chance; but in all, a great probability that their enormous riches will be very unequally distributed.

Many other circumstances, without doubt, connect themselves with these, and modify their effects. The different characters of people, the nature of their government, the greater or less extent of their information, and, above all, of their knowledge of the social art in the moments which decide their fortune, occasion like events to have very different consequences. If Vasco De Gama and his contemporaries had had the same views and misfortunes as Cook, or La Peyrouse, our relations with the Indies would be quite different from what they are. It is above all remarkable, how much influence the epoch at which a political society begins to be formed, has on the duration of its existence. Certainly empires founded by Clovis or by Cortez, or societies receiving their first laws from Locke or Franklin, ought to take very different directions; and this we clearly perceive, in every period of their history.*

It is these causes so different, and above all the last, which produce the infinite variety remarked in the destinies of nations, but the ground is every where the same. Society affording to every one security of person and property, causes the development of our faculties; this development produces

---

* This is so striking, that I imagine there is no one who does not regret that America was discovered three hundred years too soon, and who does not even doubt whether it would yet be a proper time for discovering it. It is true that these events, however deplorable, have promoted our ulterior progress; but it is buying them very dear. It appears that such is our destiny.

the increase of our riches; their increase brings on sooner or later their very unequal division; and this unequal division occasioning the inequality of power which society begun by restraining, and was intended to destroy, produces its weakness, and sometimes its total dissolution.

It is doubtless this vicious circle which historians have wished to represent to us by the youth and old age of nations, and by what they call their primary virtue, their primitive purity, then their degeneration, their corruptions, their effeminacy. But these vague expressions, against which I have already protested, paint the facts very badly, and often lead astray even those who employ them: they tell us always of the virtue of poor nations. Certainly where equality renders injustice and oppression more difficult, and more rare, they are more virtuous from the fact itself, since fewer faults are committed. But it is equality and not poverty which is their protection. Otherwise the passions are the same there as elsewhere. Why incessantly represent to us commercial nations as avaricious, and agricultural people as models of moderation? Men every where hold to their interests, and are occupied with them. The Carthaginians were not more avaricious than the Romans; and the Romans, who were the most cruel usurers at home and insatiable spoliators abroad, were quite as avaricious in what are called their best times, as under the emperors. The state of society alone was different. It is the same with the word degeneration. Certainly when a part of mankind has been accustomed to resign itself to oppression, and another part to abuse its power, we may well say they have degenerated; but, from the manner in which this expression is often employed, we should be led to believe they are no longer born the same, that nature has changed, that the race is depreciated, that they have no longer force or courage: all this is very false. We have a still greater abuse of the expressions effeminate and effeminacy. Montesquieu[1] himself tells you gravely, that the fertility of the land effeminates its inhabitants.* It nourishes them and this is all. To listen to certain authors, we should suppose that there comes a time when all the inhabitants of a country live amidst delights, as those famous Sybarites

---

* He says of it many other things. See his 18th book of laws, in the relation they have with the nature of the soil.

1. Charles de Secondat, baron de Montesquieu (1689–1755), French writer and philosopher, author of *The Spirit of the Laws* (1748).

of whom we have been told so much. This would be very happy, but it is impossible. When you are told that a nation is enervated by effeminacy, understand that there is about an hundreth part of it, at most, corrupted by the habit of power and the facility of enjoyment; and that all the rest are debarred by oppression, and devoured by misery.* Nor are we less deceived in the sense of the expression, *poor nations;* it is there the people are at their ease; and the *rich nations* is where the people are commonly poor. It is for this reason that some are strong, and others often weak. We might multiply these reflections to infinity; but all may be reduced to this truth, which has not always been sufficiently perceived; the multiplication of our means of enjoyment is a very good thing; their too unequal partition is a very bad one, and the source of all our evils. On this point still the interest of the poor is the same as that of society. I think I have said enough on the distribution of our riches; it is time to speak of the use we make of them.

---

* And those famous delights of Capua! and all those armies suddenly effeminated, by having found themselves in abundance! Ask of all the generals if their soldiers have been the worse for having plentifully enjoyed the means of life for some time, unless they have suffered them to become pillagers, and undisciplined, by setting them the example; or the chiefs, having made their fortune, are no longer ambitious. If it is this which has happened to the Carthaginians, and others, this is what should have been said, and not in vain rhetorical phrases.

CHAPTER XI

Of the Employment of Our Riches, or of Consumption.

☙

After having seen how our riches are formed, and how they are distributed among us, we are arrived at the point of examining how we use them, and what are the consequences of the different uses we make of them. This is what will complete the illustration of the whole course of society, and show us what things are really useful or hurtful, as well to the public as to individuals. If in the two first parts, we have well ascertained and explained the truth, this will unravel itself, and every thing in it will be clear and incontestible. If, on the contrary, we have imperfectly viewed the first facts, if we have not returned to first principles, if our researches have been superficial or led astray by a spirit of system, we are about to encounter difficulties on difficulties; and there will remain in all we shall say many obscure and doubtful things, as has happened to many others, and even to the most capable and learned. However the reader will judge.

We create nothing; we annihilate nothing; but we operate changes, productive or destructive, of utility. We procure for ourselves means of enjoyment, only to provide for our wants; and we cannot employ them in the satisfaction of these wants; but by diminishing and even destroying them. We make cloth, and, with this cloth, clothes, only to clothe ourselves; and, by wearing, we wear them out; with grain, air, earth, water, and manure, we produce alimentary matters to nourish ourselves; and, by nourishing ourselves with them, we convert them into gas and manure; which again produce more. This is what we call consumption. Consumption is the end of production, but it is its contrary. Thus all production augments our riches, and all consumption diminishes them. Such is the general law.

However there are consumptions of many kinds. There are some which are only apparent; others very real, and even destructive; and some which are fruitful. They vary according to the species of consumers, and the nature of the things consumed. These differences must be examined and distinguished, in order clearly to see the effect of general consumption, on the total mass of riches. Let us begin by discussing the consumers. I hazard this expression, because it well expresses the end which I propose to myself.

We agree that we are all consumers, for we all have wants for which we cannot provide but by a consumption of some kind; and that also we are all proprietors, for we all possess some means of providing for our wants, were it only by our individual force and capacity. But we have also seen, that from the unequal manner in which riches are distributed, in proportion as they are accumulated, many among us have no part in these accumulated riches, and possess in effect but their individual force. These have no other treasure than their daily labour. This labour procures them wages, for which reason we have called them specially *wage earners;* and it is with these wages they provide for their consumption.

But whence are the wages raised? Evidently on the property of those to whom these wage earners sell their labour, that is to say on funds, in advance, which are in their possession, and which are no other than the accumulated products of labour previously executed. It follows thence, that the consumption for which these riches pay, is truly the consumption of the wage earners in this sense, that it is them it subsists; but at bottom it is not they who pay it, or at least they pay it only with the funds existing in advance in the hands of those who employ them. They merely receive with one hand and give with the other. Their consumption, therefore, ought to be regarded as being made by those who pay them. If even they do not expend all they receive, these savings raising them to the ranks of capitalists, enable them afterwards to make expenditures on their own funds; but as they come to them from the same hands, they ought at first to be regarded as the expenses of the same persons; thus to avoid double reckoning of the same article in the economical calculations, we must consider as absolutely nothing the immediate consumption of wage earners, as wage earners; and to consider not only all they expend, but even the whole they receive, as the real expenditure and proper consumption of those who purchase their labour. This is so true, that to see whether this consumption is more or less destructive of the riches acquired, or even if it tends to augment them as it often does, depends entirely on knowing what use the capitalists make of the labour they purchase. This leads us to examine the consumption of capitalists.

We have said that they are of two kinds, the one idle, the other active. The first have a fixed revenue, independent of all action on their part, since they are supposed idle. This revenue consists in the hiring of their capitals, whether moveables, money or land, which they hire to those who improve them by the effect of their industry. This revenue, is, then, but a previous levy on the products of the activity of the industrious citizens; but this is not our present enquiry. What we wish to see is, what is the employment of this revenue? Since the men to whom it belongs are idle, it is evident they do not direct any productive labour. All the labourers whom they pay are solely destined to procure them enjoyments. Without doubt these enjoyments are of different kinds: For the least wealthy they are limited to the satisfaction of the most urgent wants; for the others they are extended by degrees, according to their taste and means, to objects of the most refined and unbridled luxury. But, in fine, the expenses of all this class of men are alike in this, that they have no object but their personal satisfaction; and that they support a numerous population, to which they afford subsistence; but whose labour is completely sterile. It is however true, that amongst these expenses some may be found which are more or less fruitful; as, for example, the construction of a house, or the improvement of a landed estate. But these are particular cases, which place consumers of this kind momentarily in the class of those who direct useful enterprises and pay for productive labour. After these trifling exceptions, all the consumption of this species of capitalists is absolutely pure loss, in relation to reproduction, and so far a diminution of the riches acquired. Also, we must remark, that these men can expend no more than their revenue: if they touch on their funds nothing replaces them, and their consumption exaggerated for a moment, ceases for ever.

The second class of capitalists, who employ and pay wage earners, is composed of those whom we have called *active*. It comprehends all the entrepreneurs of any kind of industry whatsoever, that is to say all the men who having capitals of a greater or smaller amount, employ their talents and industry in improving them themselves, instead of hiring them to others; and who, consequently live neither on wages nor revenues but on profit. These men not only improve their proper capitals, but all those also of the inactive capitalists. They rent their lands, houses, and money, and employ them so as to derive from them profits superior to the rent.* They have then in their hands almost all the riches of society. It is moreover to be remarked, that it is not only the rent of these riches they annually expend, but also the funds themselves; and sometimes several times in the year, when the course of commerce is sufficiently rapid to enable them to do so: for, as in their quality of industrious men they make no expenditures which do not return to them with profit, the more of them they can make which fulfil this condition, the greater will be their profit. We see then that their consumption is immense, and that the number of wage earners whom they feed is truly prodigious.

We must now distinguish two parties in this enormous consumption. All which is made by these industrious men for their own enjoyment, and for the satisfaction of their own wants and those of their family, is definitive and lost without return, like that of the idle capitalists. On the whole it is moderate, for industrious men are commonly frugal, and too often not very rich. But all which they make for the support of their industry, and for the service of this industry, is nothing less than definitive; it returns to them with profit; and, that this industry may be sustained, its profits must at least be equal not only to their personal and definitive consumption, but also to the rent of the land and money which they hold of the idle capitalists, which rent is their sole revenue, and the only fund of their annual expense. If the profits of the active capitalists were less than these

---

* Idle capitalists sometimes rent houses and money to the other idlers: But the latter pay the rent only with their own revenues; and to find the formation of these revenues we must always return to industrious capitalists. As to lands they almost always rent them to entrepreneurs of culture, for what would the idle make of them?

necessary previous levies, their funds would be encroached on; they would be obliged to diminish their enterprizes; they could no longer hire the same quantity of labour; they would even be disgusted with hiring and directing this unfruitful labour. In the contrary case they have an increase of funds, by means of which they can increase their business, and their demand for labour, if they can find a method of employing it usefully.

I shall be asked, how these entrepreneurs of industry are able to make such great profits, and from whom they can draw them? I answer, that it is by selling whatever they produce for more than it has cost them to produce it. And this is sold, first, to themselves for all that part of their consumption which is destined to the satisfaction of their own wants, which they pay for with a portion of their profits; Secondly, to wage earners, as well those in their pay as in the pay of the idle capitalists; from which wage earners they draw by this mean the whole of their wages, except the small savings they may possibly be able to make; Thirdly, to the idle capitalists, who pay them with the part of their revenue which they have not already given to the wage earners whom they employ directly, so that all the rent which they annually disburse returns to them by one or the other of these ways.

This is what completes that perpetual motion of riches, which although little understood has been very well called circulation: for it is really *circular*,* and always returns to the point from whence it departed. This point is that of production. The entrepreneurs of industry are really the heart of the body politic, and their capitals are its blood. With these capitals they pay the wages of the greatest part of the wage earners; they pay their rents to all the idle capitalists, possessors either of land or money; and by them the wages of all the remaining wage earners; and all this returns to them by the expenditures in all these ways, which pay them more for what they have had produced from the labour of their immediate wage earners, than the wages of these, and the rent of the land and money borrowed, have cost them.

But I shall be told, if this is really so, if the entrepreneurs of industry in fact reap annually more than they have sown, they should in a short time

---

* And why is it circular and continual? Because consumption continually destroys that which has been produced. If reproduction did not incessantly establish it, all would be finished after the first turn.

obtain possession of all the public wealth; and there would remain in a state but wage earners without any thing in advance, and entrepreneurs with capitals. This is true, and things would be effectively thus if these entrepreneurs, or their heirs, did not retire from business in proportion as they become rich, and continually recruit the class of idle capitalists. And, notwithstanding this frequent emigration, it happens still that when industry has operated for a considerable time in a country, without too great disturbances, its capitals are always augmented not only in proportion to the increase of total wealth, but yet in a much greater. To be assured of this, we have only to see how slender these capitals were, through all Europe, three or four centuries ago, in comparison with the immense riches of all the powerful men, and how much they are multiplied and increased at the present day, while the others have diminished. We may add that this effect would be still much more sensible, were it not for the immense levies which all governments annually raise on the industrious class by means of imposts; but it is not yet time to occupy ourselves with this subject.

It is not necessary to observe, that at the commencement of society, before riches have become very unequal, there are scarcely any simple wage earners, and still fewer idle capitalists. Every one working for himself, and making exchanges with his neighbours, is a real entrepreneur, or momentarily a wage earner when he occasionally works for another for a recompense. Even afterwards, when the different conditions have become more separate by the effect of inequality, the same man may and often does appertain to several at the same time. Thus a simple wage earner, who has some small savings placed at interest, is in this respect an idle capitalist; as is also an entrepreneur who has a part of his funds realised in leased lands; while a proprietor of like lands, or a lessor who is a public functionary, is in this respect a wage earner. But it is not less true, that those who live on wages, those who live on rents, and those who live on profits, constitute three classes of men essentially different; and that it is the last which aliment all the others, and who alone augment the public wealth, and create all our means of enjoyment. This must be so, since labour is the source of all riches, and since they alone give an useful direction to the actual labour, by a useful improvement of the labour accumulated.

I hope it will be remarked, how well this manner of considering the consumption of our riches agrees with all we have said of their production and distribution;* and, at the same time, how much light it throws on the whole course of society. Whence comes this agreement and this lucidity? From this, that we have struck on the truth. This resembles the effect of those mirrors in which objects are represented distinctly, and in their just proportions when one is placed in the true point of view; and where every thing appears confused, and disunited, when one is too near or too distant. So here, so soon as it is acknowledged that our faculties are our only original riches, that our labour alone produces all others, and that all labour well directed is productive, every thing explains itself with admirable facility; but when, with many political writers, you acknowledge no labour as productive but that of culture, or place the source of riches in consumption, you encounter in advancing nothing but obscurity, confusion and inextricable embarrassments. I have already refuted the first of these two opinions—I shall soon discuss the second. For the moment, let us conclude that there are three kinds of consumers: the wage earners, the rentiers, and the entrepreneurs; that the consumption of the first is real and definitive; but that it must not be counted, because it makes a part of the consumption of those who employ them; that that of the rentiers is definitive and destructive; and that that of the entrepreneur is fruitful, because it is replaced by a superior production.

If consumption is very different, according to the species of consumers, it varies likewise according to the nature of the things consumed. All represent truly labour; but its value is fixed more solidly in some than in others. As much pains may have been taken to prepare an artificial fire work as to find and cut a diamond; and, consequently, one may have as much value as the other. But when I have purchased, paid for, and employed the one and the other, at the end of half an hour nothing remains of the first, and the second may still be the resource of my descendants a century to come, even if used every day as an ornament of dress. It is the same case with what are

---

* In fact we here see clearly, why production is arrested, when the fruitful consumption of industry can no longer be augmented, and why the number and ease of men increase or decrease as the industry, &c. &c.

called immaterial products. A discovery is of an eternal utility. A work of genius, a picture, are likewise of an utility more or less durable; while that of a ball, concert, a theatrical representation, is instantaneous and disappear immediately. We may say as much of the personal services of physicians, of lawyers, of soldiers, of domestics, and of all those that are called employees. Their utility is that of the moment of want.

All consumable things, of what nature soever, may be placed between these two extremes, of the shortest and longest duration. From this it is easy to see, that the most ruinous consumption is the most prompt, since it is that which destroys the most labour in the same time, or an equal quantity of labour in less time. In comparison with this, that which is slower is a kind of hoarding; since it leaves to futurity the enjoyment of a part of actual sacrifices. This is so clear that it needs no proof: for every one knows that it is more economical to have for the same price a coat which will last three years, than one which will last but three months; accordingly this truth is acknowledged by every body. What is singular, is that it should be so even by those who regard luxury as a cause of wealth: for if to destroy is so good a thing, it seems that we cannot destroy too much, and that we ought to think with the man who broke all his furniture, to encourage industry.

At the point to which we are now arrived, I do not know how to approach the pretended mighty question of *luxury,* so much and so often debated by celebrated philosophers and renowned politicians; or, rather, I do not know how to show that it comprehends any matter of doubt, nor how to give the appearance of a little plausibility to the reasons of those, very numerous however, who maintain that luxury is useful: for, when preceding ideas have been well elucidated, a question is resolved as soon as stated; and this is now the case.

In effect, he who names luxury, names superfluous and even exaggerated consumption; consumption is destruction of utility. Now how conceive that exaggerated destruction can be the cause of riches—can be production? It is repugnant to good sense.

We are gravely told that luxury impoverishes a small state and enriches a large one; but what can extent have to do with such a subject? and how comprehend, that what ruins an hundred men would enrich two hundred.

It is also said that luxury supports a numerous population. Without doubt not only the luxury of the rich, but likewise the simple consumption of all the idle who live on their revenues, supports a great number of wage earners. But what becomes of the labour of these wage earners? Those who employ them consume its result, and nothing of it remains; and with what do they pay for this labour? with their revenues, that is to say with riches already acquired, of which in a short time nothing will remain. There then is a destruction, not an augmentation of riches. But let us go further. Whence do these idle men derive their revenues? Is it not from the rent paid to them out of the profits of those who employ their capitals, that is to say of those who with their own funds hire labour which produces more than it costs, in a word the industrious men? To these then we must always return, in order to find the source of all wealth. It is they who really nourish the wage earners whom even the others employ.

But, say they, luxury animates circulation. These words have no meaning. They forget then what is circulation. Let us recall it. With time a greater or smaller quantity of riches are accumulated, because the result of anterior labours, has not been entirely consumed as soon as produced. Of the possessors of these riches some are satisfied with drawing a rent and living on it. These we have called the idle. Others more active, employ their own funds, and those which they hire. They employ them to hire labour, which reproduces them with profit. With this profit they pay for their own consumption, and defray that of the others. Even by these consumptions their funds return to them a little increased, and they recommence. This is what constitutes circulation. We see that it has no other funds than those of the industrious citizens. It can only augment in proportion as they augment; nor be accelerated, which is still to be augmented, but in proportion to the quickness of their returns: for if their funds return to them at the end of six months, instead of a year, they would employ them twice a year instead of once; and this is as if they employed the double. But the idle proprietors can do nothing of this. They can but consume their rents in one way or another. If they consume more one year they must consume less another; if they do otherwise they encroach on their capitals. They are obliged to sell them. But they can only be purchased with funds belonging to industrious men, or lent to them, and who paid for labour, which they will no longer pay for, and for labour more useful than that employed by the prodigals. Thus this is not an augmentation of the total mass of expense, it is but a transposition, a change of some of its parts, and a disadvantageous change.

Thus even in ruining themselves, the men who live on their revenues cannot increase the mass of wages and of circulation. They could do it only by a conduct quite opposite, by not consuming the whole of their rent, and by appropriating a part of it to fruitful expenditures. But then they would be far from abandoning themselves, to the exaggerated and superfluous consumption called *luxury*. They would devote themselves on the contrary to useful speculations, they would range themselves in the industrious class.

Montesquieu, who in other respects understood political economy very badly,* believes the profusions of the rich very useful; "because," says he (book 7th, chap. 4th), "if the rich do not spend a great deal, the poor must die of famine." We perceive from these few words, and many others, that he did not know either whence the revenues of those whom he calls rich are derived or what becomes of them. Once more I repeat the revenues of the idle rich, are but rents levied on industry; it is industry alone which gives them birth. Their possessors can do nothing to augment them, they only scatter them, and they cannot avoid scattering them. For if they do not expend the whole for their enjoyments, unless they cast the surplus into the river or bury it, which is a rare folly, they replace it, that is to say they form with it new funds for industry, which it employs. Thus even by economising they pay for the same quantity of labour. All the difference is that they pay for useful instead of useless labour, and that out of the profits procured, they create for themselves a new rent, which will augment the possibility of their future consumption.

Luxury, exaggerated and superfluous consumption, is therefore never good for any thing, economically speaking. It can only have an indirect utility. Which is by ruining the rich, to take from the hands of idle men those funds which, being distributed amongst those who labour, may enable them to economise, and thus form capitals in the industrious class. But first this would go directly contrary to the intention of Montesquieu, who believes luxury advantageous, especially in a monarchy; and who at the same time thinks, that the preservation of the same families, and the perpetuity of their splendor is essentially necessary to this kind of government.

---

* Montesquieu was a very great man, but the science was not built in his time; it is quite recent.

Moreover we must observe with M. Say, that a taste for superfluous expenses has its foundation in vanity, that it cannot exist in the superior class without gradually extending itself into all the others; that it is there still more fatal, because their means are less, and because it absorbs funds of which they made a better use; and thus it every where substitutes useless for useful expenses, and dries up the source of riches. All this is in my opinion incontestable.

Accordingly, our politicians no longer content themselves with vaguely saying, that luxury constitutes the prosperity of the state, that it animates circulation, that it enables the poor to live. They have made a theory for themselves. They establish as a general principle, that consumption is the cause of production, that it is its measure, that thus it is well it should be very great. They affirm that it is this which makes the great difference between public and private economy. They dare not always positively say, that the more a nation consumes the more it enriches itself. But they persuade themselves, and maintain that we must not reason on the public fortune as on that of an individual, and they regard those as very narrow minds which in their simplicity believe that in all cases good *economy* is to be *economical,* that is to say to make an useful employment of his means.*
There is in all this a confusion of ideas, which it is well to dispel and to restore light.

---

* See M. Germain Garnier, in his *Elementary Principles of Political Economy Abridged.* Paris printed by Agasse, 1796. Page xii of his advertisement, he says, formally, "The principles which serve as guides in the administration of a private fortune, and those by which the public fortune should be directed, not only differ between themselves, but are often in *direct opposition* to each other." And page xiii, "The fortune of an individual is increased by saving; the public fortune, on the contrary, receives its increase from the augmentation of consumption." Page 130, in the chapter on circulation, he likewise says, "The annual production ought naturally to be regulated by the annual consumption." Also, in the chapter on public debt, page 240, he adds, "The amendment and extension of culture, and consequently the progress of industry and commerce, have no other cause than the extension of artificial wants"; and concludes from this that public debts are good things, inasmuch as they augment these wants. The same doctrine, joined to the idea that culture is alone productive, runs through his whole work, and his notes on Smith. All this is very superficial and very loose.

Certainly consumption is the cause of production; in this sense, that we only produce in order to consume, and that if we had no wants to satisfy we should never take the trouble of producing any thing. Nothing would then be to us either useful or hurtful. It is also the cause, in this sense, why industrious men produce only because they find consumers of their productions. Hence it is said, with reason, that the true method of encouraging industry is to enlarge the extent of the market, and thereby augment the possibility of selling. Under this point of view, it is also true to say that consumption is the measure of production, for where sale ceases production stops. This has also made us say, that establishments of industry cannot be multiplied beyond a certain term; and that this term is where they cease to yield a profit: for then it is evident, that what they produce is not worth what they consume. But from all this it does not follow, for a nation any more than for an individual, that to expend is to enrich; nor that we may augment our expenses at pleasure; nor even that luxury augments them, for it only changes them. We must always return to production; this is the point of departure. To enjoy we must produce; this is the first step. We produce only by availing ourselves of riches already acquired; the more we have of them, the greater are our means of producing; they are consumed in expenses of productions, they return with profit. We can expend annually but this annual profit. The more of it we employ in useless things, the less will remain for those which are useful. If we go beyond them, we break in on our capital; reproduction, and consequently future consumption, will be diminished. They may, on the contrary, be augmented if savings are made with which to form new capitals. Once more, then, consumption is not riches; and there is nothing useful, under an economical point of view, but that which reproduces itself with profit.

No sophistry can ever shake truths so constant. If they have been mistaken, it is because the effect has been taken for the cause; and, what is more, a disagreeable effect for a benificent cause. We have seen, that when a nation becomes rich a great inequality of fortunes is established, and that the possessors of large fortunes addict themselves to great luxury. It has been believed that this causes a country to prosper; and hastily concluded that inequality and luxury are two very good things. They ought, on the contrary, to have seen that these are two inconveniences attached to prosperity:* that the riches which cause them are acquired before they exist; and that if these riches continue still to increase, it is in spite of the existence of these inconveniences, and through the effect of the good habits of activity and economy which they have not been able entirely to destroy. But the strongest personal interests contribute to give credit to this error. Powerful men are unwilling to acknowledge that their existence is an evil, and that their expense is as useless as their persons. On the contrary, they endeavour to impose by pomp; and it is not their fault if we do not believe that they render a great service to the state, by swallowing up a great portion of the means of existence, and that there is much merit in knowing how to dissipate great riches.† On the other hand, those who depend on them on whom they impose awe, and who profit by their expenses, care very little whether the money they receive from them would be better employed elsewhere, or if by being better employed it would enable a greater number of men to live. They desire that this expense on which they live should be very great; and they firmly believe that if it should diminish, they would be without resources: for they do not see what would replace it. It is thus that general opinion is led astray, and that those even who suffer from it are ignorant of the cause of their evils. Nevertheless, it is certain that the vicious consumption called *luxury,* and in general all the consumption of

---

* We have already seen, in the preceding chapter, how inequality of riches is established, or rather increases in society; and, when we shall treat of legislation, we will likewise show that the excess of inequality, and of luxury, is still more the effect of bad laws than of the natural cause of things.

† It is incredible to what length of illusion self-love leads, and induces one to exaggerate to himself his personal importance. I have seen men obliged, by the troubles of the times, to quit their castles, who really believed that the whole village would want work, without perceiving that it was their farmer, and not themselves, who paid the greatest part of the wages; and sincerely persuade themselves that even if their peasants should divide their effects, or should buy them at a low price, they would only be the more miserable.

I do not pretend to say that it was well done either to drive them away, or to despoil them; nor even that such means can ever be the cause of a durable prosperity. I have made my profession of faith on the necessity of respect for property and justice in general. But it is not the less true, that the absence of an useless man makes no change in the course of things, or at most only changes the place of a part of his small personal expenses; and that the mere suppression of some feudal rights, produces more good to a country than all the benefits of him who levied them.

idle capitalists, far from being useful, destroys the greater part of the means of a nation's prosperity; and this is so true, that from the moment in which a country, which has industry and knowledge, is by any mean delivered from this scourge, we see there immediately an increase of riches and of strength truly prodigious.

What reason demonstrates history proves by facts. When was Holland capable of efforts truly incredible? When her admirals lived as her sailors did, when the arms of all her citizens were employed in enriching or defending the state; and none in cultivating tulips, or paying for pictures. All subsequent events, political and commercial, have united in causing its decline. It has preserved the spirit of economy, it has still considerable riches in a country in which every other people could with difficulty live. Make of Amsterdam the residence of a gallant and magnificent court, transform its vessels into embroidered clothes, and its magazines into ball rooms; and you will see if in a very few years they will have remaining even the means of defending themselves against the irruptions of the sea.

When did England, in spite of its misfortunes and faults, exhibit a prodigious development? Was it under Cromwell or under Charles the second? I know that moral causes have much more power than economical calculations; but I say that these moral causes do not so prodigiously augment all our resources, but because they direct all our efforts towards solid objects: Hence means are not wanting, either to the state or to individuals, for great objects, because they have not been employed in futilities.

Why do the citizens of the United States of North America double, every twenty-five years, their agriculture, their industry, their commerce, their riches, and their population? It is because there is scarcely an idler among them, and the rich go to little superfluous expense. Their position, I agree, is very favourable. Land is not wanting for their development: it offers itself to their labours, and recompences them. But if they laboured little, and expended much, this land would remain uncultivated—they would grow poor, would languish; and would be very miserable, as the Spaniards are, notwithstanding all their advantages. Their neighbours, the Canadians, do they make the same progress? They are gentlemen, living nobly, and doing nothing.[1]

---

1. The last two sentences of this paragraph are not found in the French edition.

Finally, let us take a last example, much more striking still. France, under its ancient government, was not certainly as miserable as the French themselves have represented it to be; but it was not flourishing. Its population* and its agriculture were not retrograde, but they were stationary; or if they made some small progress, it was less than that of several neighbouring nations, and consequently not proportioned to the progress of the knowledge of the age. She was involved in debt, had no credit, was always in want of funds for her useful expenses—she felt herself incapable of supporting the ordinary expenses of her government, and still more of making any great efforts without: In a word, notwithstanding the genius, the number, and the activity of her inhabitants, the richness and extent of her soil, and the benefits of a very long peace, little troubled, she with difficulty maintained her rank among her rivals; and was of but little consideration, and in nowise formidable abroad.

Her revolution takes place: She has suffered all imaginable evils: She has been torn by atrocious wars, civil and foreign: Several of her provinces have been laid waste, and their cities reduced to ashes: All have been pillaged by brigands, and by the furnishers of the troops: Her exterior commerce has been annihilated: Her fleets totally destroyed; though often renewed: Her colonies, believed so necessary to her prosperity, have been prostrated; and, what is worse, she has lost all the men and money lavished to subjugate them: Her specie has been nearly all exported, as well by the effect of emigration, as by that of paper money: She has supported fourteen armies in a time of famine; and, amidst all this, it is notorious that her population and her agriculture have augmented considerably in a very few years; and at the epoch of the creation of the empire, without any improvement in her situation as to the sea and foreign commerce, to which so great importance is commonly attributed, without having had a single instant of peace for repose, she supported enormous taxes, made immense expenditures in public works, she effected all without a loan; and she had a colossal power,

---

* I desire it to be remembered, that I do not regard the augmentation of population as a good. It is but too often a multiplication of miserable beings. I should greatly prefer the augmentation of well being. I cite here the increase of the number of men as a symptom only, and not as a happiness. The abuse of competence is a proof of its existence.

which nothing on the continent of Europe could resist, and which would have subjugated the universe, but for the British navy. What then took place in this country which could produce such inconceivable effects? One circumstance changed has done the whole.

Under the ancient order of things, the greater part of the useful labour of the inhabitants of France was employed every year in producing the riches which formed the immense revenues of the court, and of all the rich class of society; and these revenues were almost entirely consumed in the expenditures of luxury; that is to say, in paying an enormous mass of population, whose whole labour reproduced absolutely nothing but the enjoyments of some men. In a moment almost the whole of these revenues, have passed partly into the hands of the new government, partly into those of the laborious class. They fed also all those who derive their subsistence from them; but their labour was applied to useful or necessary things; and it has sufficed to defend the state from without, and to increase its productions within.*

Ought we to be surprised when we consider that there was a time, of some length, during which, by the effect even of commotion and of the general distress, there was scarcely in France a single idle citizen, or one occupied in useless labours? Those who before made coaches, made carriages for cannon; those who made embroidery and laces, made coarse woollens and linens; those who ornamented boudoirs, built parks and cleared land. And even those who in peace rioted in all these inutilities, were forced to gain a subsistence by the performance of services which were wanting. A man who kept forty useless domestics left them to be hired by the industrious class, or by the state, and himself become a clerk of an office. This is the secret of those prodigious resources always found by the body of a nation in a crisis so great. It then turns to profit all the force which in ordinary times it suffered to be lost, without being aware of it; and we are frightened at seeing how great that is.

---

* The sole suppression of the feudal rights and tythes, partly to the profit of cultivators, and partly of the state, enabled the one greatly to increase their industry, and the other to lay an enormous mass of new imposts; and these were but a small part of the revenues of the class of useless consumers.

This is the substance of all that is true in college declamations on frugality, sobriety, abhorrence of ostentation; and all those democratic virtues of poor and agricultural nations, which are so ridiculously vaunted without either their cause or effect being understood. It is not because they are poor and ignorant that these nations are strong; it is because nothing is lost of the little force they possess, and that a man who has an hundred francs, and employs them well, has more means than he who has a thousand and loses them at play. But let the same be done by a rich and enlightened nation, and you will see the same development of force which you have seen in the French nation, which has produced effects greatly superior to all that was ever executed by the Roman republic: for it has overthrown much greater obstacles. Let Germany, for example, during some years only, leave entirely in the hands of the industrious class the revenues which serve for the pageantry of all its small courts, and rich abbies, and you will see whether she will be a strong and formidable nation. On the contrary, suppose they should entirely re-establish in France the ancient order of things, that a great mass of property should return into the hands of idle men, that the government should continue to enrich favourites and make great expenditures in useless things, you would again see there immediately, notwithstanding its great increase of territory, languor in the midst of resources, misery in the midst of riches, and weakness in the midst of all the means of strength.

It will be repeated that I attribute solely to the distribution of riches, and to the employment of the labour they pay, the result of a multitude of moral causes of the greatest energy. Once more, I do not deny the existence of these causes; I acknowledge it as all others do; but I do more, I explain their effect. I agree that the enthusiasm of interior liberty and exterior independence, and the indignation against an unjust oppression, and a still more unjust aggression, have alone been able to operate these great revolutions in France; but I maintain that these have not furnished the passions with such great means of success (notwithstanding the errors and horrors to which their violence led), but because they produced a better employment of all the national force. *All the good of human society is in the good application of labour; all the evil in its loss;* which, in other words, means nothing but that when men are occupied in providing for their wants they are satisfied, and that when they lose their time they suffer. One is ashamed to be obliged to prove so palpable a truth; but we must recollect that the extent of its consequences are surprising.

One might compose a whole book on luxury, and it would be useful, for this subject has never been well treated. It might be shown that luxury, that is to say the taste for superfluous expense, is to a certain point the necessary effect of the natural dispositions of man to procure constantly new enjoyments, when he has the means; and of the power of habit, which renders necessary to him the conveniences he has enjoyed, even when it shall have become burdensome to him to continue to procure them: that consequently luxury is an inevitable result of industry, the progress of which it nevertheless arrests; and of riches, which it tends to destroy; and that for the same reason, also, when a nation is fallen from its ancient grandeur, whether from the slow effect of luxury or from any other cause, it survives the prosperity which has given birth to it and renders its return impossible, unless some violent shock, directed to this end, should produce a quick and complete regeneration. It is the same with individuals.

It would be necessary to show, according to these data, that in the opposite situation, when a nation takes for the first time its rank among civilised people, it is requisite, in order that the success of its efforts may be complete, that the progress of its industry and knowledge should be much more rapid than that of its luxury. It is, perhaps, principally to this circumstance that we should attribute the great advances made by the Prussian monarchy under its second and third king, an example which ought to embarrass a little those who pretend that luxury is necessary to the prosperity of monarchies.* It is this same circumstance which appears to me to ensure the duration of the felicity of the United States; and it may be feared that the want of the complete enjoyment of this advantage, will render difficult and even imperfect the true prosperity and civilization of Russia.

It would be necessary to say which are the most injurious species of luxury. We might consider unskilfulness in manufacturing as a great luxury, for it causes a great loss of time and of labour. It would above all be necessary to

---

  * If luxury is necessary in a monarchal state, it is for the security of the government, but not for the prosperity of the country.

explain how the great fortunes are the principal and almost only source of luxury, properly so called, for it could scarcely exist if they were all moderate. Even idleness in this case could scarcely have a place. Now this is a kind of luxury; since, if it is not a sterile employment of labour, it is a suppression of it.* The branches of industry which rapidly produce immense riches bring then with them an inconvenience, which strongly counter-balances their advantages. It is not these we ought to wish to see first developed in a rising nation. Of this kind is a very extensive foreign commerce. Agriculture, on the contrary, is greatly preferable; its products are slow and limited. Industry, properly so called (that of manufacture), is likewise without danger and very useful. Its profits are not excessive; its success is difficult to be attained and perpetuated; it requires much knowledge, and many estimable qualities; and its consequences are very favourable to the well being of consumers. The good manufacture of objects of first necessity is above all desirable. The manufactory of objects of luxury may also be of great advantage to a country; but it is when their produce is like the religion of the court of Rome, which is said to be for that court an article of exportation, and not of consumption; and there is always a fear of intoxicating ourselves with the liquor we prepare for others. All these observations, and many others, should be developed in the book of which we are speaking; but they would be superfluous here. They enter in many respects into the reflections I have made before (chapter x) on the manner in which riches are distributed in a country, in proportion as they are accumulated. Besides, my object is not to compose the history of luxury; I only wish to show its effects on general consumption, and on circulation.

I shall content myself with adding that if luxury is a great evil, in an economical point of view, it is still a much greater in point of morality; which is always much the most important, when the question is on the interests of men. The taste for superfluous expenses, the principal source of which is vanity, nourishes and exasperates it. It renders the understanding frivolous,

---

* The only idle people who ought to be seen without reprobation, are those who devote themselves to study; and especially to the study of man. And these are the only ones who are persecuted: there is reason for this. They show how useless the others are; and they are not the strongest.

and injures its strength. It produces irregularity of conduct, which engenders many vices, disorders and disturbances in families. It leads women readily to depravity, men to avidity, both to the loss of delicacy and probity, and to the abandonment of all generous and tender sentiments. In a word, it enervates the soul, by weakening the understanding; and produces these sad effects not only on those who enjoy it, but likewise on all those who serve it, or admire it—who imitate or envy it. This will all be more clearly seen when we speak of our moral interests. I could not avoid indicating it here. We must not confound things however intimately connected they may be.

For the same reason it will not be expected surely that I should now discuss the question, whether luxury being acknowledged hurtful, we ought to combat it by laws or by manners; nor that I should examine by what mean we can favour production, and give a useful direction to consumption. This would be to encroach on the province of legislation; with which I may perhaps occupy myself some day. But in all this part of my work, I ought to limit myself to the establishment of facts.

I think I have solidly established, that since one can only expend what he has, production is the only fund of consumption; and that consequently consumption and circulation can never be augmented but by an augmenting production; and finally, that to destroy is not to produce; and that to expend is not to enrich. This small number of very simple truths, will enable us to see very clearly the effects of the revenues and expenses of governments on the prosperity of nations.

CHAPTER XII

*Of the Revenues and Expenses of a
Government, and of Its Debts.*

ℰℛ

This subject is still very vast, although it is but a part of that of which we
have just treated. Many writers would divide it into three books, which
they subdivide each into several chapters: but I prefer not to separate these
matters, that I may not cause my readers to lose sight of their mutual de-
pendance; and I feel the necessity for considering them principally in mass,
and under a general and common aspect. This will not prevent me from entering also into details, and from distinguishing the particular cases which
are really different, perhaps even with more exactitude than has been hitherto done.

In every society the government is the greatest of consumers. For this reason alone it merits a separate article in the history of consumption, without
which it would be incomplete. But for the same reason, also, we can never
perfectly comprehend the economical effects of government, and those of
its receipts and expenditures, if we have not previously formed a clear and
exact idea of general consumption, of its base, and of its progress.

The same errors which we have just combated will re-appear here. Those
who think that agricultural labours alone are productive, do not fail to say
that in the end all imposts fall on the proprietors of lands, that their revenue is the only taxable matter, that the territorial impost is the only just and
useful one, and that there ought to be no others; and those who persuade
themselves that consumptions can be a cause of direct riches, maintain that

the levies made by government, on the fortunes of individuals, powerfully stimulate industry; that its expenses are very useful, by augmenting consumption; that they animate circulation; and that all this is very favourable to the public prosperity. To see clearly the vice of these sophisms, we must always follow the same track, and commence by well establishing the facts.

In the first place, there is no doubt but that a government of some sort must be very necessary to every political society; for its members must be judged, their affairs must be administered, they must be protected, defended, guaranteed from all violence; it is only for this that they are united in society. It is no more doubtful, but that this government must have revenues since it has expenses to incur. But this is not the present question. The question is, to know what effects these revenues, and these expenses, produce on the public riches and national prosperity.

To judge of them, since government is a great consumer, and the greatest of all, we must examine it in this quality, as we have examined the other consumers, that is to say we must see from whence it receives the funds of which it disposes, and what use it makes of them.

A first thing very certain is, that government cannot be ranked amongst the consumers of the industrious class. The expenditure it makes does not return into its hands with an increase of value. It does not support itself on the profits it makes. I conclude, then, that its consumption is very real and definitive; that nothing remains from the labour which it pays; and that the riches which it employs, and which were existing, are consumed and destroyed when it has availed itself of them. It remains to be seen from whence it receives them.

Since the moral person, called government, does not live on profits, it lives on revenues. It derives these revenues from two sources. It possesses estates in land, and it lays imposts.

As to its estates in land, it is absolutely in the same situation as the other capitalists whom we have called *idle*. It leases them and receives a rent; or if they are forests, it annually sells the timber cut. The care taken of forests, and which principally consists in preserving them, does not merit the name of industrious labour. The real labour which gives them a value is that which consists in felling them, in selling and transporting them. If they belonged to him who fells them, he would receive all the profit. The price annually paid for the privilege of felling them ought to be regarded as a rent levied on the industry of the person who fells them: a rent absolutely similar to that derived from a fishery, yearly rented to him who has the industry to take the fish. Thus the revenues, derived from the estates belonging to government, are, like those of all other rural property, created by the industrious men who work them, and levied on their profits.

Many politicians do not approve of government having landed estates: it is very true, that as it is by no means a careful proprietor its managers must necessarily be very expensive and little faithful. Thus it does, with much unskilfulness, what another proprietor would do better. But it must be remarked, that this unskilfulness does not diminish, or diminishes very little, the total mass of the production of these estates: for the quantity of the production of the lands depends little on those who manage them, but almost entirely on those who work them. Now nothing prevents these lands being as well cultivated, and their timber cut down and sold, with as much intelligence as those of an individual. The defect in their management consists in employing a few more men than is necessary, and in paying them a little too dear. Now this is no very great inconvenience.

I, on the contrary, see many advantages in the governments having possessions of this kind. First, there are some kinds of productions which it alone can preserve in great quantity: such are forests of large timber, the productions of which must be so long waited for, that for the most part individuals prefer the same, or even a smaller quantity of more frequent returns. Secondly, it may be good that the government should possess cultivated lands. It will be better able to know more perfectly the resources and the interests of different localities; and, if it is wise and benevolent, it may even profit by this to diffuse a useful knowledge. Thirdly, when a great mass of landed property is in the hand of government, less remains at market. Now as this kind of possession is always greatly desired, all things otherwise equal, the less there is to be sold the dearer it will sell, that is to say that for a sum of one hundred thousand francs the buyer will be contented to receive four or even three thousand francs of revenue instead of five; and this will reduce the rate of interest of money in its various employments, which is a great advantage. Fourthly, and this consideration is the most important of all, all that the government annually draws from these estates is a revenue, which it levies on no one. It comes to it from its own property, as to all other proprietors; and it is so much in diminution of what it is obliged to procure by imposts. In fine, in a case of necessity it may, as an individual, find a resource in the sale of its estates without having recourse to loans, which are always a great evil, as we shall soon see.

For all these reasons I think it very happy for government to be a great proprietor, especially of forests and large farms. One circumstance only would be to be regretted, that this would prevent these estates from falling into the hand of the industrious class. But we have seen on the subject of agricultural industry, that from the nature of things property of this kind can seldom be in the possession of those who work them, because this would take from them too great a portion of their funds. Now I had rather they should belong to government, than to any other capitalist living on revenue.

On the whole, our modern governments in general possess but little landed property. It is not that they have not almost all declared their domains inalienable, but they have also almost all sold or given a very great part of them. The true revenue on which they calculate is that of imposts; it is then this which we should take into consideration.

By means of imposts, the government takes from individuals the wealth which was at their disposition, in order to expend it itself; these then are always sacrifices imposed on them.

If this sacrifice bears on the men who live on their revenues, and who employ the whole of them on their personal enjoyments, it would make no change in the total mass of production, consumption and general circulation. All the difference would be, that a part of the wages which these men paid, would be paid by government with the money taken from them: this is the most favourable case.

When the impost falls on industrious men, who live on profits, it may only diminish their profits. Then it is that part of these profits which these men employ in their personal enjoyments which is attacked. It is these enjoyments which are diminished; and the impost has the same effects as in the preceding case. But if it goes so far as to annihilate the profits of the industrious men, or even to touch on the funds of their industry, then it is this industry itself which is deranged or destroyed; and consequently production, and in the end the general consumption are diminished by it. Suffering prevails every where.

Finally, where the impost falls on the wage earners, it is evident they begin to suffer. If the loss rests entirely on them, it is a part of their consumption which is suppressed; and which is replaced by that of those whom the government pays with the money taken from them. If they are able to throw it on those who employ them by raising the price of their wages, it is then necessary to know by whom they are employed; and, accordingly as they are in the employ of idle or industrious capitalists, this loss will have one of the two effects which we have just described in speaking of these capitalists.

I think this preliminary explanation must appear incontestable, after the elucidations we have given in speaking of consumption. At present the great difficulty is to find on whom the loss occasioned by the impost really falls: for all imposts do not produce the same effects, and thus are so multiplied that it is impossible to examine every one separately. I think it best to arrange under the same denomination all those which are essentially of the same nature.

All imaginable imposts, and I suppose they have all been imagined, may be divided into six principal kinds,* viz. First, The impost on the revenues of lands, such as the *real tax,* the twentieth the manorial contribution in France, and the *land tax* in England. Second, That on the rent of houses. Third, That on the annuities due from the state. Fourth, That on persons, as the capitation and poll tax, sumptuary and furniture contributions, on patent rights, on charters and freedom of corporations, &c. &c. Fifth, That on civil acts and certain social transactions, as on stamps, and registers, on changes in property ownership, the hundredth penny, reductions in debt, and others; to which we must add the annual impost on annuities charged on one individual by another, for there are no means of knowing of these investments, donations, or transmissions, but by the depositories which preserve the acts establishing them. Sixth, That on merchandise, whether by monopoly or sale, exclusive, or even forced, as formerly of salt and tobacco

---

* This is in my opinion the best method of classing them, to give a clear account of their effects.

in France; or at the moment of their first production, as the taxes on salt ponds and mines, and part of those on wines in France and on breweries in England; or at the moment of consumption, or on their passage from the first producer to the ultimate consumer, as the customs interior and exterior: the tolls on roads, canals, postage, and at the entrance of cities, &c. &c.*

Each of these imposts has one or several manners, peculiar to itself, of being burdensome.

At the first glance, we may see that the tax on revenues from land has the inconvenience of being difficult to assess with justice, and of annihilating the value of all those lands whose rent does not exceed the tax or exceeds it by too little, to determine any one to incur the inevitable risk, and the expenditures requisite for putting these lands into a state for cultivation.

---

* A note communicated to the Editor. Our author's classification of taxes being taken from those practised in France, will scarcely be intelligible to an American reader to whom the nature as well as names of some of them must be unknown. The taxes with which we are familiar class themselves readily according to the basis on which they rest. 1. Capital. 2. Income. 3. Consumption. These may be considered as commensurate; consumption being generally equal to income; and income the annual profit of capital, a government may select either of these basis for the establishment of its system of taxation, and so frame it as to reach the faculties of every member of the society, and to draw from him his equal proportion of the public contributions. And if this be correctly obtained, it is the perfection of the function of taxation. But when once a government has assumed its basis, to select and tax special articles from either of the other classes is double taxation. For example, if the system be established on the basis of income, and his just proportion on that scale has been already drawn from every one, to step into the field of consumption, and tax special articles in that, as broadcloth or homespun, wine or whiskey, a coach or a waggon, is doubly taxing the same article. For that portion of income, with which these articles are purchased, having already paid its tax as income, to pay another tax on the thing it purchased, is paying twice for the same thing. It is an aggrievance on the citizens who use these articles in exoneration of those who do not, contrary to the most sacred of the duties of a government, to do equal and impartial justice to all its citizens.

How far it may be the interest and the duty of all to submit to this sacrifice on other grounds, for instance, to pay for a time an impost on the importation of certain articles, in order to encourage their manufacture at home, or an excise on others injurious to the morals or health of the citizens, will depend on a series of considerations, of another order, and beyond the proper limits of this note. The reader, in deciding which basis of taxation is most eligible for the local circumstances of his country, will of course avail himself of the weighty observations of our author.

The tax on house rent, has the defect of lessening the profit of speculations in building; and so of deterring from building houses to rent, so that every citizen is obliged to content himself with habitations less healthy, and less convenient, than those he might have had at the same rent.*

A tax on annuities due from the state is a real bankruptcy, if established on annuities already created, since it is a diminution of the interest promised for a capital received; and it is illusory if established on them at the moment of their creation, for it would have been more simple to have offered in the first instant an interest lessened by the amount of the tax, which would have come to the same thing.

A tax on persons gives occasion to disagreeable scrutinies to assess it justly, according to the fortune of every one; and can never rest but on arbitrary bases and very uncertain knowledge, as well when attempted to be assessed on riches already acquired as when intended to bear on the means of acquiring them. In the latter case, that is to say, when it is predicated on the supposition of any kind of industry whatever, it discourages that industry, and obliges it to rise in price or to be abandoned.

The tax on civil acts, and in general on social transactions, cramps the circulation of real property, and diminishes their market value, by rendering their transfer very expensive; augments so much the expenses of justice that the poor dare no longer defend their rights; renders all business perplexing and difficult; occasions inquisitorial researches, and vexations by the

---

* I do not avail myself against this impost of the pretentions of some economists, that the rent of houses ought not to be taxed, or at least but in proportion to the nett revenue which would be yielded by the cultivation of the land occupied by these houses, all the rest being only the interest of the capital employed in building, which according to them is not taxable.

This opinion is a consequence of that which considers agricultural labour as alone productive, and that the revenue of land is the only thing taxable, because there is in the produce of land a part purely gratuitous and entirely due to nature; which portion, according to these authors, is the only legitimate and reasonable subject of taxation.

I have shown that all this is false, therefore I cannot avail myself of it either against this or any of the following imposts; which are all not only reprobated in this system, but are declared illusory, as never being nor possible to be, any thing but an impost on the revenue of lands, disguised and additionally charged with useles expenses and losses. Such a theory is untenable when we know what is production.

agents of the revenue; gives rise in these acts to concealments, and even to the insertion of deceptious clauses and valuations, which open the door to much iniquity and give rise to a multitude of contentions and misfortunes.

As to taxes on merchandise, their inconveniences are still more numerous and complicated; but are not less disagreeable nor less certain.

Monopoly, or a sale exclusively by the state, is odious, tyrannical, contrary to the natural right which every one has of buying and selling as he pleases, and it necessitates a multitude of violent measures. It is still worse when this sale is forced, that is to say when government obliges individuals, as has sometimes been done, to buy things they do not want, under pretext that they cannot do without them, and that if they do not buy them it is because they have provided themselves by contraband.

A tax, levied at the moment of production, evidently requires on the part of the producer an advance of fund, which being long without returning to him greatly diminishes his means of producing.

It is not less clear that all imposts levied either at the moment of consumption or during the transportation from the producer to the consumer, cramp or destroy some branch of industry or of commerce; render scarce, or costly, necessary or useful articles; disturb all enjoyments, derange the natural course of things; and establish, between the different wants and the means of satisfying them, proportions and relations which would not exist but for these perturbations, which are necessarily variable, and which render the speculations and resources of the citizens inevitably precarious.

Finally, all these taxes whatsoever on merchandise occasion an infinity of precautions and embarrassing formalities. They give place to a multitude of ruinous difficulties, and are necessarily liable to be arbitrary; they oblige actions indifferent in themselves to be constituted crimes, and inflict punishments often the most cruel. Their collection is very expensive, and calls into existence an army of officers, and an army of defrauders, men all lost to society, and who continually wage a real civil war, with all the grievous economical and moral consequences which it brings on.

When we attentively examine each of these criticisms on the different taxes, we see that they are well founded. Thus, after having shown that every impost is a sacrifice, we find that we have also shown that every impost has, besides, a manner peculiar to itself of being hurtful to the contributors.

This is already a great deal, but it does not yet teach us on whom precisely falls the loss resulting from the impost, nor who it is that really and definitively supports it. Yet this latter question is the most important, and absolutely necessary to be resolved in order to judge of the effects of taxes on the national prosperity. Let us examine it then with attention, without adopting any system, and adhering scrupulously to an observation of facts, as we have done hitherto.

As to the tax on the revenues of land, it is evident that it is he who possesses the land, at the moment in which the tax is established, who pays it really without being able to throw it on any one. For it does not give him any means of augmenting his productions, since it adds nothing either to the demand for articles, or to the fertility of the soil; and does not in any degree diminish the expense of cultivation. All assent to this truth. But what has not been sufficiently remarked, is, that this proprietor ought to be considered less as having been deprived of a portion of his yearly income, than as having lost that part of his capital, which would produce this portion of income at the current rate of interest. The proof is, that if a farm, yielding annually five thousand francs nett rent, is worth an hundred thousand francs, the day after it shall have been charged with a perpetual tax of a fifth, all other things equal, it will not command more than eighty thousand if offered for sale; and it will be stated but at eighty thousand francs, in the inventory of an inheritance which contains other articles whose value have not been changed. In effect, when the state has declared that it takes in perpetuity the fifth of the income of lands, it is as if it had declared itself proprietor of the fifth of the capital, for no property is worth but the utility which may be derived from it. This is so true, that when, in consequence of a new impost, the state opens a loan, for the interest of which it pledges the revenue it has seized, the operation is consummated; it has really received the capital, it had appropriated, and has made away with the whole at once, instead of annually expending its income. It is as when Mr. Pitt took at once from the proprietors the capital of the land tax with which they were charged: they were liberated and he swallowed his capital.[1]

---

1. William Pitt, the Younger (1759–1806), British prime minister (1783–1800, 1804–6). Pitt had sought to eliminate the national debt by raising taxes.

From hence it follows, that when once all the land has changed owners since the establishment of the tax, it is no longer really paid by any one. The purchasers having bought only what was left, have lost nothing; the heirs having succeeded but to what they found, the surplus is to them as if their predecessors had expended or lost it, as in effect they have lost it. And, in case of inheritances abandoned as of no value, it is the creditors who have lost the capital taken by the state from the property which was security for their debt.

It follows likewise from this, that when the state renounces the whole or part of a territorial tax, anciently established as a perpetuity, it purely and simply makes a present to the actual proprietors of the lands of the capital of the revenue which it ceases to demand. It is as to them a gift absolutely gratuitous, to which they have no more right than any other citizens. For none of them calculated on this capital, in the transactions by which they became proprietors.

It would not be absolutely the same, if the impost had been originally established only for a determinate number of years. Then there would really have been taken from the proprietor but a part of the capital corresponding to this number of *years*. The state, likewise, would have borrowed but this value from the lenders, to whom it might have pledged this impost for the payment of their principal and interest; and the lands would have been considered in the transaction but as deteriorated to this amount. In this case when the tax ceases, as when the corresponding dividends of the loan are exhausted, it is on both sides a debt extinguished, because it is paid. On the whole the principle is the same, as in the case of a tax and of a perpetual rent.

It is then always true, that when a tax is laid on land, a value equal to the capital of this tax is taken at once from the actual proprietors, and that when all have changed owners, since the establishment of the tax, it is really no longer paid by any one. This observation is singular and important.

It is absolutely the same with the tax established on the rent of houses. Those who possess them at the moment it is established support the entire loss, for they have no means of indemnifying themselves. But those who buy them afterwards pay for them but in proportion to the charges with which they are incumbered. Those who inherit them, reckon them, in like manner, but at the value which remains; and as to those who build subsequently, they make their calculations according to the state of things as they are established. If no room is left for useful speculation they defer building until the effect of scarcity raises rents. As, on the contrary, if it was extremely advantageous there would soon be funds enough employed therein to make it no longer preferable to any other employment of them. We conclude again that the proprietors on whom the impost falls, lose the entire capital, and that when all are either dead or expropriated, this impost is paid but by those who have no right to complain of it.

We may say the same of the taxes which governments sometimes permit themselves to impose on annuities which they owe for capitals formerly furnished. Certainly the unfortunate creditor from whom this deduction is made suffers the entire loss, not being able to throw it on any one; but he moreover loses the capital of the sum retained. The proof is that if he sells his annuity he gets so much the less, as it is more encumbered if otherwise the general rate of interest on money has not varied. Whence it follows that subsequent possessors of this annuity no longer pay any thing: for they received it in this condition and for its remaining value in virtue of a purchase freely made or of successions voluntarily accepted.

The effect of a tax on persons is not at all the same. We must distinguish between that which is supposed to bear on acquired riches, and that which is meant for the means of acquiring them, that is to say on industry of some sort. In the first case it is certainly always the person taxed who supports the loss resulting from it, for he cannot throw it on any other. But as the tax on every one ceases with his life, and every one is successively subject to it, in proportion to his presumed fortune, the first person taxed loses only the dues which he pays, and not the capital, and does not liberate those who come after him; thus at whatever epoch the tax ceases, it is not a pure gain to those who are subject to it, it is a burthen weighing really on them and which ceases to be continued.

As to a tax on persons, which has for its object industry of some sort, it is equally true that he who first pays it does not lose the capital nor liberate those who are subjected to it after him; but it gives room for considerations of another kind. The man who exercises a branch of industry at the moment in which it becomes burthened with a new personal tax, such as the establishment or increase of patent rights, the freedom of corporations, masterships, or other things of the same kind, this man I say has but two courses to pursue, either to renounce his occupation, or to pay the tax and support the loss resulting from it, if notwithstanding this it still holds out a prospect of sufficient profits. In the first case he certainly suffers, but he does not pay the tax; therefore I shall not now occupy myself with it. In the second case, it is he assuredly who pays the imposition, since neither augmenting the demand, nor diminishing the expense, it does not give him any immediate mean of increasing his receipts or lessening his expenditures. But taxes are never all at once laid so heavy as to oblige inevitably all of the same occupation to quit it: for all industrious professions being necessary to society, the total extinction of any one would produce general disorder. Thus after the establishment of a tax of the kind we speak of, none but those who are already rich enough to consider a diminished profit as no object, or those who exercised their profession with so little success, that no profits would remain to them after paying the tax, would renounce their occupation. The others continue it; and these, as we have said, really pay the tax at least until rid of the competition of many of their brethren, they could avail themselves of this circumstance to levy it on the consumers by making them pay more for the articles than before.

It is thus with those who exercised the profession at the moment of the establishment of the tax. The case is different with those who embrace it after the tax has been once established. They find the law made; we may say that they engage themselves on this condition. The tax is for them among the expenses required by the profession, as the necessity of renting a particular situation, or of buying a particular utensil. They only enter on this profession because they calculate that, notwithstanding these changes, it is still the best employment they can make of the portion of capital and industry they possess. Thus they certainly advance the tax, but it does not really take any thing from them. Those to whom it is a real loss are the consumers, who without this change could at less expense have made up the income with which they are contented, and which was the best in their power to procure in the present state of society. From hence it follows, that, if the tax be removed these men really make a profit on which they did not calculate, at least until this advantage produces new competitors. They find themselves gratuitously, and fortuitously, transported into a class of society more favoured by fortune than that in which they were placed; while to those who exercised it previously to the tax, it is but a return to their first state. We see that a tax on persons, founded on industry, produces very different effects; but its general effect is to diminish the enjoyments of consumers, since their furnishers do not give them merchandise for that part of their money which goes into the public treasury. I cannot enter into more details; but we cannot too much accustom ourselves to judge of the different reverberations of a tax, and to follow them in thought, in all their modifications. Let us pass to the imposts on papers, deeds, records, and other monuments of social transactions.

This requires also a distinction. The portion of this impost, which goes to augment the expenses of justice, and which makes a part of it, is certainly paid by the parties on whom the judgment throws the expense; and it is difficult to say to what class of society it is most hurtful; however, it is easy to see that it burdens particularly the kind of property most liable to contention. Now, as this is landed property, the establishment of such an impost certainly diminishes its market value. Whence it follows that those who have purchased lands, since the existence of the tax, are a little compensated, in advance, by the smaller price of their purchase; and that those who possessed them before bear the entire loss if they have any lawsuit, and even sustain a loss without any law contest, and without paying the tax, since the value of their property is diminished. Consequently if the tax ceases, it is but a restitution for the latter; and there is a portion of gratuitous gain for the others, for they find themselves in a better situation than that on which they had calculated, and according to which they had made their speculation.

All this is yet more true, and is true without restriction, of that portion of the tax on transactions which regards purchases and sales, such as fines on alienation, the hundredth penny, reductions in debt, and others. This portion of the tax is entirely paid by him who possesses the property at the moment it is thus encumbered: for he who buys it subsequently pays him but accordingly, and consequently pays really nothing. All that can be said, is that if this tax on deeds of sale of certain possessions is accompanied by other taxes on other transactions which affect other kinds of property, other employments of capitals, it will happen that these possessions are not the only ones lessened in value; and consequently that proportion is preserved, at least in part, and that thus a part of their loss is prevented by that of others, for the market price of every kind of revenue is relative to that of all the others. Thus, if all these losses could be exactly balanced, the total loss resulting from the impost would be exactly and very proportionably distributed. This is all that can be asked: for it must necessarily exist, since impost is always a sum of means taken from the governed, to be placed at the disposition of those who govern.

Imposts on merchandise have effects still more complicated and various. To unravel them well, let us recollect that all merchandise, at the moment it is delivered to the consumer, has a natural and necessary price. This price is composed of the value of what has been necessary for the subsistence of those who have fabricated and transported this merchandise, during the time which they were employed about it. I say that this price is natural because it is founded on the nature of things independently of all convention; and that it is necessary, because if the men who execute a labour whatsoever do not obtain subsistence they perish, or apply themselves to other occupations, and this labour is no longer executed. But this natural and necessary price has scarcely any thing in common with the market or conventional price of the merchandise, that is to say with the price at which it is fixed by the effect of a free sale. For a thing may have cost very little trouble, or if it has required much labour and care it may have been found or stolen by him who offers it for sale; in these two cases he may sell it very low, without losing; but it may at the same time be so useful to him, that he will not part with it but for a very great price; and, if many people want it, he will obtain this price, and make an enormous gain. On the contrary it is possible that a thing may have cost the vendor infinite trouble, that not only it may not be necessary to him, but that he may have a pressing call to dispose of it, and that yet no body is desirous of buying it. In this case he will be obliged to part with it for almost nothing, and will sustain a very great loss. The natural price is then composed of anterior sacrifices made by the vendor, and the conventional price is fixed by the offers of buyers. These are two things, in themselves foreign to one another. Only when the conventional price of any labour is constantly below its natural and necessary price, it ceases to be performed. Then the produce of this labour becoming scarce, more sacrifices are made to procure it, if it is still desired, and thus however little it is really useful the conventional or market price re-ascends to the level of the price which nature has attached to that labour, and which is necessary to a continuance of its execution. It is thus all prices are formed in a state of society.

It follows hence that those who exercise a labour, the conventional price of which is inferior to its natural value, ruin themselves or disperse, that those who execute a labour, or in other words exercise an industry whatsoever, the conventional price of which is strictly equal to the natural price, that is to say, those whose profits balance nearly their urgent wants, vegetate and subsist miserably and that those who possess talents the conventional price of which, is superior to absolute necessaries, enjoy, prosper, and in course multiply. For the fecundity of all living, even among vegetables is such, that nothing but a want of nourishment for the germs disclosed arrests the increase of numbers of the individuals. This is the cause of the retrograde, stationary or progressive state of population, in the human kind. Momentary calamities, such as famine and pestilence have little effect. Unproductive labour, or productive in an insufficient degree, is the poison which deeply infects the sources of life. We have already made nearly all these observations, either in the fourth paragraph of our introduction, in speaking of the nature of our riches, or in the chapters in which we have spoken of values and population. But it was well to bring them again into view in this place.

Now it is easy to perceive that imposts on merchandise, affect prices, in different ways, and in different limits, according to the manner in which they are levied, and according to the nature of the articles on which they bear. For example in the case of monoply or exclusive sale, by the state, it is clear that the impost is paid directly immediately and without resource by the consumer, and that it has the greatest extension of which it is susceptible. But this sale, if forced cannot however, either in price or quantity exceed a certain term, which is that of the possibility of paying it. It stops whenever it would be useless to exact it, or when it would cost more than it would bring in. This is the point at which the tax on salt was in France and it is the *maximum* of possible exaction.

If the exclusive sale, be not forced it varies according to the nature of the merchandise, if it be on articles not necessary in proportion as the price raises the consumption diminishes; for there is but a certain sum of means in the whole society, which is destined to procure a certain kind of enjoyment: it may even happen, that a small increase of price may greatly diminish the profit because many renounce entirely this kind of consumption, or are even able to replace it by another. But the impost is always effectively paid by those who persevere in consuming.

If on the contrary the exclusive sale made by the state, but by mutual agreement bears on an article of the first necessity, it is equivalent to a forced sale, for the consumption, diminishes truly in proportion as the price rises, that is to say, people suffer and die, but as in fine it is necessary, it always rises with the means of paying, and it is paid by those who consume.

After these violent means, if we examine others, more mild, we shall find their effects analagous, with a less degree of energy. The most efficacious of these is a tax imposed on merchandise at the moment of production, for no part escapes, not even that consumed by the producer himself, nor even that which may be damaged or lost in warehouses, previously to being employed. Such is the tax on salt levied on the salt ponds; that on wine at the instant of the vintage, or before the first sale, and that on beer at the breweries. We may also range in the same class the impost on sugar, coffee, and other such articles levied at the moment of their arrival from the country which produces them: for it is not till this moment they exist, for the country which cannot produce them and which is to consume them.

This tax levied at the moment of production, if established on an article little necessary is as limited as the taste we have for it. Thus, when it was wished to derive a great revenue from tobacco, pains were taken to render it a necessary to the people. For if society is instituted for the more easy satisfaction of the wants given us by nature, and from which we cannot withdraw ourselves, it seems that fiscality is destined to create in us artificial wants, in order to refuse us one part, and make us pay for the other.

When this same impost, at the moment of production, is established on an article more necessary, it is susceptible of a greater extension; however, if this article costs much labour and expense in its production the extent of the impost is likewise soon stopped, no longer through want of a desire to procure the article, but by the impossibility of paying for it: for there must always reach the producers a sufficient portion of the price for their subsistence; thus there is less remaining for the state.

But an impost displays all its force when the article is very necessary and costs very little, as salt for example: there all is profit for the treasury; accordingly its agents have always paid a particular attention to salt. Very rich mines produce also the same effect to a certain point, but in general governments have taken the property to themselves, which saves the trouble of taxing, and is equivalent to the process of exclusive sale. Air and water, if they could have appropriated them would have been objects of taxation very heavy and very fruitful for the treasury; but nature has diffused them too widely. I do not doubt but, in Arabia, revenue farmers would draw great profit from a tax on water, and so that no one should drink without their permission. As to air the window tax accomplishes as much on that as is possible.

Wine is not a gratuitous present from nature. It costs much trouble, care and expense; and, notwithstanding the necessity and the strong desire we have to procure it, we should with difficulty, believe it could support the enormous charges with which it is burthened at present in France, at the moment of its production. If we were not apprised that a part of this burden falls directly on the land planted in vines, and operates only as a great reduction of the rents paid. In that way it has the effect of a land tax, which is, as we have seen to take from the proprietor of the soil a portion of his capital, without influencing the price of the products or encroaching on the profits of the producer. Thus the capitalist is impoverished, but nothing is deranged in the economy of society, and this capitalist is obliged to sustain this loss, whenever the land would yield him still less by a change of culture.

Corn, like wine, might be the object of a very heavy tax, levied at the moment of production, independently even of the tenth, with which both are burthened almost every where. A part of this impost would operate in like manner in diminution of the rent of the land, without touching the wages of the production, and consequently without increasing the price of the article. If in general they have abstained from this tax, I am persuaded it is not from a superstitious respect, for the principal nourishment of the poor, which has otherwise been charged in many ways which enhance the price, but because they have been prevented by the difficulty of superintending the entry into every barn, a difficulty which in effect is still greater than that of entering every cellar. In other respects the similitude is complete.

Let us observe, in finishing this article, that an impost thus levied, at the moment of production, on an article of indispensable use all over the world, is equivalent to a real capitation; but of all capitations it is the most cruel, for the poor. For it is the poor who consume the greatest quantity of articles of the first necessity, there being for them no other substitute; and they constitute almost the whole of their expenses, because they can only provide for their most pressing wants. Thus such a capitation is distributed, in proportion to misery and not to riches in the direct ratio of wants and the inverse of means. In this way we may appreciate imposts of this kind. But they are very productive: for it is always the poor who constitute the great number, and by this great number great sums. They little affect those who could make their complaints be heard; and this determines in their favour. It cannot be dissembled, that these are the two only causes of the preference given to them.

As to imposts levied on different merchandises, either at the moment of consumption or at their different stations, as on the public roads, in the markets, in ports at the gates of cities, in shops, &c. &c. their effects have been already indicated by those we have just seen resulting from exclusive sale, or from a tax at the moment of production. These are of the same kind, only they are commonly less general and less absolute; because they are more various, and seldom embrace so great an extent of country. In fact the greatest part of these imposts are local measures. A toll affects only the goods which pass along the road or canal on which it is established. At the entrance of towns it affects directly only the consumption made within their interior. (I suppose its *transit* exempt from duty.) A tax levied in a market or shop does not affect what is sold in the county, or at extraordinary fairs. Thus it deranges prices and industry more irregularly, but always deranges them in the points on which they bear. For so soon as an article is charged the condition either of the producer or the consumer is deteriorated.

It is here that we meet again relatively to products and the effects of taxation, the consequences of two important conditions proper to all merchandise, the one being of the first necessity, or only agreeable or of luxury, the other that their conventional or market price be greater than their natural or necessary one, or merely equal to it, as to being lower, we already know that impossible in the long run.

If the article taxed be of the first necessity it cannot be dispensed with, it will always be bought while there are means; and, if its conventional price be only equal to the natural one, the producer can make no abatement; thus all the loss will fall on the consumer. Whence we are to conclude, that if the sale and the product of the tax diminishes, it is the consumer who suffers and perishes.

We must remark that in our old societies occupying a territory circumscribed long ago, and able to acquire only lands already appropriated, this is the case with all merchandises of the first necessity; for, by the effect of the long contention between the contrary interests of the producer and consumer, every one is posted in the social order according to his degree of capacity. Those who possess some talent, in sufficient demand to enable them to exact payment beyond their absolute necessities, will devote themselves to the employment so preferred. None but those who cannot succeed in them devote themselves to the indispensable productions; because these are always in demand. But they are not paid more than is strictly necessary; because these are always inferior persons, who can do nothing else. It is even necessary it should be so: these articles of first necessity are the urgent wants of all, and especially of the poorest of all the other classes who consume without producing them, being occupied in other productions; thus the poor can subsist only in proportion as these articles are easy to be procured. The more indispensable then a profession is, the more inevitable it is that those who devote themselves to it for want of other capacity should be reduced to the strictly necessary. The only direct means of ameliorating the condition of these men, the last in rank in society from their want of talent, would be to persuade them to multiply less, and to leave them always free to go and exercise their feeble talent whenever it would be the most profitable. For this reason expatriation should always be permitted. There are still some other political measures which might indirectly concur in defending extreme weakness against extreme misery; we will speak of them elsewhere. On the whole these men, whom we compassionate with justice, suffer still less than they would in the savage state. The proof is that they vegetate in greater numbers, for man extinguishes but through excess of suffering.

We have already said all this elsewhere, as occasions presented themselves; but it was very necessary to repeat it here on the subject of taxation. For the history of the revenues and expenses of government is the abridgment of the history of production and consumption of the whole society; since under this point of view government is but a very great rentier, with whom authority stands instead of capital. Without too much forcing the similitude between the circulation of riches and that of the blood, we might say that the circulation operated by government in society, resembles entirely the pulmonary circulation in an individual. It is extracted from the total mass, and returns to diffuse itself there again after having performed its functions separately; but in a manner absolutely similar.

If the article taxed is not of the first necessity, and if nevertheless its conventional price is but equal to its necessary one, it is a proof that the consumers hold feebly to this enjoyment. Then, the tax supervening, the producer has no choice but to renounce his occupation, and endeavour to find wages in some other profession; in which he will increase misery by his concurrence, and in which he likewise is under disadvantage from it, not being his own. Thus they perish, in a great measure at least. As to the consumer, he loses but an enjoyment, to which he was little attached apparently, because he easily replaces it by another; which gives occasion to other wages. But the produce of the tax becomes null.

If, on the contrary, merchandise of little necessity, stricken by a tax, has a conventional price greatly superior to its necessary one, and this is the case with all articles of luxury, there is scope for the treasury without reducing any one precisely to misery. The same total sum is expended for this enjoyment, unless the taste diminishes which has occasioned it to be desired: and it is the producer who loses almost the whole of what the impost takes from this total sum; but, as he gained more than the necessary, he is not yet below it. However it must be observed that this is only true in general. For in this trade, supposed generally advantageous, there are individuals who through want of skill or good fortune, obtain only the slender necessary; and the impost supervening, these are obliged to abandon their profession; which is always a great suffering.

It is thus we may represent to ourselves with sufficient accuracy the direct effects of the different imposts, local and partial, levied on merchandise in their passage from the producer to the consumer. But, besides these direct effects, these imposts have others that are indirect, foreign to the first, or which mix with and complicate them. Thus a heavy duty on an important article, levied at the entrance of a city, diminishes on one hand the rent of its houses, by rendering its habitation less desirable, and on the other it diminishes the rent of land which produces the dutied article, by rendering the sale less considerable or less advantageous. Here then idle capitalists, although they should be absent and not consumers of any thing, are affected in their capital, as by a land tax while it is believed that only the consumer or producer is affected. This is so true, that these proprietors, if it were proposed to them, would make sacrifices to pay off a part of the funds of this impost, or directly furnish a part of their annual produce. This we have seen a thousand times.

What is more, in our economical considerations we often regard as real consumers of an article those only who effectively consume it for their personal satisfaction; yet they are by no means the only buyers of the article. Often the greater part of those who procure it purchase it as a first material of other productions, and as a material of their industry. Then the tax on these articles affects all these productions, and all these occupations. It is what particularly happens to articles of very general use, or of indispensable necessity. They make a part of the expenses of all producers, but in different degrees.

Finally, we must likewise observe, that the imposts of which we are speaking never fall altogether on a single article. They are at the same time levied on many different kinds of goods, that is to say on many species of productions and consumptions. On each, according to its nature, they operate some of the effects we have just explained; so that all these different effects reciprocally clash, balance and resist each other. For the new expenses, with which any kind of industry is burdened, lessen the promptitude to engage in it, in preference to another which has also experienced an injury of the same kind. The burden which oppresses one kind of consumption, prevents its becoming a substitute for that which we wish to renounce. Whence it results, that if it were possible so completely to foresee all these reverberations as to be able perfectly to balance all the weights and to place them all at the same time, so as to produce every where an equal pressure, no proportion would be changed by them. They would produce all together no other effect than the general one inherent in all imposts, namely that the producer would have less money for his labour and the consumer less enjoyment for his money. We might consider imposts as good when to this general and inevitable evil they do not join particular evils too distressing.

I shall follow no farther this examination of the different kinds of imposts. I think I have said enough to enable all to judge of them, and especially to show as clearly as that is possible on whom the loss occasioned by them really falls.

In effect, we see first, that the tax on annuities due by the state and that on the income of land, are not only annually paid by those on whom they fall without their being able to throw any part of them on others but that they lose even the capital; so that after them nobody really pays any thing. Secondly, that it is the same with the tax on the rent of houses; but that moreover it restrains speculations in building, and diminishes the comfort of tenants. Thirdly, that a personal tax, having acquired riches for its object does no wrong but to those from whom it is demanded; but does not liberate those who are to pay it after them. Fourthly, that the loss resulting from a tax on the instruments of social transactions is really supported by those from whom it is demanded, whenever the occasion of paying it occurs; but that its existence alone is injurious to others, by reducing the price of several things and shackling several kinds of industry. Fifthly, that a personal tax which has for its object any kind of industry whatsoever, and all taxes on merchandise, burden first all those from whom they are demanded; and, moreover, that they derange all prices and all kinds of industry; and that, by the effect of their numerous reverberations they end by falling on all the consumers, so as that we cannot precisely ascertain in what proportions.

I know that these results, separated, distinguished, modified, will appear less satisfactory than a very dogmatical decision which, treating the series of the interests of men as a row of ivory balls, should affirm that which ever is touched the last only is put in motion; but I could only represent things as I see them, and not as they may be imagined. If extreme simplicity pleases the understanding by relieving it, if even it is for this that it creates abstractions, a good understanding ought not to forget that this extreme simplicity is found only in itself; and that even in mechanics, as soon as there is a question of real bodies, it is necessary to have regard to many consider-ations, which have no place so long as we reason on mathematical lines and points. Nevertheless, urged by the desire of arriving at a positive principle, I shall be asked perhaps, as I have been already asked on a similar occasion, what is my conclusion, and what is the tax which I prefer. Having exposed the facts, I might leave to the reader to draw his own consequences. But I will give my opinion with its reasons, warning however beforehand that it will never be absolute, but always relative; for a tax is never good when it is exaggerated, nor even when it is not in proportion to all others.

First I repeat, that the consumption of industrious men, that which I have called productive consumption, being the only one that reproduces what it destroys, and being therefore the only source of riches, is that above all which we ought to endeavour not to derange.

Setting out from this truth, the tax on the annuities due by the state would appear to me the best of all; but it is impossible to think of it, since we have seen that it is a true bankruptcy. It is not that I think it useful to cherish the public credit. I think, on the contrary, it is an evil for the government to have credit, and to be able to borrow; I will give the reason when I shall speak of its debts. Moral considerations alone determine me invincibly. Society being entirely founded on conventions, it is impossible that it should not be pernicious to give an example of the violation of plighted faith. No pecuniary calculation can counterbalance such an in-convenience. Its consequences are immense and fatal. The true method of taxing rentiers is to administer well. This causes them to receive but a low interest for their money.

After this tax, of which we cannot think, the best in my opinion are those which resemble it the most, that is to say the taxes on the income of land, and on the rent of houses, to which we may join that personal tax which has for its object riches already acquired. It will be seen, that if I prefer the tax on the income of land, it is not for the reasons of the ancient economists. It is on the contrary, because I regard the proprietors of land as strangers to reproduction. Moreover, I consider these three imposts, which bear princi-pally on the rich, as a compensation for the imposts on merchandise, which necessarily oppress principally the poor. I have no need to say that the tax on land ought not to be such that much land would be neglected.

The tax on deeds and social transactions, notwithstanding its inconveniencies, appear to me admissible also, provided it be not exaggerated. Extending to many things, it bears on many points, which is always an advantage; and it does not press immediately on the first wants of the poor, which is also a great good.

As to taxes on merchandise, to which we must join the personal tax which has presumed industry for its object, I begin by rejecting absolutely all exclusive sales; and yet more, all forced sales, as well as every measure tending to shackle the freedom of labour, and to injure individual property, that is to say the entire disposition of personal faculties. These excesses provided against, I see nothing to forbid the establishment of taxes on merchandise. First, all those on articles purely of luxury are excellent, and have nothing but advantages without any inconveniencies. They diminish the effects of the excessive inequality of fortunes, by rendering more costly the enjoyments of extreme luxury. They are the only sumptuary laws which can be approved. But these are the taxes against which powerful men exclaim the most; besides they are always of very slender product, for in all cases it is the great number, though too much despised, which constitutes the force. We must therefore have recourse to taxes on more useful merchandise, and even on those of first necessity: for, in short, there must be a public revenue. These, as we have said, bear principally on the poor; but, as we have also said, they are balanced by those which bear solely on the proprietors of land, and they justify them. Besides, levied at the gates of cities, they contribute to desseminate the population over the whole extent of the territory, levied at the frontiers, they may be useful on some diplomatic combinations, so long as sound policy has not their entire direction. I do not think then we should blame these impositions. I confine myself to the recommendation, that they never be so heavy as to crush any kind of industry; and that they be very various, that they may bear on all. All are taken care of when all are so charged as that each will sustain its part of the common burden, for it must not be forgotten that our only question here is ever how, to do the least evil possible; and that when we have well distributed the necessary evil, we have attained the *maximum* of perfection in this art.

The expense of collection and the necesity of punishments are likewise two accessory evils of taxation, to which, some it is true are more subject than others; but on which I have nothing to say. But that neither the one nor the other are carried to extremes when the taxes are not excessive and when not enforced by tyrannical forms. Thus I regard them only as secondary considerations.

This is what I think of imposts. But is a more precise conclusion desired? Here it is. The best taxes in my opinion are, first, the most moderate, because they occasion fewer sacrifices, and less violence. Second, the most various, because they produce an equilibrium of the whole. Third, the most ancient, because they have entered into all prices and that all are regulated in consequence.

Once more I fear that this decision will not be satisfactory. It is not sufficiently striking to be brilliant; but except in its moderation (which is often wanting through necessity), it is sufficiently conformable with what is practised every where; and if it be just as I think it is, it will be a new example of an intellectual phenomenon very common, but which has not always been sufficiently remarked: that in matters somewhat difficult the practice is, provisionally, sufficiently reasonable long before the theory becomes so; and, when the subject is thoroughly examined, we perceive that the good sense of the public (I might almost say the general instinct) has less wandered from the right road than the first scientific speculations. The reason is simple. In practice we are close to the facts; they present themselves every moment, they guide us, they retain us, they continually bring us back to what is, to the truth. Whereas in speculative combinations, which consist all in deductions, one first false supposition suffices to lead us very consequently into the greatest errors, without any thing apprizing us of it. This is the cause of the blind attachment so generally manifested for whatever is in use, and the great distrust inspired by every new truth too contrary to it. This disposition is without doubt exaggerated, but it is sufficiently founded in reason. However this may be, we have said enough on the revenues of government. Let us occupy ourselves with its expenses.

We have little to say on this subject. We have seen that government in every country is a very great consumer, and a consumer of the kind of those who live on revenues, and not on profits; that it is a very great rentier with whom authority is instead of capital. Consequently all we have said of this species of consumers is applicable to it. Its expense does not re-produce itself in its hands, with an increase of value, as in those of industrious men. Its consumption is real and definitive. Nothing remains from the labour it hires. The riches it employs, and which did exist before they passed into its hands, are consumed and destroyed when it has made use of them. In effect, in what consists the much greater part of its expense? In paying soldiers, seamen, judges, and officers of every kind, and in defraying all the expenses required by these different services. All this is very useful without doubt, and even necessary in the whole, if the desirable economy is employed in it; but nothing of all this is productive. The expenditure which government may incur to enrich the favourites of power is equally sterile, and has not the excuse of necessity nor even of utility. Accordingly it is still more disagreeable to the public, which it injures instead of serving. It is quite otherwise with funds employed in public labours of a general utility, such as bridges, ports, roads, canals, and useful establishments and monuments. These expenses are always favourably regarded, when not excessive. They contribute in effect very powerfully to public prosperity. However they cannot be regarded as directly productive, in the hands of government, since they do not return to it with profit and do not create for it a revenue which represents the interest of the funds they have absorbed, or if that happens, we must conclude that individuals could have done the same things, on the same conditions, if they had been permitted to retain the disposal of the sums taken from them for this same use; and it is even probable that they would have employed them with more intelligence and economy. Finally, we may say the same things of what the government expends, on different encouragements of the sciences and arts. These sums are always small enough and their utility is most frequently very questionable. For it is very certain that in general the most powerful encouragement that can be given to industry of every kind, is to let it alone, and not to meddle with it. The human mind would advance very rapidly if only not restrained; and it would be led, by the force of things to do always what is most essential on every occurrence. To direct it artificially on one side rather than on another, is commonly to lead it astray instead of guiding it. Nevertheless let us also admit the constant utility of this kind of expenses; not very considerable in relation to money, it is not the less true that, like all the preceding, they are real expenses which do not return.

From all this I conclude, that the whole of the public expenses ought to be ranged in the class of expenses justly called *sterile and unproductive,* and consequently that whatever is paid to the stake, either under the title of a tax or even of a loan, is a result of productive labour previously executed, which ought to be considered as entirely consumed and annihilated the day it enters the national treasury. Once more I repeat it, this is not saying that this sacrifice is not necessary, and even indispensable. Without doubt it is necessary that every citizen, from the product of his actual labour, or the income of his capital which is the product of more ancient labour, should give what is necessary to the state; as it is necessary to keep up his house, that he may lodge in it in safety. But he should know that it is a sacrifice he makes; that what he gives is immediately lost, to the public riches, as to his own; in a word, that it is an expense and not an investment. Finally, no one should be so blind as to believe that expenses of any kind are a direct cause of the augmentation of fortune; and that every person should know well that for political societies, as well as for commercial ones, an expensive regimen is ruinous, and that the best is the most economical. On the whole, this is one of those truths which the good sense of the people had perceived for a long time before it was clear to the greatest politicians.

If, from the examination of the ordinary expenses of government, we pass to that of its extraordinary expenses and of the debts which are their consequence, the same principles will guide us. This is likewise a subject on which the general good sense has greatly preceded the science of the pretended adepts. Simple men have always known, that they impoverished themselves by spending more than their income, and that in no case is it good to be in debt; and men of genius believed and even wrote, not long since that the loans of government are a cause of prosperity, and that a public debt is new wealth created in the bosom of society. However, since we are convinced, first, that the ordinary expenses of government add nothing to the general mass of circulation, and only change its course in a manner most often disadvantageous; Secondly, that they are of such a nature, also, as to add nothing to the mass of riches previously produced, from which they are taken, we ought to conclude that the extraordinary expenses of this same government being of the same nature as its ordinary expenses, are equally incapable of producing either the one or the other of these good effects. As to the ridiculous idea, that in issuing certificates of dues from the state a new value is really created, it does not merit a serious refutation: for if those who receive these certificates possess a certain sum the more, it is evident that the state which issues them must possess an equal sum, the less; otherwise we must say that as often as I subscribe an obligation of a thousand francs, I augment the total mass of riches by a thousand francs, which is absurd. Thus it is very certain, that in no case have we reason to rejoice at the increase of the consumption of government, and the greatness of public expenses.

But, finally, when these expenses are very considerable, ought we to felicitate ourselves on being able to meet them by loans, rather than taxes? or, in other words, is it happy for the governed, that the government should make use of its credit, or even that it should have credit? This is the last question which remains to be treated, before finishing this chapter. I know it is resolved for many statesmen, and even for many speculative writers, who firmly believe that public credit constitutes the force and safety of the state; that it is a great cause of prosperity in ordinary times, and the only efficacious resource in urgent necessities; and thus that it is the true palladium of society. Yet I think I have good reasons for combatting their opinion. I will say nothing of the grevious effects of loans on the social organization, of the enormous power they give to the governors of the facility they afford them of doing whatsoever they please, of drawing every thing to themselves, of enriching their creatures, of dispensing with the assembling and consulting the citizens; which operates rapidly the overthrow of every constitution. These things are not now my subject. I consider in loans at this moment but their pure economical effects; and it is solely under this point of view that I am going to discuss their advantages and inconveniencies.

The first thing said in favour of loans is, that the funds procured by these means are not taken involuntarily, from any one. I think this an illusion. In effect it is very true, that when government borrows it forces no one to lend; for we must not regard forced loans, as loans, but as contributions. When, therefore, the lenders carry their money to the public treasury it is freely and voluntarily; but the operation does not end there. These capitalists have lent, not given; and they certainly intend to lose neither principal nor interest. Consequently, they force the government to raise, one day or other, a sum equal to that which they furnish and to the interest which they demand for it. Thus, by their obligingness, they burthen without their consent not only the citizens actually existing, but also future generations. This is so true, that the kind of easement, which their service produces for the present moment, only amounts to a rejection of a part of the burden on future times.

This circumstance, in my opinion, gives room for a great question; which I am astonished to have seen no where discussed. A government of any kind, whether monarchical or polyarchical, in a word of men now existing, has it a right thus to burden men not yet in existence, and to compel them to pay in future times their present expenses? This is not even the case of a testament; against which it has been said, with reason, that no man has the right of being obeyed after his death. For, in fine, the society which for the general good takes so many different powers from its individual members may well grant them this, and guarantee it if it is useful to them; and the heirs of the testators are always at liberty to accept or to refuse their inheritances, which at bottom belong to them only in virtue of the laws which give them, and under the conditions prescribed by the laws. But when there is a question of public interest the case is quite different. One generation does not receive from another, as an inheritance, the right of living in society; and of living therein under such laws as it pleases. The first has no right to say to the second, if you wish to succeed me, it is thus you must live and thus you must conduct yourself. For from such a right it would follow that a law once made could never be changed. Thus the actual legislative power (whatever it be), which is always considered as the organ of the actual general will, can neither oblige nor restrain the future legislative power, which will be the organ of the general will of a time yet to come. It is on this very reasonable principle that it is acknowledged in England that one parliament cannot vote a tax but until the commencement of another, or even until a new session of the same parliament. I know well that to apply this principle generally to the debts of a country where it is not admitted, and where prior engagements have been entered into bona fide, would be to violate public faith; and I have heretofore sufficiently manifested my profound belief that such an act can never be either *just* or *useful*, two terms for me absolutely equivalent to *reason* and *virtue*. But it is not the less true,

to return to the example of England, that it is contradictory, and consequently absurd that a parliament should think it could not vote taxes but
for one year, and should think it could vote a loan on a perpetual annuity
or on long reimbursements: for this is to vote a necessity for taxes sufficient
to pay these annuities or these reimbursements, without a right to refuse
them. I find the principle formerly admitted in Spain much more sensible
and honourable, that the engagements of one king are not binding on his
successor. At least those who contract with him know the risks they run and
have no room for complaint of what may happen to them. We shall soon
see that this principle, put in practice, is as beneficial as it is reasonable.

For the present I only maintain, that, since definitively the principal and
interest of a loan can never be paid but by taxes, the funds which government procures by this mean end always in being involuntarily taken from
individuals; and, what is worse, from individuals not obliged, because they
have never engaged either by themselves or by their legitimate or legal representatives. I call *legal,* those whom the existing law authorizes; and whose
acts are valid, even if the law is not just.

The second advantage which is found in loans, is that the sums which
they furnish are not taken from productive consumption: since it is not entrepreneurs of industry who place their funds in the hands of the state; but
idle capitalists only living on their revenue, who choose this kind of annuity
rather than another. I answer that this second advantage is not less illusory
than the first. For although it be true that those who lend to government
are not, in general, the men who have joined their personal industry to
their capital, to render them more useful in productive employments; yet it
happens that there are many of these lenders whom the facility of procuring
a sufficient existence, without risque or fatigue, has alone disgusted from
labour and thrown them into idleness. Besides, even admitting that all were
equally idle if the state had not borrowed, it is certain that if they had not
lent it their money they would have lent it to industrious men. From that
time these industrious men would have had greater capitals to work on,
and, by the effect of the concurrence of lenders, they would have procured
them at a lower interest. Now these are two great goods of which the public
loans deprive them. In fine it cannot be denied that without a bankruptcy,
when a sum is borrowed it must be repaid; and, to repay it, it must be levied

on the citizens. Thus, sooner or later, it affects industry as much and in the same manner as if it had been levied at first. Moreover, there must be added to this all the interest paid by the state till the moment of reimbursement; and it is easy to see that in few years these interests have doubled the capital, and consequently the evil.

But at this day, in Europe, we are so habituated to the existence of a public debt, that when we have found the means of borrowing money on perpetual annuities, and of securing payment of the interest, we think ourselves liberated and no longer owing any thing; and we do not or will not see that this interest absorbing a part of the public revenue (which was already insufficient) since we have been obliged to borrow, is the cause that this same revenue still less suffices for subsequent expenses; that soon we must borrow again to provide for this new deficit, and load ourselves with new interest; and that, thus in but a short time it is found that a considerable portion of all the riches annually produced is employed, not for the service of the state, but to support a crowd of useless rentiers. And to fill the measure of our evils, who are these lenders? Men not only idle, as are all rentiers; but also completely indifferent to the success or failure of the industrious class to which they have lent nothing: having absolutely no interest but the permanence of the borrowing government, whatsoever it be or whatsoever it does; and at the same time having no desire but to see it embarrassed, to the end that it may be forced to keep fair with them and pay them better. Consequently natural enemies to the true interests of society, or at least being absolutely strangers to them. I do not pretend to say that all the rentiers of the state are bad citizens; but I say that their situation is calculated to render them such. I add further, that life annuities tend moreover to break family ties; and that the great abundance of public effects cannot fail of producing a crowd of licentious gamblers in the funds. The truth of what I advance is manifested in a very odious and fatal manner in all great cities without commerce; and especially in all the capitals in which this class of men is very numerous and very powerful; and has many means of giving weight to their passions, and of perverting the public opinion.

It is then as erroneous to believe that the loans of government are not hurtful to national industry, as it is to suppose that the funds which they

produce, are not taken from any individual involuntarily. In truth these
are not the real reasons which cause so much importance to be attached
to the possibility of borrowing. The great advantage of loans, in the eyes
of their partisans, is that they furnish in a moment enormous sums, which
could only have been very slowly procured by means of taxes, even the most
overwhelming. Now I do not hesitate to declare that I regard this pretended
advantage as the greatest of all evils. It is nothing else than a mean of urg-
ing men to excessive efforts, which exhaust them and destroy the sources
of their life. Montesquieu perceived it well. After having painted very en-
ergetically the state of distress and anxiety to which the exaggeration of the
public expenses had already, in his time, reduced the people of Europe, who
ought by their industry to have been the most flourishing, he adds, "And,
what prevents all remedy in future, they no longer count on the revenues;
but make war with their capital. It is not unheard of* for states to mortgage
their funds even during peace, and employ to ruin themselves means which
they call extraordinary; and which are so much so that an heir of a family
the most deranged could with difficulty imagine them."†

It will not fail to be said that this is to abuse its credit, and not to use it;
and that the abuse which may be made of it does not prevent its being good
to have it. I answer, first, that the abuse is inseparable from the use, and
experience proves it. It is scarcely two hundred years since the progress of
civilization, of industry, of commerce, that of the social order, and perhaps
also the increase of specie, have given to governments the facility of making loans; and in this short space of time these dangerous expedients have
led them all either to total or partial bankruptcies, sometimes repeated, or
to the equally shameful and more grevious resource of paper money, or to
remain overburdened under the weight of a load which daily becomes more
insupportable.

But I go farther. I maintain that the evil is not in the abuse; but in the use
itself of loans, that is to say that the abuse and the use are one and the same
thing; and that every time a government borrows it takes a step towards its

---

* He ought to have said, "it is frequent."
† Spirit of laws, book 13th. Chap. 17.

ruin. The reason of this is simple: A loan may be a good operation for an industrious man, whose consumption reproduces with profit. By means of the sums which he borrows, he augments this productive consumption; and with it his profits. But a government which is a consumer of the class of those whose consumption is sterile and destructive, dissipates what it borrows, it is so much lost for ever; and it remains burdened with a debt, which is so much taken from its future means. This cannot be otherwise. In several countries they have commenced, by being long without feeling the bad effects of these operations; because the progress of industry and the arts being very great at this epoch, their advance has been found more rapid than that of the debt; and the means of the government have not failed to augment also. Many have even concluded that a public debt was a source of prosperity, while it only proved that individuals did more good than the government did evil; but this evil was not the less real; and nobody now undertakes to deny it.

These cogent reasons are answered by the excuse which is usual where no other remains. *Necessity;* but I insist, and affirm, that in the present case necessity itself is no excuse: for it is this very remedy which creates the obligation we are under to have recourse to it. I will explain myself. When a nation is once engaged in a perilous situation there is no doubt but that there is a necessity for it to make the greatest efforts to free itself from it. But a body politic does not naturally find itself placed in such a situation. Always some anterior cause has brought it to this. Or it has very badly managed its internal affairs; and thereby encouraged some unquiet neighbour to attack it, to profit by its weakness; or, if it has well conducted its own affairs, it has sought to avail itself of it to meddle unreasonably with those of others: it has abused its own prosperity to trouble that of others, to undertake too great enterprises, to raise exaggerated pretensions; or merely to assume a menacing attitude, which provokes hostile measures and produces hatred. These are, in effect, the faults which commonly bring on the necessity of making excessive efforts, and of having recourse to loans; and if it is true that it is by the foolish confidence inspired by this pernicious resource, that governments have been led into these faults, it will be agreed that the credit which is regarded as a remedy to these evils is their true cause. Now history teaches us that it is in fact since governments have had what is called credit, that is to say the possibility of employing in an instant the funds of several years, that they have no longer set bounds either to their prodigality, or their ambition, or their projects, that they have augmented their armies, multiplied their intrigues, and that they have adopted that intermeddling policy with which it is impossible to avoid war or enjoy peace. These are the effects of this public credit which is regarded as so great a good. But, at least, is it useful in imminent dangers? No. There is no imminent danger for a nation, except a sudden invasion of its territory. In this extreme case it is not money which saves it, it is the concourse of force, it is the union of wills. Requisitions supply necessaries, conscription furnishes men; loans are of no use. The end answered by credit is the maintenance of distant wars, that is to say their prolongation. It also fails when they become disastrous, that is to say in the moment of necessity. Then peace is made. It would have been sooner made if the government had not had credit, or rather there would have been no war. And, when this tardy and forced peace is signed, it is perceived that of all the losses sustained, that most to be regretted, after the useless sacrifice of men, is that of the sums they would have preserved had they not had the unfortunate facility of borrowing them. The conqueror himself is never indemnified by his successes for the sacrifices they have cost him, and the debts with which he remains burdened. From all this I conclude anew, that what is called *public credit,* is the poison which rapidly enough destroys modern governments.

I will not, however, advise a law which should forbid a government ever to borrow, and the governed ever to lend. Such a law would be absurd and useless: absurd, for it would be founded, like the evil which it is meant to destroy, on this false principle: that the actual legislative power can bind the legislative power of futurity, useless because the first thing that would be done by those who, in the sequel, should wish to borrow would be to abolish the law which forbids them; and thus would have a right to do it. I should wish then quite a different course to be pursued. I should wish them, on the contrary, to recognise and proclaim this principle of eternal truth: *that whatsoever is decreed by any legislature whatsoever, their successors can always modify, change, annul;* and that it should be solemnly declared, that in future this salutary principle shall be applied, as it ought to be, to the engagements which a government may make with money lenders.

By this the evil would be destroyed in its root: for capitalists, having no longer any guarantee, would no longer lend; many misfortunes would be prevented, and this would be a new proof that the evils of humanity proceed always from some error, and that truth cures them. It is by this wish that I will terminate what I had to say of the revenues and expenses of government, and that I will finish this first part of the treatise on the will. Only, before passing to the second I will yet present to the reader some reflexions on what we have so far seen.

CHAPTER XIII.

Conclusion.

❧

We are now arrived at a remarkable point on the road over which I had proposed to travel. I ask permission to stop here for a moment. I will again repeat to the reader, that what he has just read is not properly a treatise on political economy. It is the first part of a treatise on the will, which ought to have two other parts; and which is itself but the sequel of a treatise on the understanding. Every thing here then ought to be co-ordinate with what precedes, and what will follow. Thus it ought not to excite surprize that I have not entered into the details of political economy; but it should have done so if I had not ascended to the origin of our wants and of our means, if I had not endeavoured to show how these wants and means arise from our faculty of willing, and if I had neglected to point out the relations of our physical with our moral wants.

It is that I may not merit these reproaches that I have commenced by a very general introduction, which no more belongs to economy than to morality or to legislation; but in which I have endeavoured clearly to explain what are the ideas for which we are indebted to our faculty of willing, and without which these three sciences would not exist for us. I shall be told that this introduction is too metaphysical. I answer that it could not be otherwise, and that it is precisely because it is very metaphysical that there is no bad metaphysics in the rest of the work. For nothing can so effectually preserve us from sophisms and illusions, as to begin by well elucidating the principal ideas. We have not been long without proofs of this.

In fact after having well observed the manner in which we know our wants, our original weakness, and our propensity to sympathy, we were no longer in any doubt on the nature of society. We have seen clearly that it is our natural and necessary state, that it is founded on personality and property, that it consists in conventions, that these conventions are all exchanges, that the essence of exchange consists in being useful to both the contracting parties, and that the general advantages of exchanges (which constitute the social state) are to produce a concurrence of force, the increase and preservation of knowledge, and the division of labour.

After having examined in like manner our means of providing for our wants, we have also seen that our individual force is our only primitive riches; that the employment of this force, our labour, has a necessary value, which is the only cause of all the other values; that all our industry consists in manufacturing and transportation; and that the effect of this industry is always and solely to add a degree of utility to the things on which it is exercised, and to furnish objects of consumption and means of existence.

Ascending always to the observation of our faculties, since personality and property are necessary it is evident that inequality is inevitable. But it is an evil. We have seen what are the causes of its exaggerated increase, and what its fatal effects. These have explained to us in a very precise manner what has commonly been said very vaguely of the different states through which the same people successively pass.

Since we all have means, we are all proprietors; since we all have wants, we are all consumers. These two great interests always re-unite us. But we are naturally unequal; from whence it happens, in process of time, that some have property in advance, and many others have not. These latter can only live on the funds of the former. From thence two great classes of men, the hired and the hirers, opposed in interest in the respect, that the one selling their labor wishes to sell dear, and the other buying it wishes to buy cheap.

Amongst those who buy labour, some (the idle rich) employ it only in their personal satisfaction; its value is destroyed. The others (these are the entrepreneurs of industry) employ it in a useful manner, which reproduces what it has cost. These alone preserve and increase the riches already acquired; these alone furnish to the other capitalists the revenues which they consume, since doing nothing, they can derive no benefit from their capitals, whether move-able or immoveable, but by hiring them to industrious men in consideration of a rent, which the latter pay out of their profits. The more the industry of the latter is perfected the more our means of existence are augmented.

In fine, we have remarked that the fecundity of the human species is such, that the number of men is always proportionate to their means of existence; and that wheresoever this number does not continually and rap-idly augment, it is because many individuals daily perish for want of the means of life.

Such are the principal truths which follow so immediately from the ob-servation of our faculties, that it is impossible to dispute them. They lead us to consequences no less certain.

After having seen what society is, it is impossible not to reject the idea of foregoing it absolutely, or of founding it on an entire renunciation of one's self, and on a chimerical equality.

After having well unraveled the effects of our industry, it is impossible not to see that there is nothing more mysterious in agricultural industry than in any other, but we discover the inconveniences which are proper to it, and which are the cause of the different forms which it takes according to times and places.

When we have recognized the necessary cause of all values, we must conclude that it is absurd to pretend that money is but a sign; and odious to undertake to give it an arbitrary value, or forcibly to replace it by an imaginary value; and that every establishment which tends towards this end is dangerous and pernicious.

When we have seen how the formation of our riches is operated and their continual renovation, which we call *circulation,* we necessarily see that consumption in itself can never be useful, and that the exaggerated con-sumption, called *luxury,* is always hurtful; and we cannot otherwise than find rediculous, the importance ascribed to men who have no other merit but of being consumers, as if that were a very rare talent.

Just views of consumption give necessarily just ideas on that greatest of consumers, *government;* on the effects of its expenses, its debts, and the dif-ferent imposts which compose its revenues, and lead us clearly to trace the different reflections of these assessments, and to estimate the greater or less evil they do, according to the different classes of men on which they fall.

All these consequences are rigorous. They will not be the less contested. It was necessary then, to arrive at them methodically. But those above all, which will experience the greatest opposition, are what lead us to determine the degrees of importance of the different classes of society. How persuade the great rural proprietors, so much cried up, that they are but lenders of money, burdensome to agriculture and strangers to all its interests? How convince these idle rich, so much respected, that they are absolutely good for nothing; and that their existence is an evil, inasmuch as it diminishes the number of useful labourers? How obtain acknowledgement from all those who hire labour, that the dearness of workmanship is a desirable thing; and that, in general, all the true interests of the poor are exactly the same as the true interest of the whole society. It is not merely their interests, well or ill understood, which oppose these truths, it is their passions; and among these passions, the most violent and antisocial of all, *vanity*. With them demonstration, or at least conviction is no longer possible; for the passions know how to obscure and entangle every thing; and it is with as much reason as ingenuity, that Hobbes has said, that if men had a lively de-sire not to believe that two and two make four, they would have succeeded in rendering this truth doubtful; we might produce proofs of it.

On many occasions, then, it is still more difficult to conciliate to truth than to discover it. This observation discovers to us a new relation between the subject we have treated of, and that which is next to occupy us, between the study of our actions and that of our sentiments. We have perceived, and said, that we should know well the consequences of our actions, to appreciate justly, the merit or demerit of the sentiments which urge us to this or that action; and now we see that it is necessary to analyze our sen-timents themselves, submit them to a rigorous examination, distinguish those which being founded on just judgments always direct us well, and those which having their source in illusions, and rising from the obliquities of our minds, cannot fail to lead us astray and form within us a false and blind conscience, which always removes us further from the road of reason, the only one leading to happiness. This is what we shall next investigate, and if we have well exposed the results of the actions of men, and the effects of their passions, it seems that it will be easy to indicate the rules which they ought to prescribe to themselves. This would be the true spirit of laws and the best conclusion of a treatise on the will.

Index

government (*continued*)
  entrepreneurs, privileges granted to,
  167; expenses of, 241–43; financial
  companies, loans from, 158–59; as
  land owner, 218–20; paper currency
  and, xviii, 23, 24, 145–52, 159. *See
  also* public credit and public debt;
  taxation
grain or corn taxes, 233–34
Grammaire (Destutt de Tracy, 1803),
  xii–xiii, 9, 31
Great Britain. *See* England
great farmers or great culture, 122–23,
  127

happiness, liberty equated with, 78,
  79, 80
Helvétius, salon of widow of, x
historical development of nations,
  194–96
Hobbes, Thomas, 88
Holland: population in, 173;
  prosperity, circumstances of, 210;
  wage-related unrest in, 183
horses, 127
houses, taxation on rent of, 223,
  226–27, 238, 239

ideas and perceptions, 57–58
Idéologues, x–xii
ideology and *Idéologie proprement dite*
  (Destutt de Tracy, 1801), xii, 9, 31
idle rich, 253; capitalists, idle versus
  active, xvii, 27, 200; consumption
  by, 199, 202, 209–10; lack of
  production by, 107; luxury and,
  205, 206, 210, 215; money and, 153;
  taxation of, 220, 239; uselessness of,
  209n*, 215
immigration, 184
imposts. *See* taxation
income. *See* capitals; production; wages
  and wage earners

incompatibilities in logic, 35, 41
India (Indostan): English colonization
  of, 194; money in, 142
inequality, xviii, 26, 193–96, 253. *See
  also* wealth and poverty
inflation resulting from paper money,
  149–52
Institut National, xi–xii
interest of money, 152–54
isolation, state of, 86–88, 93–94, 133
Italy: population in, 172; wage-related
  unrest in, 183

Jefferson, Thomas: Destutt de Tracy
  compared, xiv; love essay sent to,
  xviii; Montesquieu critique and,
  xiv–xv, 3; opinion of *Treatise,*
  xv–xvi, 3, 5–8; on taxation, 5, 222n*;
  translation of *Treatise* by, xv, xxi, 3
John of Leyden, 183
judgment: reliability of, 13–14, 32, 34;
  suspension of, 42
justice and injustice, 87–88

labor: importance of good application
  in providing for wants, 208–14;
  production resulting from, 20, 107,
  109; value of, 17, 21, 73–75, 109–12;
  will as source of, 16, 70–72
laborers or workmen, 21, 107,
  114–16; agricultural, 119, 128, 129;
  commercial, 137. *See also* wages and
  wage earners
Lafayette, Marquis de, xv
La Fontaine, Jean de, 71
land, taxation of, 222, 225–26, 229–30,
  238, 239
La Pé[y]rouse, Jean-François de
  Galaup, comte de, 19
laws, origins of, 87–89
legal interest, 152–53
lenders, 157

The Theory of Moral Sentiments (Smith, 1759), 100
tolls, 222, 234
trade: commercial industry, 22, 133–38, 186–89, 193; exchanges, economic society as series of, 95–97, 100–101, 113, 133; merchants, 107, 133–34, 136–37
transportation of goods, value of, 107, 155
A Treatise on Political Economy (Destutt de Tracy, 1815): completion and publication in France, xv; main arguments of, xvi–xviii; modern revisions to Jefferson's translation, xxi–xxii; original title page, 2; translation and publication in United States (1817), xv–xvi, xxi, 3; will, as first part of treatise on, xii–xiv, 10–11, 24, 29, 160, 252
A Treatise on Political Economy, or the Production, Distribution and Consumption of Wealth (Say, 1803), 103n2
Turgot, Anne-Robert-Jacques, 5, 103

undeveloped nations, wealth and poverty in, 153n*, 167
United Kingdom. *See* England
United States: availability of agricultural land in, 153n*; development of, 169n*; luxury in, 214; population of, 171, 172; prosperity, circumstances of, 210; publication of *A Treatise on Political Economy* in, xv–xvi; slavery in, 182–83; wage levels in North and South of, 182
utility or value. *See* value or utility

value or utility: of agricultural land, 153n*; of labor, 17, 21, 73–75,

109–12; of liberty, 80; measure of, 20–21, 108–12, 139; of transportation of goods, 107, 155. *See also* money
vegetative force, 104
vineyards, 128, 130
Voltaire, 65n†

wages and wage earners, 25–26, 107; in agricultural industry, 117; constancy of wages and commodity prices, 184–86; consumption by, 198–99, 203; employers and, 166–67, 177–78; sufficiency of wages, 181–83; taxation of, 221, 222n*; in undeveloped societies, 202
wants. *See* desires or wants
war, state of, 86–88
wealth and poverty, xviii, 24–25, 161–69; common and opposed interests of, 25–26, 164–67, 180, 191; extreme inequality, avoidance of, 191–96; national increase of riches, means of, 193–94; natural inequality of property, 163–64; population, effects of, 25, 131, 165, 169, 170–75; respect for interests of poor, importance of, 179–80, 189; will as origin of ideas of, 16–17, 72–77. *See also* production; progress of society
The Wealth of Nations (Smith, 1776), 100
will: feeling or sensibility, as mode and consequence of, 53–58; labor, as source of, 16, 70–72; liberty and constraint, as source of concepts of, 17, 77–81; perception, relation to faculty of, 15; property and, 15–16, 61–66, 160; rights and duties, as source of concepts of, 18, 55, 81–89; self or personality, as origin of idea of, 15, 16, 58–66; *A Treatise on*

This book is set in Adobe Garamond Pro, a modern adaptation by Robert Slimbach of the typeface originally cut around 1540 by the French typographer and printer Claude Garamond. The Garamond face, with its small lowercase height and restrained contrast between thick and thin strokes, is a classic "old-style" face and has long been one of the most influential and widely used typefaces.

Printed on paper that is acid-free and meets the requirements of the American National Standard for Permanence of Paper for Printed Library Materials, z39.48-1992. ∞

Book design by Louise OFarrell
Gainesville, Florida
Typography by Apex CoVantage
Madison, Wisconsin
Printed and bound by Sheridan Books, Inc.
Ann Arbor, Michigan